STATUS OF WOMEN AMONG THE LEPCHAS

STATUS OF WOMEN AMONG THE LEPCHAS

D. C. ROY

AKANSHA PUBLISHING HOUSE
NEW DELHI-110002 (INDIA)

AKANSHA PUBLISHING HOUSE
4649-B/21, Ansari Road
Darya Ganj, New Delhi - 110 002
Ph.: 23263193 / 9811582579 / 09435116718
Fax: 011-23263193
Email: ektabooks@yahoo.com
www.akanshapublishinghouse.com

Status of Women among the Lepchas

First Published 2017

Reprint 2026

ISBN 978-81-8370-210-2

PRINTED IN INDIA

Published by Akansha Publishing House, New Delhi and Printed at Mehra Offset Press, Delhi.

In the Loving Memory of
My Grand Mother
Late Binodinee Roy

Contents

Preface

Participation of women is sine qua non of any development. Without adequate concern of women the developmental efforts, so far taken by the government, will be derailed. Integrating women in the main developmental process is of vital importance for the overall development of the country. It has been realized and accepted, both theoretically and legally, that equal standing of women with their male counterpart is the only key of success of human development.

Women play a very important and significant role in the tribal society. The actual status of women in the society depends upon the type of the society. In a matriarchal society, the status of women is comparatively higher than that of in a patriarchal society. Again, women under all matriarchal society do not enjoy same social status. Even they enjoy higher social status; they may not enjoy similar type of political or economic status.

The position of women in any tribal society can be viewed mainly from three angles—social, political and economic. All the three aspects are so closely and mutually correlated that only an integrated approach can reveal the actual position of women in their respective societies.

The social status can be identified from the role of women in the family and in the society, rights and duties to other members of the family and society, customs in selecting mates etc. Political status in the traditional tribal society depends upon the possibility of performing the role of a chief who happened to possess both physical strength and the power of army. The chief remained the head of the judiciary system which is guided by tribal rules and customs. All fellow tribes are to be royal to and carry out the decision of the chief. But in the present day, political involvement of women is represented by their participation and engagement in different types of peoples' representatives like Panchayat, MLA, MP etc. The economic status of the women connects them with their participation and involvement in productive and distributive activities. Primitive tribes subsist on hunting and food gathering is a story of the past. In modern days most tribal economy is agriculture based. Tribal agriculture may better be identified as tribal peasantry. The economic status of women now depends upon their involvement and active participation in different types of agricultural activities including their role in decision making process.

As per West Bengal Human Development Report 2004, Darjeeling ranks 4th position among the 17 districts of the state. This encouraging HDI is also matched with increasing sex ratio in favour of women per thousand men. As against 914 in 1991 it increased to 943 in 2001. In 2001, the proportion of female per thousand male in the district remains higher than that of in West Bengal (934) and all India (933). The HDI comprises of three indices — health index, income index and education index. The corresponding ranks for the district in health, income and education indices are 4th, 2nd and 5th respectively. The overall status of women in the district is appreciable. In GDI estimation, the position of Darjeeling is 2nd in the state of West Bengal. As per the individual indices of GDI, the district ranks 1st, 5th and 6th in respect of income index, health index and education index respectively. So women are placed highly in the district of Darjeeling. The high ranking of the district in the state has no doubt been contributed by the women through their participation and contribution in all the three indices. Economy of Darjeeling is basically based on agriculture and plantation. The area east of Teesta is agriculture based while western bank of Teesta is based on tea and cinchona plantation. In 1991 the proportion of agricultural worker to total worker is 36.50 while it is about 21.01 percent for plantation worker. But both agriculture and plantation are labor intensive and absorb huge number of female labour. The participation of female in agriculture is as high as 69.69 per cent while it is 51.21 per cent for plantation and other allied activities.

The percentage of ST population to the total population of the country has slightly been increased from 8.08 to 8.20 over the decade 1991 and 2001. But their respective percentage for the state of West Bengal has decreased from 5.59 to 5.50 over the same period. This is more so for the district of Darjeeling where the percentage figures has decreased from 13.78 to 12.69 over the last decade. In this category Darjeeling ranks fourth (12.69 per cent) after Dakshin Dinajpur (16.12 per cent), Purulia (18.27 per cent) and Jalpaiguri (18.89 per cent). But in respect to the absolute number of ST population (204167 person in 2001), the position of Darjeeling is 8th among all the districts of the state. The percentage of ST to the total population of Darjeeling has decreased from 14.75 to 13.78 and further to 12.69 for the census periods 1981, 1991 and 2001. This constant decrease in percentage figure of ST to the total population of the district is a matter of great concern.

Economically 39.41 per cent ST population of Darjeeling is engaged in the category of main worker in 1991. Among the main workers, 31.52 percent are cultivators, 19.41 percent agricultural labour and 20.73 per cent are engaged in livestock, forestry and plantation activities. The percentage of ST engaged in other categories of industrial workers is very negligible.

Among the main workers 62.34 per cent are male and 37.66 per cent are female. The ratio of male to female among the cultivators is 67.96:32.04. The proportion of female as agricultural labor is 38.45. But female plays an important role in the category of livestock, forestry, fishing and plantation where their percentage to total persons engaged in this category is 48.73. It is to note that 55.88 per cent of ST female remained in non-worker category. Thus it can be inferred that the ST society in Darjeeling is economically dominated by the males.

Lepchas are the aboriginals of the hilly region of the district of Darjeeling and the state of Sikkim. In 2001 the total Lepcha population in West Bengal is 32377 while their number is 31210 in the district of Darjeeling where they comprise 96.40 per cent of their total population of the state. They constitute 15.29 per cent of the total ST population and 1.94 per cent of total population of the district in 2001. In Darjeeling their main concentration is in the sub-division of Kalimpong.

Lepchas are not new to the academicians and the researchers and a few research works have been carried out on them. But most of the works are either travelogues or based on socio-ethnographic in character. No work has so far been carried out on the status of women in the Lepcha society. Lepchas are matrilineal and women are placed highly in the society in respect of bride price, inheriting mother's *moo*, right to worship etc. But the variables and factors which act and react in different stages of social development have never been attracted by the scholars and researchers. Absolutely no work has ever been tried regarding the political and economic status of women in the Lepcha society.

Women are the better half of any society and no development of the society can be achieved without developing the women. Most of the tribal society are either matriarchal or matrilineal and at present are facing some sort of crisis.

The position of women is in transition. The traditional women dominated society finds a jolt when it reacts with the male dominated outside world. Land ownership is in the names of male members although India has accepted legal equality of property between man and woman through equal right of inheritance. Properties are distributed among sons and not equally to the daughters. In the light of these apparent contradictions, the present study aims to examine the pattern of harmony or tension, if any, in the Lepcha tribal society.

Two Constitutional Amendments have been done for giving more political power to the women. The 73rd and 74th Amendments reserve 1/3rd seat for the women in Panchayet and Municipality elections respectively. The National Policy for the Empowerment of Women (2001) ensures equal right of women in social, political and economic life of the nation. The Ministry of Tribal Affairs has undertaken a number of schemes for the development of the tribes in respect of their income generation and infrastructure development, educational development and literacy, employment-oriented scheme, ensuring fair price and food security, support of entrepreneurship etc. But except construction of hostel for the girls (since 1962-63), educational complex in low literacy pockets (since 1993-94) etc. no special drives have been taken for the development of tribal women. It is reported that absolutely no projects have ever been carried out by the Ministry of Tribal Affairs for the development of the Lepcha women of the region.

Economic development, political empowerment and social status are inseparable to each other. To integrate women in general and the tribal women in particular in the mainstream of national development, overall development of the women in the fields of economic, political and social sectors is not only necessary but indispensable. A multi-faceted approach integrating different departments can examine the actual status of women in the society.

There are many other Lepcha friends and students who helped and accompanied me during the field survey. They were my host in the village and act as my interpreter, narrator and guide wherever I visited. I would like to thank Dorjee Tshering Lepcha, Songden Lepcha, Ren O.T. Lepcha, Remue Sankit Lepcha of Mani Gumba; Gyanthup Lepcha, Ezra Lepcha, Sevesten Lepcha and Renue Sangmit Lepcha of Tashiding Busty; Nima Lepcha of Khambung; Kuldeep Lepcha of Lower Beyong. I would like to thank, without mentioning names and making a long list, all the respondents and the heads of each 154 households of all the four villages, for sparing their time and responding with smile all my quarries. I like to acknowledge the role of each of the 816 members and especially all the 402 female members of the four villages and express 'all the best' and 'thank you' for them.

I am extremely thankful and indebted to Dr Bani Prasanna Misra, retired Professor and Director, Centre for Himalayan Studies and Dr. Rajat Subhra Mukhopadhya, Professor, Department of Sociology, North Bengal University for their blessing, advice and guidance. Special mention is due to Mr Abhijit Mukherjee of Rockvale Academy for taking the painstaking job of proof-reading the entire manuscript.

During my engagement in collecting data, tabulating, writing and typing them, Ranju, my wife; Dona, my daughter and Rishi, my son were always by my side, encouraging and sparing me to carry out the study. I am thankful to all of them.

Dr D. C. Roy

1

Introduction

"One of the difficult fields of 'food battle' is that of intra-family divisions. While economic models are often constructed on the assumption that the distribution of commodities among different members of the family is done on the basis of equalizing wellbeing or need-fulfillment, there is considerable evidence intra-family divisions often involve very unequal treatments." (Dreze, J & A. K. Sen ,1989: pp. 50 - 51). Nobel Laureate Amartya Sen entered in the kitchen to see the prevalence of inequality in division of food among the male and female members in most developing countries.

Family is the unit which receives maximum service from the women who in their capacity of a daughter, wife, and mother contribute their best for the family. In under-developed countries, women satisfy themselves by extending their service for the family and serving the family members. They remained confined themselves within the four walls of the family and spend most of their time in carrying out the household activities. Kitchen is the temple, place of worship for other members of the family, where they spend most part of their life in preparing food for the family members but they themselves suffer from malnutrition, anaemic, low life expectancy etc. The irony of the fact that they prepare the food without even knowing its taste; they supply nutritional food for other members keeping themselves in the stage of severe malnutrition stage; they give birth the future generation but themselves remain uneducated. ill health and ignorant. They enjoy by sacrificing and not by receiving or consuming.

Society may be considered as an extended family. By society here we mean the unilateral type of social formation comprising of only one community. In a mono community society, the social status of women is the reflection of their status in the family. The community status may be compiled together to get the national status of women. In the chain relation between family and the country, there exists a number of steps each of which has been influenced and affected by a number of factors.

In order to evaluate the status of women in any society particularly in the tribal society, one has to consider their status from different angles – social, economic and political. All the three aspects are so closely and mutually correlated that only an integrated approach can reveal the actual position of women in the society. This is more important in case of tribal society where the activities of any individual are so integrated and interrelated that no compartmentalization and separation is possible. The concept of division of labour is a modern phenomenon and is applicable in case of capitalized social structure. It has very negligible relevance to a tribal society. A comprehensive approach covering different aspects and [illegible] of engagement is suitable for the study of status of women in the society.

As family is the basic unit of any society, the social status of women can only be known from the role of women in the family and the rights and duties women enjoy and perform at different stages of day to day family life. The rights and duties of women during the pre and post marital stage are sharply different. Her position and relation with other members of the family as daughter, sister, wife and mother reveals the status of women in the family. The role and involvement in the main social organizations like marriage, religion, education etc determine the comparative weight of women vis-à-vis men in the family. The social functions, culture, customs, taboos etc are some of the markers of social status of women.

Economic status may be considered as one of the important aspect to determine the overall status of women in the society. A higher economic status automatically places the women in higher social position. Economic status connects them with their participation and involvement in productive and distributive activities. Primitive tribe, subsist on food gathering and hunting, is the story of the past. In modern days most tribal society are based on agriculture which may better be identified as tribal peasantry. The economic status of women in the society can better be judged from their involvement and participation in different types of agricultural operations including their role in decision-making processes.

Political status in the traditional tribal society depends upon the possibility of performing the role of a chief who happened to possess both physical strength and the power of army. The chief remained the head of the judiciary system which is guided by tribal rules and customs. All fellow tribes are to be royal to and carry out the decision of the chief. Now, political involvement of women is judged by their participation and engagement in different types of peoples' representatives like Panchayat, MLA, MP etc. Participation and engagement in different political organizations with decision making power has been discussed in terms of political empowerment. But the nature and system of public institutions in any tribal society are different from those of the civil society. For tribal society political status rather than political empowerment may be more useful.

Status: A Theoretical Orientation

There is no unanimity among the social scientists and researchers about the definition of the term 'status'. By crossing the boundary of sociology and anthropology the term has got an inter-disciplinary relevance in its present use for the gender study. Different authors like Henry Maine, Robert E. Park, Ernest W. Burgess. Ralph Linton. Robert K. Merton, Whyte, Max Waber and others have defined the term differently.

The term status is used in relative term and may be used to mean how much importance a society confers as women's versus men. It may also be used to mean how much power and authority women have relative to men in the society. It may again be used to examine how much power and right women or men enjoy in the society. To examine economic status one should know how many right men or women possess on property, asset, income earning activity etc. The political status can be viewed from the angle of right to vote, elect or take part in political activities and policy making body. In fact, the term status is an issue based term and need to be compared and interpreted as per the issue or base of the concept used.

In his illuminating cross cultural study, M. Whyte (1978) could not arrive at any definite conclusion about the status of women. He rated 52 different items used in defining the relative status of the sexes. He found very few items are related and concluded that the term can not be used as a single concept. He preferred to talk about relative status of women in different sphere of life.

However, the sociologists and the social anthropologists use the term in different senses.

Status was initially used to mean 'ascribed' status while later the concept started using in wider sense of 'achieved' status. Ralph Linton distinguished between ascribed and achieved status. Ascribed status refers to the inhered one while those status resulting from personal attainment of goal set forth by the culture, is treated as achieved one.

In all societies certain items/things are selected as reference points for the ascription of status such as age, sex, occupation. family relationship etc.

Ralph Linton (1936) opines that the term status is used with a double significance. "A status, in the abstract, is a position in a particular pattern. It is thus quite correct to speak of each individual as having many statuses, since each individual participates in the expression of a number of patterns. However, unless the term is qualified, the status of any individual means the sum total of al the statuses which he occupies. It represents his position with relation to the total society." (1936: p. 113).

By status Floian Znaniecki identified social status which depends on the role of an individual in the society. He said "A person who is needed by a social circle and whose self possesses the qualities required for the role for which he is needed has a definite social status". (1940: p. 14). A person occupying a certain status is granted certain rights by his social circle. The rights granted to an individual in a particular social circle, are indicative of his specific social status.

E.C. Huglus (1944) mentioned about the dilemmas, contradictions and confusions in regards to personal attributes and status. There are some individual positions which remain fixed for long. But social change, technical change, appearance of new individual creates new change in the status of an individual. This makes contradictions, confusions and dilemmas of status of an individual in the society.

R.H. Lowie (1948) mentioned four aspects of examining status of tribal women. They are: i) actual treatment attained,

ii) legal status, iii) opportunities for social participation, and iv) character.

The two concepts status and role are inseparable but they are two separate concepts. Status is a collection of rights and duties and can be expressed through a medium of an individual. Role represents the dynamic aspects of status. The individual occupy the status socially assigned to him. He does so with relation to other statuses. Further the individual is said to perform the role when the rights and duties associated with status are put into effect. In practice there are no roles without statuses or statuses without roles.

According to Robert K. Merton social statuses and social roles comprise major building blocks of a social structure. He wrote "each social status involves not a single associated role, but an array of roles. This basic feature of social structure can be registered by the distinctive but not formidable term, role-set. By role-set I mean that complement of role relationships in which persons are involved by virtue of accompanying a particular social status." (1976: p. 294). It is thus clear that the concept status can neither be used in any specific meaning nor can be used uniformly for all societies. It is society or community specific. The status of women in any society depends on the rights and duties as conferred to the women by the respective socio- cultural pattern and organization.

Status of Women in Indian Society

Women were placed at a very high position in the Indian Hindu mythology. The three important Hindu Goddesses – *Parvati*, Goddess of power; *Lakshmi*, Goddess of wealth; *Saraswati*, Goddess of learning -- are all female. Manu, the great Hindu sage, author of *Manusmriti* wrote: "Where a woman is honoured, God feels delighted."

Indian mythology sets the women on a pedestal but the history speaks about their oppression, inequality, unjust and other derogatory practices against women. Raja Rammohun Roy (1772 – 1833), father of modern India and champion of women's rights and a feminist had to fight hard in stopping Satidaha and introducing remarriage of widows. Iswar Chandra Vidyasagar was the champion in female education and legalized widow remarriage. Keshab Chandra Sen, a leader of Brahmo Samaj, gave a modern touch among women through schools, prayer meetings etc. Swami Vivekananda tried to inculcate power among the women. Swami Dayananda Saraswati, founder of Arya Samaj encouraged women education and condemned those customs which degraded women. Lokmanya Tilak and Mahatma Gandhi took up the cause of women in the promotion of female education, remarriage of widows etc. There are many male social reformers and activists who fought for women's right and justice in the male-dominated Indian society.

After Independence, India showed a remarkable change in respect of women's status in our society. UN General Assembly passed a number of resolutions advocating equal rights and dignity of women. The Indian Constitution was framed and amended with an objective of ensuring equal status of women in the country. Some changes in the women's status can be marked in the fields of economic, social and political arenas after Independence. But sixty years of independence is found to be insufficient in improving the position of women as per their expectation and balancing them at par with the men members of the society. In spite of Constitutional guarantee, the Indian women are the victims of inequality in economic, social and political fields. Enactment of laws by the Parliament and Legislature are and amendment of the Constitution shows the presence of inequality in the country even in the twenty first century.

Status of Women in Tribal Society

Women are indispensable part of every social setup — be

it primitive or tribal or modern. Women's status and role in any tribal society is different than among the non-tribals. During food gathering and hunting stage, a group or band of people used to move together from one place to another in search of food. Women not merely accompanied the group but took active part in hunting and collecting fruits, roots, and animals in the forest. With the change in social structure, the status and role of women has changed but even then their status in the tribal society remains significant and different than that of other civil society. It may be noted that the type of matriarchal and matrilineal society can be found only among the tribals.

Modern civil societies are largely patriarchal where economic and social resources are mainly controlled and possessed by the males. Sociologically matriarchal civil society is almost nil. But tribals are generally either matriarchal or matrilineal. Women in such cases usually play a vital role in economic, social and political organizations. Beside owning and inheriting movable and immovable properties, women's involvement in primary occupation is no less important than the males.

Higher economic status placed the women at a higher social status in the tribal milieu. Bride price, staying of groom in the bride's house is some of the customs which place the women in a socially advantageous position. In many religious beliefs women are regarded next to God and are worshipped.

Their economic and social status keeps the tribal women politically better than others. A tribal woman not only take part in family decision-making but has been found to take key role in social and communal activities. History witnesses a number of tribal movements where the role of women has been well recognized.

The wave of modernization and the intended change in all-round social and economic sphere has changed the role of women among the tribes. The slogan of the day, 'to bring the tribes in national main stream', is more materialistic and in the changed complex system, women started loosing their earlier position to their male counterpart.

Writings pertaining to historical, economic, social and political perspective of tribal women are very scanty. A composite write-up covering socioeconomic and political aspects of any tribe has never been attempted. To work among the tribes is more challenging and difficult which might have diverted the social scientists to avoid tribal women study.

Malinowski assessed the status of women in tribal society "after taking into consideration the mutual duties between the sexes and the safeguards provided for the protection of each sex against the high handedness of the other. (Malinowski.1920: p. 20). Here status is used as synonym for role. "Madan and Majumdar (1956) have explained that status of women in all types of societies, particularly in patriarchal, is determined by various types of taboos that are attended to women generally. In another occasion Madan and Majumdar argued that it would be a scientific error to approach the women of a society with a rigid bias to the view that they have either a low or a high status. And those dichotomics are generally misleading. There can be so many intermediate statuses and there can be polarity, though it may not be very striking. The tribes, differing in life and culture patterns, accord status to the women as per their respective purview. Use of a single concept may not make the position clear" (K. Mann:1987: pp. 16-17).

The status of women is community specific and depends on the specific socio-economic and political environment of the community. Women's status can only be known and discussed within the environment in which they grow, interact, work, serve and live as a daughter, wife, mother, grandmother and so on. All societies are influenced and affected by the external factors. The culture, custom, habit, style of livelihood of the dominating neighbouring community slowly but steadily enter in other community and thereby give a mixed shape of the two. The influence of the modern electronic and other media like TV, cinema, magazine, newspaper etc. can no way be ignored in influencing and shaping the position of an individual in the society.

Before the advent of the British in the region, Lepchas were totally unknown to the out side world. They lived in the forest which provided them with food and shelter. They also practiced shifting cultivation during Tibetan rule. In course of time they had to settle down to terraced based settled cultivation due to forest reservation policy of the British. They were absorbed in different works for extending both physical and mental services. At present the Lepchas are mostly agriculturists producing food crops for subsistence and some cash crops to meet other requirements. Women were a part and parcel of Lepcha economy. During the food gathering and hunting stage the whole group including the women not only moved together but also took part in day to day activities along with men. Even at the present settled cultivation, the role and involvement of the women in different agricultural operation is very important and indispensable.

Lepcha religion got influenced by the British and the Tibetans. Lepchas were originally nature worshippers but were first converted into Buddhism by the Tibetans and later into Christianity by the British. Mun, the Lepcha female priest lost her prestigious position and role in the changed socio-cultural situation. All natural items were the objects of worship but the changed religious situation took them away from their deep association and feelings with the nature. The changed religion, custom, taboos etc are some of the factors which are responsible for changing the position and status of women in the Lepcha society.

Objectives

The threefold objectives of the present study are:

(a) to identify the social status of women in the Lepcha society. The basic purpose of the study here is to identify the areas and factors that make the prestigious position of the girl child in the society. A comparison between the traditional and present ethnic values, customs, and rules will help us to know the dynamism of social status of the women in Lepcha society.

(b) to identify the political status of the women in the society. Participation of women in decision-making bodies during the traditional system and modern democratic setup identifies the political status of women in the Lepcha society. The traditional customs, judiciary system along with participatory role as voter and contesting candidate in different tiers of election will identify the dynamism of political status of women is the Lepcha society.

(c) to know the economic status of women in Lepcha society. Involvement and role of women in productive and distributive activities during the traditional and modern society symbolize the type of economic dynamism among the Lepchas.

Hypotheses

The proposed project has been planned to carry out with two sets of hypotheses – working hypothesis and scientific hypothesis. The working hypotheses or preliminary hypotheses are made when sufficient information is not available to establish any hypothesis and it is a step towards formulating the final research hypothesis. Our working hypothesis is that the Lepcha society has undergone some sociopolitico and economic change over the decades. With this working hypothesis, we seek to test three scientific hypotheses from the surveyed data.

Firstly, we hypothesized that in the social front Lepcha women have lost some of their days old prestigious position in the society to their male counterpart.

Secondly, we hypothesized that in the political front Lepcha women have gained their position in decision making bodies through their active participation in all types of democratic government formation.

Thirdly, we hypothesized that in economic front Lepcha women continued to play their key role in both production and distribution of agricultural produce.

Incidentally in the course of our study we will automatically test some hypotheses like the maintenance of matriarchal society, the role of priestess, role and number of women political leader, existence of bride price/ dowry, inequality of wage distribution, nature and type of work for the females, taboo in women's participation in work etc.

Methodology

Both primary and secondary data have been used for examining the dynamics of the status of women in the Lepcha society.

Secondary data have been collected from government, non-government sources and from the existing literature on the Lepchas. Various government publications, reports, census documents are the main source of data. The existing literature, although very meagre in number, written by the foreign and domestic writers, academicians, travelers, and administrators are used and referred as and when necessary. Some local government officials like Sub Divisional Officer, Block Development Officer, and SC, ST Development Officer have been consulted. The dignitaries and other members of the Indigenous Lepcha Tribal Association are found to be of great help in carrying out the study. But the basic primary data have been collected personally through field survey. We take the help of investigators and interpreters from among the Lepchas who acted as bridge between the common Lepchas and the researcher. These investigators were engaged not only in collecting quantitative and qualitative data but they helped in conducting different tour programs.

In Darjeeling district of West Bengal, Lepchas mainly live in Kalimpong sub-division. A list of Lepcha dominated villages was prepared with the help of block level data. Only those villages which are absolutely dominated by the Lepchas are selected. Before finally selecting villages, a primary survey was conducted to gather some first hand information about the village. The officials of the Association were consulted and a sort of permission was obtained to avoid any later confusion and contradiction. Most of the Lepcha dominated villages are located at far-flung hilly areas without any proper communication facilities. So it is decided that four such villages would be sufficient for collecting data for the present study. Proximity to the town, religion, education, type of crops produced etc. have been used as the basic criterion for selection of the villages. In the hilly region villages are sparsely populated so complete enumeration rather than sample survey has been considered as the better method of collecting data. During our conduct of household survey we have used the observation technique for recording some of the events, practices, material conditions etc. We knew that participant observation method is the best for this type of study but for obvious reason we preferred and used close observation method.

Both qualitative and quantitative data have been collected for the study. A questionnaire has been prepared and used for quantitative data while qualitative data have been gathered through close observation and involvement. The investigators, employed from within the Lepchas of the concerned villages helped in collecting both qualitative and quantitative data. We, as invitee or non invitee, participated in all types of social religious, ethnic, political, economic functions as and when possible and practicable.

Tools Used

Primary data have been collected from two different sources: village level and institutional level.

Village level primary data have again been collected from two different sources: a) from selected Lepcha dignitaries, elderly persons of the concerned village, members of the Indigenous Lepcha Tribal Association etc. and b) household data from the selected villages. Some cross check of the data/information has been made from different households of the respective village. Revisit of the village has been carried out to solve the confusions and to make scrutiny of the inconsistency in data.

Institutional data have been collected from among the Lepcha girl students studying in the two colleges of Kalimpong. A schedule has been used for the purpose of gathering quantitative data. Students were taken into confidence and a close relation was established with them for the purpose of examining and assessing their mentality about the status of women in their society.

Women participation in political affairs particularly in contesting, winning and taking part casting votes in Panchayet, legislative and parliamentary elections or any other local governmental organization have been planned to collect from Sub Divisional and Block Development Offices.

Photographic information regarding women participation in social, political and economic activities has been collected as and when available. Different cultural, social, ethnic, religious, economic and political functions and programs are attended and documentations have been done and moments are clicked and recorded through photographs.

Beside the adult women labor, proper care has been taken for collecting data on child labor. Some information are considered to be very relevant e.g. women education, women literacy rate, women health care, women mortality rate, women participation in political activities, women participation in decision making, women participation in the types of social activities etc.

Qualitative data have been collected through participation and observation. All ethnic, social, political and economic activities, both as invitee or non invitee, were attended and observed closely.

Period of Study

One full calendar year, from March 2006 to April 2007, has been spent in collecting primary data from the villages. All major sociocultural and religious events within the study period have been covered. Two main social events – one marriage and one funeral ceremony have been attended as close observer. Some cultural events like Birth anniversary of King Gaeboo Aackuk, Muk-Zik-Ding Rum Faat, Naam Boon, etc. have been observed very minutely. Revolt of the Lepchas against construction of Hydro electricity power project at Dzongu and the connected relay hunger strike at Kalimpong has been noticed from very close. The year does take into consideration a complete agricultural calendar year and the agricultural operations for the entire major crop within the year have been examined. A complete crop circle has been investigated and the pattern of women participation has been marked for the present study.

2

Review of Existing Literature

2.1. INTRODUCTION

The present study aims at examining the status of women among the tribes in general and among the Lepchas in particular. At the outset it is to be mentioned that absolutely no literature has been available on the status of women among the tribes in general and among the Lepchas in particular. Three words have been considered relevant for the purpose of consulting the existing literature for the present study. They are: a) Lepchas, b) tribe and c) women. The present chapter has, thus, been divided in three sections.

In the first section we examined the status of women in the Lepcha society from the available literature written on the Lepchas in general. Although no work has been attempted solely on the women among the Lepchas but some scholars, researchers, writers have contributed on the study of the Lepchas in general and thereby mentioned something about the role and status of women in their society.

The second section deals with the review of existing literature on tribes in general and on tribal women in particular. It is to note that Indian tribes remain the central source of study to both the Indian and European social scientists and anthropologists. Even then no work has been undertaken on the study of women in the tribal society in general and among the Lepchas in particular. Existing tribal study highlights history, culture, social and anthropological aspects of tribal life and society in general without separating the status of women in their respective society. In our brief review on the available literature on tribal study, we examined only those aspects which relate to the status of women in their respective society.

In the third section we reviewed those literatures which deal with the women study. It may be noted that women study is a recent phenomenon but by this time a good number of works have been published and made available on them. Different problems and their solutions have been focused on the women issues from political, social, anthropological, historical and economic angles. But absolutely no work has been conducted on the status of women among the tribes in general and among the Lepchas in particular.

2.2. LITERATURE ON THE LEPCHAS :

Absolutely no written document is available on the status of women in the Lepcha society. In fact, works on the Lepchas are very scanty and piecemeal. Some works on them are available but most of them are neither systematic nor sufficient for the present study. Documentation on the Lepchas has been started after British occupied Darjeeling track. But the earlier writings were not focused absolutely on the Lepchas rather they just mentioned, used and documented the case of the Lepchas as a bi product of their main work. So most works are piecemeal in character and guided by administrative objectives. After independence, some independent studies have been carried out by the scholars, researchers. Some Lepcha scholars have also documented their insiders view about their social structure.

The first systematic study on the Lepchas was carried out by A.K.Das (1976) for his Ph.D. degree from Calcutta University. He gave a detailed account of the demographic profile of the people with their social, economic and domestic life. Religion of the Lepchas, their myths, songs, tales, proverbs, marriage, customs, and language take separate chapters in his study. Although the study does not give any specific focus on the women in particular but one can pick up some aspects of women from the general discussion of the tribe. Sex-wise breakup of the Lepcha population for the district of Darjeeling as per Police Station and for the state as a whole as per district for the year 1961 have been analysed in the chapter on demography. Industrial classification of the Lepchas shows the involvement of the women in different categories of work. He observed that "males and females both equally play their parts in sowing.... In these days actual planting is done by women but it is of no significance." (p. 51). Das quoted Morris in finding the importance of female labour in Lepcha agricultural operations. He noticed the involvement of women in construction work. "Male members' share in the constructional activities is much more than that of the females, though females also contribute their might even in labourious jobs". (p. 62). In the family set up Das noticed a bit decreasing role of wife compared to her husband. "In the family husband and wife look upon each other as help mate and partner in different spheres of activities. Wife has a definite say in every affair of domestic or otherwise. The husband generally consults the wife regarding any problem that arises from time to time. No difference in status exists between the sexes in these activities. Among the advanced, educated and economically well placed section, the husband plays a dominant in every day's say and the wife is gradually becoming submissive to him losing thereby her hold from day to day's say" (pp. 99, 100).

Sonam Wangdi Lepcha (1979), a Lepcha by himself, presented an insiders view in his research on the Lepchas for his Ph.D. degree from Bhagalpur University. He conducted his study on sociological aspects of modernization and change among the Lepchas of Darjeeling and Sikkim. The scholar made an elaborate description about the changes in different social and cultural life of the Lepchas. Origin of the tribe, their language details, demographic details, social aspects like family, marriage, religion etc, economic change in occupation, agricultural practice etc. are some of the items which have been discussed at length in the study. But very little regarding the role and status of women in the Lepcha society has been discussed by the scholar. After writing the general information about the Lepchas regarding their origin, language, demography, etc., Wangdi mentioned about the family of he Lepchas. He wrote: "owing to the lack of systematic social or religious system among the Lepchas, we find an admixture in the family traditions also. Both father and mother share the position of "family head' and the children descend through both mother and father side. This, coupled with the institution of 'Mun' – the female priest being more powerful than the 'bongthing', i.e. the male priest, indicates that once there was prevalence of 'matriarchal' families" (p. 176). The author mentioned four types of marriage – arranged marriage, sorrorate and levirate, marriage by service, and love marriage but he has given more importance on marriage by elopement where the wish of the boy and girl is final. The author gives some accounts on Lepcha Mun and Bongthing and writes that a Mun can be either a male or a female but Bongthing is always a male.

Veena Bhasin (1989) conducted a comparative study on ecological and cultural change between two major tribes of Sikkim: Lepchas and Bhutias. The main items of comparison are sociopolitical system, religious beliefs and rituals, education and their economic life. The study made a comparative analysis between the Lepchas of Dzongu and the Bhutias of Lachen and Lachung areas of North Sikkim.

Different socio – economic and cultural aspests of the region and of the two communities have been analysed at length but not much about the status of women in the Lepcha society. Hence the study is not much relevance for the present study.

In his study Sumit Ghosal (1990) made a study on cultural, ecological and social change in the Lepcha society and acquired his Ph.D. degree from the Department of Sociology, North Bengal University. Among other things like physical setting of the district, village set up, etc the study comprises ethno history of the Lepchas of the region, their material culture, economic behaviour, social organization, political organization, religious beliefs etc. Ghosal observed the important role played by the women in shifting cultivation. He wrote "in shifting cultivation women's participation is much more intensive at operational level than that of men. In Lepcha shifting cultivation women's work is in fact slow and continuous, evenly distributed throughout the agricultural season. The men's share, namely the cleaning, lasts a limited time and forms no part of the actual process of cultivation. But in contrast with the more intensive cultivation system, slash and burn agriculture requires high level inputs to crop tending, especially weeding, and watching the crop against the animals. In Lepcha shifting cultivation most of these operations are done by women. These include sowing, weeding and harvesting of crops" (p. 84). The author believed that the presence of polygyny in the elpcha society is due to the important role played by the women in the shifting cultivation. "Since the women play an important role in Lepcha shifting cultivation, it can, be assumed that it will lead to increased degree of polygyny in Lepcha society. In other words the presence of polygyny in the Lepcha society can be predicted as a consequence of its high degree of female participation in shifting cultivation. That is why the incid of polygyny is still found among the Lepchas of Dzo...

because they still practices some amount of shifting cultivation even in these days" (p. 85). The author also noted a sort of division of labour among the Lepchas. "Animals must never on any account be killed by a woman. This is the only complete and absolute sex linked prohibition of any form of activity imposed upon the women. There are some acts which are more commonly or indeed exclusively practised by men or by women only, but except this there is no sort of prohibition for members of the fairer sex doing them if they feel so inclined. For example, only women transplant the seedlings and only men plough but there is no reason why a man should not transplant if he wants to and similarly a woman can plough, but her relative lack of strength prevents her from doing so." (pp. 142, 143).

Rip Roshina Gowloog (1995), a Lepcha by herself, carried out her research of diachronic study on the Lepchas of Lingthem, a village in Dzongu, North Sikkim. The work compares the changes in respect of economic, social and religious organizations in the same village after 50 years of original study conducted separately by Geoffrey Gorer and John Morris both in 1938. The work does deal not much about the activities and involvement of the females in the Lepcha society. It is a comparative study on general information about the Lepchas as observed by the author after fifty years time. Anyway, Gowloog made very sporadic and negligible comparison on the activities of women. However she substantiate the view of Gorer that females were the better weavers of mats, blankets and cloths etc than the males and these articles they produce only for domestic consumption and not for sale. "Only two women were found weaving cloth for commercial purposes in 1987 (p. 62)". She further comments "the Lepcha women seem to have a natural flair for weaving but they have not so far received much encouragement to excel in this activity. Instead the refugee women from Tibet are given a lot of incentives in this regard.

This is probably because the latter are urban based and with no alternative to livelihood as the Lepcha women have" (p. 63). Without mentioning the contemporary situation Gowloog quoted Gorer in finding distinction and treatment towards male and female babies in Lingtham village. "The distinction between male and female babies was clearly maintained in the village then. For instance, on the fourth day of the child's birth a ceremony called *Pa-gong Chi-tong* took place in which if the child is a boy, particularly the first born, an ox or a pig, or a goat was sacrificed but if the child was a girl no such sacrifices took place. The few well-off Lepchas however bought some meat and gave each guest a piece as a sort of gift. Again if the child was a boy, the guest brought one rupee and a ceremonial scarf whereas in case of a girl no scarf was brought and the amount was six *annas* or a chicken only.... There is no evidence, either in Gorer's or Morris's book, to show that male and female children were given differential love and care by their parents. The difference in ceremonial importance attached to male and female children could probably taken as a remnant of a tradition in which the males were more important" (pp.70 - 71).

Jenny Bentley (2007) conducted a field survey in two Lepcha villages of North Sikkim and submitted a dissertation for her Master degree in the University of Zurich. The basic purpose of the study was to analyse the cultural revival and indigenous right movements in the Lepcha community of Sikkim. After putting research questions, methodology etc the scholar uses survey technique to discuss the history, original and contemporary cultural aspects and then analyses the role of different Lepcha Associations in reviving their indigenous culture in Sikkim. Status of women among the Lepchas of Sikkim can only be found through the role of Mun in different rituals. The author identifies the Lepcha cultural problem through intermarriage with the neighboring classes like Nepalese and Bhutias. The appendix of the study is more relevant for the present analysis where the scholar recorded details about the moo, Lepcha rituals, myths, role and types of Mun etc. Jenny Bentley focused her attention with the Lepchas of Sikkim but in a number of cases she compares with their counterpart in Kalimpong. It is interesting to note that before finally decided to work with the Lepchas of Sikkim, Jenny like Gorer (in 1938), Rene De Nebesky (in 1950), Hofdon Siiger (in 1967) also visited, stayed sometime and acquired enough knowledge about the Lepcha from Kalimpong.

In addition to the above mentioned full fledged research work, a good number of write ups written by different scholars, and authors starting from British period until today are available in the form of books, articles, reports, travelogues, references etc. These works can be found in the form of gazetteers and government reports, travelogues, journals, magazines and newspapers, folk tales and folklores, ethnic affinity, linguistic and sociological and academic work etc.

'Note on the Lepchas of Sikkim' by A. Campbell, Esq. Superintendent of Darjeeling has published his popular documentary article in the *Journal of Asiatic Society of Bengal* in 1840. This can be recognised as the first hand written document on the Lepchas of undivided Sikkim-Darjeeling areas and has been used and quoted by almost all writers on Lepchas in the later period. Campbell has presented an overall picture of the Lepchas considering their social, anthropological, economic, religion and a list of vocabulary of Lepcha language. It was so authentic that writers like E.T. Dalton (1872), W.W. Hunter (1876), H.H. Risley (1876). A.K. Das (1962) and others in a number of occasions quoted Campbell for their individual study. Although there was not much scope to the author to discuss about the activities and status of women among the Lepchas

but Campbell did not forget in mentioning the identifying dress of Lepcha women. He spent one paragraph in narrating the day to day activities of women in Lepcha society. "The women are less handsomely dressed than the men; a piece of plain unbleached cotton cloth, or the cloth of the castor oil insects, rolled to form a sort of petticoat, with a loose bed gown of the same, and a profusion of mock coral and coloured bead necklaces, from their entire wardrobe. They are the domestic and farm drudges of the men, performing all out – and in-door work along with their husbands, and much besides. It is not unusual to meet a stout and active man bow in hand, sauntering along the road followed by his wife and sisters heavily loaded with grain or merchandise. It is the delight of a Lepcha to be idle, he abhors the labour of practicing any craft, but he expects that while he is amused and unemployed, the female part of the household shall be busily engaged in the field, or in looking after the pigs and poultry" (pp. 383-84).

L.S.S.O'Malley has prepared a full fledged comprehensive District Gazetteer of Darjeeling in 1907. He gave a detailed description of history of the region, its demographic set up, and all the physical and administrative set up of the district. Lepchas, as the aboriginal race of the region occupies a pivotal position and has been discussed in a number of occasions. But no specific discussion whatsoever are made in the study on the status, role and activities of women as relevant for the present study. E.C.Dozey, the first political Officer of Sikkim and Bhutan analysed the position of Lepchas in his *'History of Darjeeling'* in 1922. The book is authentic and has been well received by the scholars, researches and common readers but for obvious reasons it fails to fulfill the requirements of the present purpose.

Another interesting work also publisher in the Asiatic Society of Bengal was carried out by C.De Beauvoir Stocks in 1925. Lack of written document compels the author to choose alternative method of folk lore and folktales to know the culture, custom, socioeconomic life and history of the Lepchas of Sikkim. Although nothing details about the status of women are available but one can notice sporadic mention about some activities and role of women in the Lepcha society. Some Lepcha customs like family life, birth, marriage, death, burial etc are also noted by the author. The role of women in the family life was narrated as "they (both male and female members) go to the work in the fields, first sharpening their knives, (ban) on a stone slab. The remains of the breakfast are taken with them which they finish when hungry. In the evening they collect weeds, leaves, ferns, vegetables, fruit and yams and returned home. The men of the house sit down to rest, while the women either make sour buckwheat bread from the plant called *ka-hru-khu*, or sweeter bread from flour, which is called *ka-hret-khu*, or boil Indian corn (*kung chum*). The women give the men '*chi*', also taking it themselves; while supper consists of the same food they had in the morning" (p. 461). Stocks narrated details about the laws and taboos in connection to Lepcha marriage.

For the first time a Lepcha, Lyangsong Tamsang, has compiled, translated and edited a 'Lepcha Folklore and Folksongs' in 2008. From the compilation one can find both contemporary and present position of women in the Lepcha society. It discusses about the origin of moo, origin of Lepcha marriage, love story of river Teesta and Rangeet, story of clever women etc. All these speak highly about the position of women in their society. L.S.Tamsang identifies four moos as per geographical location where the Lepchas are residing. They are: i) Renjyong moo (the inhabitants of Sikkim, Darjeeling, Kurseong and Siliguri), ii) Illammoo (the inhabitants of Nepal), ii) Damsangmoo (the inhabitants Kalimpong) and iv) Promoo (the inhabitants of Bhutan). But separate moo for the women as present among the Lepchas and which are relevant for the present study are not available in the study.

H.H. Risley (1928) prepared an account of Sikkim in his *Gazetteer of Sikkim*. As the original inhabitant of the place one can find the early history of the land, their rulers, geographical boundary, demographic account and some other information about the Lepchas. It accounts that in 1891, Lepchas (5762) comprises 18.91 per cent of total population of the state. The sex ratio was 1016 female per thousand male. Beside sex ratio no other information are available on the status of women among the Lepchas.

'Himalayan Village: An Account of the Lepchas of Sikkim' by Geoffrey Gorer (1938) can be considered as the first complete anthropological account of the Lepchas of Sikkim. The author visited and stayed among the Lepchas of Zongu to collect information for his study. Although the book was not well accepted by the Lepchas but the author has narrated a number of aspects on Lepcha women. On economic activities the author observed that "until the beginning of the century Lepchas used to weave all their own cloth, but nowadays only a couple of women bother to weave; people wear instead readymade and fairly shoddy clothes."(p. 53). Women are also entrusted with the task of weaving mats and blankets. "This weaving is ideally men's work, as the weaving of thread is women's, but a certain number of women are as good mat makers as any of the men, and there is felt to be no disgrace in employing articles made by women" (p. 67). He noticed Lepcha women to work even in construction of houses. The author used some photographs as evidence to show the women at work in clearing the ground and planting dry rice. A detailed description of Lepcha marriage and religion are also available in the study. The main defect which the educated Lepchas object and could not accept is the over emphasis of sexual life of the Lepchas in the narration.

Chi Nakane (1966) published his article 'A Plural Society in Sikkim' in C.V.Furer Haimendorf (ed) 'Caste and Kin in Nepal, India and Cylon'. The work is based on field work from three villages of Sikkim; Pabyuk (5 miles south-east of Gangtok), Phodang and Phensong (15 mile north of Gangtok). The work contains history of Sikkim, settlement pattern in each of the three villages, role of Lama in Monastery, kinship ties, Lepcha-Bhutia intermarriage etc. He prepared a list of clan or Moo as present in the study villages without making any specific distinction between the male and female moo. Here clan is not a sex linked phenomena and '98 per cent of the male members remained in the community after their marriage'. He noted that "as male members have a strong coherence in terms of a patrilineal kin group, most marriages are virilocal" (p. 235). Out of 46 cases of marriage in the study area 16 are within the community. Although the study recognizes the importance of clan in the Lepcha society it does not consider the existence of separate clan for the women in Sikkim.

Holdon Siiger's (1967) *The Lepchas: Culture and Religion of A Himalayan People* was published in two volumes. This ethnographic work is brilliant but very fragmented and based on folktales and oral versions from a few Lepchas of Sikkim and Kalimpong. It is widely used by the later anthropologists but from the context of women status, the work is not that relevant.

The only book written in Bengali *'Sikkimer Adibasi Lepcha'* (Lepcha: The Aboriginal Tribes of Sikkim) by A. Maitra (1974) has referred in nut sell a number of Lepcha accounts which includes their early history, present habitation, physical structure, socioeconomic position, language, marriage custom, religion, folk culture etc. Although over the period Lepcha society has changed from its earlier matriarchal to patriarchal structure due to the influence of the neighbouring dominant communities but the women could retained a higher position in their society. The author could notice use of mother's moo by the girl child and restrictions on marriage within the moo only in the village areas. He detailed out the marriage system of the Lepchas and the existence of bride price. The author mentions that either Boongthing or Mun performs death rituals but it is only Mun who can purify the spirit after death.

A.K. Banerjee and others (1980) prepared a detailed description of contemporary situation of the district of Darjeeling in his *District Gazetteer*. Among other things it also discussed the position of the Lepchas in the past and during the study period but not much about the role and position of women in the community and hence is not much relevant for us.

A.R. Foning, a Lepcha by himself put different aspects of Lepcha life including their beliefs, convictions, and such other matters of the Lepchas in 1987. *'Lepcha: My Vanishing Tribe'* can be considered as widely circulated and popular book on the Lepchas. The author gives an insiders view about the religion, clan, marriage etc of the tribe. Although the basic purpose of his study was not to assess the status of women solely but in course of describing the social system, the author in a number of places has mentioned the role and status of women in connection with the religious belief particularly their position as Mun and customs of marriage as performed by *Peeboo*, the go between. The position of women can be assessed from their mythology, folk tales and legends as used by the author.

Very recently J.R. Subba, an administrator turned writer, after gathering vast experience about the people of Sikkim during his long 32 years service in different departments of the state has come out with a book 'History, Culture and Customs of Sikkim' in 2008. It deals with the cultural history of each of the specific communities of Sikkim i.e. Lepcha, Bhutia, Limbu, Rai, Kiraties, etc. In the general historical part, Lepchas comprise an important place before the advent of the Tibetans in the country. One can gather a first hand knowledge about the demography, food habit, kinship, social organization, dress, folk songs, festivals, religious beliefs, marriage system etc of the Lepchas from the book. The author quoting Singh (1983) spares a full paragraph on the women folk of the Lepchas. "Women have no right of inheritance. They have a great role however in the agricultural operation from sowing to harvesting. They feed and nurture the animals, but women must never on any account kill an animal. They collect fuel and fodder for the family, and portable water from the spring. Women can spin and the men weave. Women have a role in other economic activities and social functions too. Women prepare the meal and distribute it in the family. They have a role in religious and ritual spheres. The Lepcha women can become a Mun (1983: 90: p. 253).

Beside all these, a good number of written materials on Lepchas are available in shape of article, report, government publication, periodicals, documentation etc. But none of these literature deals solely with the Lepcha women and in some very occasional cases mentions are made on different aspects of the Lepcha women. Without reviewing them thoroughly we prefer to mention some such works. G.C. Bagchi (1982), *From Semi Nomadism to Settled Agriculture*; L.B. Basnet (1974), *Sikkim: A Short Political History*; C.A. Bell (1905), *Final Report on the Survey and Settlement of the Kalimpong Government Estate in the District of Darjeeling – 1901-1903;* T.Chattopadhyay (1990), *Lepchas and Their Heritage;* D.D. Dahal (1984), *Sikkim Ko Rajnaitik Itihas* (in Nepali); E.T. Dalton (1872), *Descriptive Ethnology of Bengal*; A.K. Das and S.K. Banerjee (1962), *The Lepchas of Darjeeling District*; F.Donaldson (1900), *Lepcha Land or Six Weeks in the Sikkim Himalayas*; P. Lepcha (1999), *A Study of the Scottish Mission Work in Kalimpong Sub-division with Special Reference to the Lepcha Tribe*; H.H. Maharaja and Maharano Dolma of Sikkim (1908), *History of Sikkim*; G.B. Mainwearing (1876). *A Grammar of the Lepcha (Rong) Language*; R.V.W. Nebesky

(1956), *Where the Gods are Mountains : Three Years among the People of the Himalayas*; B.P. Niroula (1988), *Caste/Ethnic Composition of Population of Nepal;* H.H.Risley (1891), *Tribes and Castes of Bengal Ethnographic Glossary*; R. Sankrityanayan (1950), *Darjeeling Parichay (in Hindi);* R.N.Thakur (1988), *Himalayan Lepchas*; L.A.Waddell (1899), *Among the Himalayas and others.*

Literature of Tribal Study

India is the second largest country for the tribes in the world next to Africa. Nearly 8.00 per cent Indians are identified as tribal. In the Vedic and Sanskrit literature it is mentioned that some indigenous human group were living in India before the arrival of the Aryans. But the term tribe or tribal is the legacy of British rule in India. In the tribal literature a number of terms synonymous of tribe have been used. They are: primitive, indigenous, aboriginals, native, naïve, savage, adivasi, janajati. uncivilized, barbaric, depressed class, simple society, backward Hindus etc.

Beside the demographic strength, India is also the home-land of large variety of tribes. The diversity among the Indian tribes is so much so that it is yet to have a proper cataloging of the Indian tribes on the basis of their social and anthropological character. It is often roughly stated that there are around 450 – 500 variety of tribal community in India, But the Constitution of India identified as much as 747 entries of ST categories in different state's ST list. It is to note that some ST community are overlapping in more than one lists and at the same time there are some broad categories under which so many sub groups are merged together and which constitute around 1800 entries. Releasing the overlapping cases, Indian constitution has identified around 1200 variety of tribes.

The large number of population and their diverse groups make India as a fertile and virgin field of study for the sociologists and the anthropologists. Since British rule write ups on the tribes are made available by the administrators. researchers. travelers, etc. Existing literature on the tribals can be categorized from different angles: administrative, social, cultural, political, anthropological, economic, demographic and so on. Some studies are region specific, while others are community specific. Some works are carried out by examining the details about the individual community while others are connected with the tribal problems of the country as a whole. But almost no work have been attempted to unveil the status, position and role of women in any tribal society in particular and for all the tribes in general. Any way, the followings literatures are worth reading in connection with the tribal study.

T.Bagchi (1994), *Profile of Some Indian Tribes*; D.N. Bakse (1987), *Tribal Society of West Bengal*. (in Bengali); A.Bateille – (i) (1974), *Six essays in Comparative Sociology*. (ii) (1977), *The Definition of Tribe*, *(iii)* (1986), *The Concept of Tribe with Special Reference to India*; A.Bose, U.P.Sinha & R.P.Tyagi (ed), *Demography of Tribal Development*; N. K.Bose - (1980), *Tribal Life in India*; N.P.Chambe (ed). *Tribal Techniques, Social Organisation and Development*; K.D.Chattapadhyay- (i) (1978), *Tribalism in India*,*(ii)* (1978), *Tribalism in India*; B.Choudhuri (ed) (1990), *Tribal Development in India*; A.K.Danda (i) (1973). *Tribal Economics And Their Transformation*, (ii) (1988), *Tribes in India;* A.K.Das, B.K.Roy & M.K.Raha (1966), *Hand Book of Scheduled Castes and Scheduled Tribes of West Bengal*; A.K.Das. M.K.Raha & S.Dey (1990), *Tribal Situation In West Bengal*.; A.R.Desai (1971), *Tribes in Transition;* S.C.Dube (1977), *Tribal Heritage of India;* V.Elwin (1943), *The Aboriginals;* G. S.Ghurte (i) (1943), *The Aboriginals So Called And Their Future*, (ii) (1959), *The Scheduled Tribes;* C. V. F. Haimendorf (1982), *The Tribes of India: The Struggle for Survival;* J.J. Kattakayan (1983), *Social Structure and change among the Tribes : A Study among the Uralies of Idukki District of Kerala*; P.L. Mehta (1999), *Constitutional Protections to Scheduled Tribes in India in Retrospect and Prospect;* L.K.Mahapatra (1994), *Tribal Development in India: Myth And Reality*; D.N.Majumdar (i) (1937), *A Tribe In Transition: A Study in Cultural Pattern*, (ii) (1950), *Affair of A Tribe: A Study in Tribal Dynamics*; M.Miri (1997), *Continuity And Change In Tribal Society*; J.Pathy (1984), *Tribal Peasantry : Dynamics of Development*; B.K.Roy Burman, B.Chudduri &K. K.Mishra (ed) (2004), *Encyclopedia of Indian Tribes and Castes;* U.K. Roy,A.K.Das & M.K.Choudhuri (1982), *Planning for the Scheduled Tribes and Scheduled Castes: A West Bengal Perspectives*; Sachachidananda (1964), *Culture Change in Tribal Bihar: Munda And Oraon*; S.P.Sahay (1988), *Tribal Women Labours: Aspects of Economic and Physical Exploitation;* M.D.Sahlins (1968), *Tribesmen;* B.D.Sharma (i) (1978), *Tribal Development,(ii)*(1984), *Planning for Tribal Development;* K. S.Singh (i) (1982), *Transformation of Tribal Society: Integration vs Assimilation*,(ii) (1983), *Tribal Movement in India*,(iii) (1985), *Tribal Society in India: An Anthropo—historical Perspective, (iv)* (1982), *Economics of Tribes, (v)* (1993), *The Scheduled Tribes. People of India*; L.P.Vidyathi (i) (1964), *Cultural Contours of Tribal Bihar*,(ii) (1981), *Tribal Development And its Administration, (iii)* (1968), *Study Of Tribal Labours - Both Agricultural And Industrial In And Around Ranchi;* V. Xaxa (2003), *Tribes in India.*

Literature on Women Study

Women study has actually started after the UN Declaration of 1975 as International Women Year and 1975-85 as women's decade. The history of women study in India has its origin in different seminars, conferences, and workshops organized by different institutions and organizations after UN declaration of Women Year. The development of women study rests on the series of periodical conduct of such seminars, workshops and conferences. Literature on women study in India, thus, can be analyzed by dividing the source materials in two broad groups: a) seminar, workshop and conference and b) existing literature.

Seminar, Workshop and Conference

"In 1979, the first discussion on the nature and scope of women's study called it 'the new academic search to organize gather knowledge on various aspects of women's situations' (Mazumdar and Sharma, 1979). In 1981, a few concerned scholars decided to convene the first National Conference on Women's Studies. This conference started a serious debate on the objectives of Women's Studies and tried to outline alternative approaches to the development of the discipline in India. ...the UNESCO Conference on Women's studies in South and South East Asia (1983) attempted to expand the definition of Women Studies and described it as 'an instrument for social science development.'

In April 1985, a joint seminar co-sponsored by Indian Association of Women's Studies (IAWS) and UGC undertook the exercise to identify the purpose and objectives guiding the incorporation of Women's Studies in the University system." (Kumud Sharma,2002 in Malashri Lal ed. p. 42).

From 1986 women's study centers have started in different Universities and Colleges in India. At present UGC supports 36 such centres and 6 cells to study women perspectives country wide. All such study centers through regular periodic seminars, conferences and published works continued adding materials on women study in India. The major works of Indian women study are carried out by such sponsored centres and cells.

National Workshop on Women's Studies organized by ICSSR (1988) observed that Women's Studies can be introduced in the university system as distinct discipline.

The Indian Association of Women's Studies in collaboration with UGC organized a seminar on Women Studies in Chandigarh in 1999. It was decided that Women Studies should be considered as multidisciplinary in both teaching and research purposes.

The UGC and ICSSR have been recognized as apex bodies in the sphere of Women Study in India.

The UNESCO Conference on Women's Studies in South and South East Asia was organize in New Delhi during 4 – 8 October 1983 added new momentous to the Women Study in India. The conference identified some problems in connection with Women's study and tried to solve them.

Different Universities, colleges and institutions either of their own or under the sponsorship of different parent organization, conducted seminars, workshops etc on Women Study.

The SNDT University, Mumbai made a Report of the National Conferences on Women's Studies in 1981. SNDT Women's University Mumbai established a Women's Study Unit in 1974. This Women's Study Unit under the support of UGC organized a National Conference on Women in Bombay in 1980. Baroda centre for Women's Studies, Chandigarh presented a Seminar on Women's Studies under the joint sponsorship of IAWS and UGC in 1999.

The SNDT University and Delhi University are successful in establishing International linkages on Women issues in the academic circle. The Indian Institute of Advanced Study, Shimla organized a Workshop on 'Women's Studies Research and Curriculum in, October, 2001. Dr Malashri Lal and Dr Sukriti Paul Kumar came out with an edited copy of the workshop proceedings in 2002.

Among the established popular Indian Journals publishing articles on women's issue, *Economic and Political*

Weekly (EPW) is important. During late 1980's and 1990's a number of historical works on women have been published in *EPW*. It published its biannual *Review of Women's Studies* in April 1986. Since then EPW has become one of the important Indian Journal which concentrates on academic research work on women's studies.

Anyway, the present study concentrates on the status of women in tribal society particularly among the Lepchas. It is thus considered to be relevant to review the activities of the Centre for Women's Study (CWS), North Bengal University which locates with in the jurisdiction of Darjeeling district of West Bengal and Sikkim, the homeland of the Lepchas.

The Centre for Women's Studies, North Bengal University since its inception has been organizing periodical seminars, conferences, workshops, training programs on women issues. Some research works have also been carried out by the scholars and faculty members. The Centre has also coordinated in publishing books on women issues. In 2005 the Centre in collaboration with Northern Book Centre, New Delhi published six books on women of North Bengal. They are: 'Women Workers in Brick Factory' by Amal Mandal; 'Belief in Witch- Witch Killing in Doors' by Ananya Baruya; 'Facets of Feminism' by Raghunath Ghosh; 'Rural Muslim Women' by Seikh Rahim Mandal; 'Micro Finance for Women' by Samirindra Nath Dhar; 'Tribes Education and Gender Question' by Sanjay Roy. Among all these published works, Sanjay Roy made an elaborate study on tribal women in tea gardens of Doors areas of Jalpaiguri district. Although the study discussed at length the issue of tribal education particularly among the women but the areas of action does not cover the Lepcha dominated zone.

The Centre for Women Studies, North Bengal University at regular interval organizes seminars and conferences Although women remain the centre of discussion in all such seminars but no seminar so far was targeted for the tribal women. But in the multi dimensional issues, few research papers have been presented on tribal women. The paper entitled 'Story of Three Unknown Women Personalities in the Lepcha Society' presented by D.C.Roy at the UGC sponsored International Seminar on Women's Situation and Women's Studies: A South Asian Perspective during 18 -- 20 December, 2006 is relevant for the present study. It deals with some aspects of political status of women in the Lepcha society.

Existing Literature

Studies on Indian women date back to British period when the rulers on their own interest and some revolutionists worked with the women. The pioneering of them was Raja Rammohun Roy who was identified as 'Father of modern India', 'Champion of women's Rights', 'First Feminist in India'. He was very vocal and was against the system of Sati, a custom of burning the wife along with her husband.

There is a long list of social reformers who not only worked for the cause of the women but used their pen for expressing their independent concern about women. "In Bengal, Iswar Chandra Vidyasagar championed female education and led the campaign to legalize widow remarriage, and Keshub Chandra Sen, a leader of the Brahmo Samaj, sought to bring women into new roles through schools, prayer meetings, and experiments in living. By the turn of the century, Swami Vivekananda, the leader of an activist order of Hindu monasticism, was arguing that women could become a powerful regenerative force. In North India, Swami Dayananda Saraswati, the founder of the Arya Samaj, encouraged female education, condemned customs he regarded degrading to women: marriages between partners of unequal ages, dowry, and polygyny. At the same time, Rai Salig Ram (known as Huzur Maharaj), a follower of the

Radhasoami faith, advocated female emancipation in his volume of prose, *Prem Patra*. Among Muslims, Khwaja Altaf Husain Hali and Shaikh Muhammad Abdullah introduced education for girls. In western India, Mahadev Govind Ranade founded the National Social Conference to focus attention on social reforms. At the same time, the Parsee journalist Behramji Malabari captured the attention of the British reading public with his articles in The Times on the evils of child marriage and the tragedy of enforced widowhood for young women. Dhondo Keshav Karve offered a practical solution with his institutions in Poona to educate young widows to become teachers in girl's schools. In South India, R. Venkata Ratnam Naidu opposed the *devadasi* system while Virasalingam Pantulu worked for marriage reform. Both sought to increase opportunities for female education. (G. Forbes, 1998, pp. 19-20). During those periods the social reformers were more in action than in writings. More over the nature and pattern of social set up has changed a lot over the century. Indian society is fast dynamic and the problems with the women never remained the same.

The year 1975 is the critical year for the history of Indian women studies. "Between 1975 and 1979 thirty books on women were published, as many as the total produced over the previous several decades."(Forbes, F. 1998. 255). Within a decade or so the Indian market is flooded with a variety of works on Indian women but absolutely no work has been conducted on the status of women among the tribes in general and on the Lepchas in particular. As no books are directly related to our focused theme of tribal study, we prefer to just mention some of them and as such the purpose of review does not arise but the existing literature on women has been divided in two parts: a) Literature on Women and b) Literature on Tribal women.

However the following literature on women may be worth mentioning for the present study:

A. Agarwal & S.Narain - (1985), *Women and National Resources*; M.Allen & S.N.Muhkerjee - (2006), *Women in India and Nepal* ; T.A. Baig - (1976), *India's Women Power*; A. Baruya - (2005), *Belief in Witch – Witch Killing in Doors* ; A. Basu - (1976), *Indian Women*; Z. Bhatty - (1981), *The Economic Role and Status of Women in the Beedi Industry in India* ; P.K. Bhowmick - (1993), *Dynamics of Tribal Development* ; R. Choube & K. Saini (ed) - (2002), *Status of Women in Rural Societies* ; B. Chouduri (ed) -(1992), *Tribal Transformation in India* ; A.N. Das - (1992), *India Invented: A Nation in the Making*: N.Desai - (1967), *Women in Modern India* ; R.P.Devadas - (1999), *Women and Development*; M.P. Dodkey - (1999), *SHG's and Micro Credit Sustaining Rural Women*; G. Fobres - (1998), *Women in Modern India*; D. Jain (ed) - (1975), *Indian Women*; U.S. Jha & P.Pujari - (ed) (1996), *Indian Women Today, Tradition, Modernity and Challeng;* M. Lal and S.P.Kumar (ed) - (2002), *Women Studies in India*; A. Mandal - (2005), *Women Workers in Brick Factory;* K.Misra & J.H.Lower (ed) - (2007), *Recent Studies in Indian Women.: Empirical Work of Social Scientists*; R.K. Moorthy - (2001), *Capacity Building for Women*; S. Narasimham - (1999), *Empowering Women: An Alternative Strategy for Rural India;* R.N.Pati & L.Jagatdev (ed) – (1991), *Tribal Demography in India*; K.Prasad (ed) - (2006), *Women in Rural Development. Contemporary Social Policy and Practice;* S.Roy Mukherjee (ed) - (2006), *Indian Women: Status, Participation and Empowerment;* S. Roy - (2005), *Tribes Education and Gender Question;* R.K. Samanta (ed) - (2005), *Empowering Rural Women: Issues, Opportunities and Approaches;* P.R. Sanday - (1973), *Towards a Theory of Status of Women*; P. Sengupta - (1960), *Women Workers in India*; S.Singh - (2001), *Empowerment of Women: Miles to Go*; J. K. Soni - (2006), *Women Empowerment: Exploring the Fact;* M.N. Srinivas - (1978), *The Changing Position of Indian Women;* G.Tiwari - (2006), *Role of Women in Family.*

3

Overview of the People and the Region

Introduction

The present chapter intends to introduce the people and the study area. The chapter is divided in four sections: etymological meaning of the name Lepcha, boundary of the Lepcha land, short history of the land and the demographic profile of the Lepchas. Each section has further been divided in different parts as per the requirement of the study and the availability of the data. Apparently the chapter has nothing much in its direct relation with the status and role of women in the Lepcha society but it introduces the background of the study area and the people whom we are dealing with. The chapter is based solely on the available literature on the Lepchas and secondary data published by different authorities including the modern electronic media of internet facilities.

Etymological Meaning of Lepcha

Etymologically most tribes in the world are known by two sets of names – a) exoethnonym, the name by which the neighbors or the outsiders recognize the tribe and remained popular in the outside world and b) endoethnonym, the name the tribe use to identify themselves. Both types of names are generally referred to certain common characteristics or qualities to any tribe. Some of the characteristics may glorify the tribe while others may at the same time used in derogatory sense. Study of etymological, both exoethnonym and endoethnonym, meanings of tribe names from the prevailing tradition, legends, folktales and folklores help to unveil the history of the society with its self recognition and identity.

The exoethnonym name of the tribe under study is 'Lepcha' by which they are popularly recognized in the outside world. Their endoethnonym name is Mutanchi Rongkup Rumkup or in short Rong.

Exoethnonym Meaning:

There is no unanimity among the writers, social scientists and the researchers regarding the exoethnonym name 'Lepcha' given to the tribe. Some say that it is a derivation from the Nepali word 'Lapche' means 'vile speaker'. Regarding the derivation of the term Mainwaring was not sure but says "it may be considered to have become Auglicised; I do not know the origin of the word, but it is doubtless a denomination of the Gorkhas." (G.B.Mainwaring, 1876, P- VII).

The term 'Lapchey' given by the Nepalese has out rightly been rejected by K.P.Tamsang, the Lepcha scholar. In his view, "it is most derogatory and unfavourable to the Lepchas, for, the Lepchas are in truth not scurrilous speakers. Because their language is the most simple and pure... one and not a single abusive, indecent, obscene, slang or vulgar word exists in the language as commonly found in all the other languages of the world." (K.P..Tamsang, 1983, P- 2).

Das and Banerjee are of the view that the word is not derogatory but credit worthiness for their 'submissive temperament'. It is also said that the name came from its similarity with a fish found in Nepal, 'Lapche' which is very submissive like that of the Lepcha people who are very mild and quite disposition.

The Limbu version of the term does not mean a complementary but it means a person who instead of bringing presentation of pig brought presentation of fowl to his father-in-laws. Hence, the term Lepcha i.e. who 'uses animal having feathers'.

Sonam Wangdi Lepcha could find some other derivation of the term. He opined that 'Lepchas were animists' by tradition who used to worship nature from such mounted places they call 'Lapcho'. Hence it is natural to draw a similar word for the people who use it. 'Lapcho' and 'Lepcha' are so similar that it is difficult for the outsiders to differentiate between the two words. The author could find that 'Lapcho' do not necessarily mean 'worshipping place' but instead 'a place to take rest'.

In Lepcha the term also means 'to wait or to observe'. Since the 13th century the motherland of the tribe has been ruled by the Tibetans, Bhutanese, British but no one could stay permanently in the divine land. So the term indicates to wait and observe what comes next. It relates to the basic nature of the tribe who talks less and observes more about the happenings all around. It is believed that Lepchas will survive in this region so long bamboo grows in this part of the land.

Whatever may be the exoethnonym meaning of the term, the outside world popularly recognizes the tribe by the name 'Lepcha'. In modern days when the fellow tribe introduce themselves to the outsiders, they do use this exoethnonym name only. It is so much popular among them that they have started using it as their surname. In the earlier days Moo, the clan name or the place of origin, was used as surname but recently most of them irrespective of their sex have started using 'Lepcha' as their surname.

Endoethnonym Meaning

The endoethnonym meaning of the tribe is *Mutanchi Rongkup Rumkup* or in short *Rong*. This means the son of the snowy peak and the son of God. This meaning of the tribe relates to their divine origin. According to their folklore Lepchas originated from the peak of Kanchanjunga. God first created *Fodongthing*, the male out of the snow by his left hand and then created *Nazaongnyo*, the female by his right hand as his partner from the pure snow of Kanchanjunga. The Lepchas proclaim themselves as *Rongkup*, which means son of snowy peak. As God is their creator, they identify themselves as *Rumkup* that means the son of God. In Lepcha *Rong* means mountain and Rum means God.

Quoting *Namthar* (Lepcha religious writings in manuscript form), R.N.Thakur says "human being is the last creation of God. Rum, God out of pure snow from the top of the mount Kanchanjunga made shape of a man into which He infused nine *Nongyong* and then life appeared. That person was named '*Fudongthing*'. Perceiving his state of loneliness God thought of creating his partner. Then God made another shape of a woman from the body of *Fudongthing* (thus causing only eight *Nongyong* in case of a male). She was named '*Nuzong Nyu*'. They started living like friends in the place known as '*Ne Mayel Kyong*', a place near Kanchanjunga. But when they started behaving like husband and wife God angered upon them and send them nine steps down to the world.". (1988: pp. 24-25).

Boundary of Lepcha Land

From various sources both written and oral, hearsay accounts and folktales, customs,and tradition, R.N. Thakur (p. 37) demarcates the boundary of original Lepcha land. In the north it was extended up to Kanchanjunga while Jalpaiguri in the south. In the east it was extended up to river Rudok at Paro valley under Ha province of Bhutan and the western boundary was spread up to Ruchong and Runga (Arun and Tambur) river making boundary with Nepal. Lyangsong Tamsang opined that Lepcha land was extended up to Titalia now in Bangladesh. Titalia is a Lepcha word means 'to retreat'. In a battle between Sikkim Raj and Nepal Raj, the Lepcha battalion chased the Gorkha force up to Titaliya from where they had to come back. Lepchas used to call their own land *Ne Mayel Lyang* or *Mayal Lyang* – the land of the holy and eternal purity having the rule of the honorable people.

Observation of different scholars and authors [like Dozey, O'Malley, Donaldson, Bell, Mainwaring etc.] regarding the intimate relation of Lepchas with all the animate and inanimate objects of Sikkim Himalayas, unequivocally establish that Lepchas are the indigenous people of the region. They were completely dependent on forest for their day-to-day life and were using land without any restrictions imposed from any side. But different alien communities like Tibetan, Bhutanese, Europeans, and Nepalese etc. had overrun the indigenous group, in different periods of time. In the process they have been scattered, cornered and become minority in their own land.

At present, Lepchas, the autochthonous people of the Eastern Himalayas, spread over the hilly regions of Darjeeling, Sikkim, Eastern Nepal and Western Bhutan. Majority of them reside in Sikkim; in Darjeeling spatial concentration is found in Kalimpong sub-division; in Bhutan and Nepal the proportion of Lepchas are very negligible.

Short History of Lepcha Land

The spread of Lepcha population over the three different countries India, Nepal and Bhutan, is not due to their migratory character but due to the political history of the region. Political change and corresponding reshuffling of boundaries forced the Lepchas to be ruled by different authorities at different times or at the same time by different authorities at different places. Let us discuss in brief the political change in the region historically and see how the Lepchas in their own land got separated among themselves.

Lepcha king *Turvey* or *Turvey Punu* (king), the notable figure in Lepcha history reigned the *Ne Mayal Lyang* during 1420 approximately. After *Turvey Punu*, another if not the last leading spiritual figure was *Thi-Kung-Tek*. The 'Blood Treaty' signed between *Thi-Kung-Tek* and *Khye-Bumsa*, Tibetan counterpart, paved the way for long lasting Tibetan suzerainty over Sikkim. This treaty ultimately smoothed the way for Phuntso Namgyal who officially ascended the throne of Sikkim in 1642. The historical Blood Treaty, thus, coolly arrested the Lepchas, the yeoman of the soil, under the reign of the Tibetans, the first alien ruler of the region.

With some ups and downs in their relation with the monarch, Lepchas still inhabited in their own land obviously under the rule of Namgyal dynasty, the Tibetan rulers. The Bhutanese made the first artificial cleavage between Lepchas of Sikkim and Kalimpong. Bhutan attacked Sikkim and fought with Lepcha king *Punu Gaeboo-Achyok* at Damsang area and ultimately occupied the entire land including the Kingdom from 1700 to 1707. Later on at the request from Dalai Lama, the religious supreme of Bhutan and Sikkim, Bhutan returned from Sikkim but refused to evacuate the Damsang area i.e. east of Teesta presently known as Kalimpong. Thus, since 1707 Lepchas of Kalimpong permanently came under the Bhutanese rule while the Tibetans ruled their brothers and relatives on the other part of Teesta. Lepchas, although ruled by the Tibetans, were the dominant community in Sikkim while in Bhutan their proportion was very negligible and were treated second-class citizen by the ruler.

The third division among the Lepchas of Sikkim occurred in 1835 through an agreement between the East India

Company and the King of Sikkim. Through this agreement, the Rajah of Sikkim presented Darjeeling to the company out of friendship to construct a sanatorium for the British soldiers. All the lands south of the Great Rungeet River, east of the Balasur, Kahail, and Little Rangeet Rivers, and west of Rungno and Mahanuddi Rivers came under the control of East India Company. This grant not only further divided the Lepcha land but also its inhabitants particularly the Lepchas. This political division again segregated Lepchas in their own land. The Lepcha as a community came under three different alien rulers – Tibetans in Sikkim, Bhutanese in Damsang area and British in Darjeeling area.

The fourth political reshuffling occurred in 1865 when Kalimpong and the adjoining areas were taken over by the British from the Bhutan through a war. The British Company administered the entire area of Darjeeling including Kalimpong from its Head quarter at Darjeeling. Due to this political change, Lepchas of Kalimpong and Darjeeling areas came under the same political authority. But some Lepchas across the boundary on the Bhutan still remain under the rule of Bhutanese. They still remain separated from their counterpart residing in present Darjeeling including Kalimpong and Sikkim. Lepchas in Bhutan became insignificant compared to other community. At this stage also three foreign rulers – Tibetans in Sikkim, Bhutanese in Bhutan and British in Darjeeling including Kalimpong ruled the Lepchas.

Another political change occurred in August 1947 when India acquired independence. Darjeeling became a district under the state of West Bengal and the Lepchas remained insignificant (population wise). Even in their own homeland Darjeeling, by this time they became minority due to the then British policy of inviting Nepalese from Nepal. Calcutta or Delhi became the administrative headquarter for the Lepchas of Darjeeling, Gangtok for Lepchas of Sikkim and Thimpu for the Lepchas of Bhutan. Lepchas have no role at all to play in any of these administrative headquarters.

It has been reported that some Lepchas are residing along the western part of Bhutan where the country borders with Kalimpong sub-division of India. But no details regarding the strength of population, attitude of the monarch towards the community, role of the community in administration etc. are available. Hence, we leave any further discussion on Lepchas of Bhutan by recognizing their presence in that country.

Lepchas witness another political change when the state of Sikkim from its monarchical rule merged with India as a separate state in 14th May 1975. Sikkim is the only state in India where majority of Lepchas reside. But their population compared to the total population of the state is not appreciable because of immigration of Nepalese and Tibetans during the monarchical rule. Considering the original homeland of Lepchas, the state of Sikkim has reserved Dzongu, an area of 15,845 hectares specifically for the Lepchas. No other community, tribal or non-tribal, is allowed to reside permanently in Dzongu. In true sense, Dzongu is the present day *Mayal Lyang* for the Lepchas where land had not been alienated to any other community. They also use their own language at home and observe most of traditional customs and culture. The total area under the present day *Mayal Lyang* thus confined to 15,845 hectares with a population of 7745 including 3414 seasonal labors from Nepal as per 1981 census. Dzongu falls in the north district of Sikkim, which is bounded, by Nepal in the west, Tibet in the north and other three districts of Sikkim in the south. Lepchas of Sikkim, thus, politically changed from monarchical rule to a democratic system. But they are under the same union government like those of Darjeeling areas. At this stage Lepchas were residing in India in the states of West Bengal and Sikkim.

In the recent past Lepchas of Darjeeling district had to face another change when the three sub-divisions came under the direct administration of Darjeeling Gorkha Hill Council (DGHC) since 1988. After violent agitation, DGHC was formed through democratic procedure within the state of West Bengal. In case of policy-making and administration, Lepchas of Darjeeling are at present in a different position than the Lepchas in Sikkim. Here in Darjeeling under DGHC, Lepchas are facing Panchayet at the village level, DGHC at the district level, State Government at the state level and ultimately the Central Government at the all India level.

Beside all these, since long some Lepchas are residing in Illam areas of Nepal. Illam is situated on the extreme eastern Nepal bordering with Darjeeling and Sikkim.

Three arguments may be put for the existence of Lepchas in Nepal. Firstly, it may be inferred that once upon a time the Lepcha land, *Mayal Lyang* might have been extended up to Illam. Several attacks by the Gorkhas and counter attacks by the Lepchas or Namgyal Dynasty constantly changed the geographical boundary of both the monarchical states of Sikkim and Nepal. History of the region also witnessed a number of wars organized mainly by the Gorkhas to encroach the neighbouring lands. The Sikkim Puttee Rajah presented the Lepcha populated areas of Illam or it might have been seized by the Gorkhas from Sikkim before the Darjeeling area was gifted to East India Company in 1835. All the lands of Illam including its inhabitants, thus, separated from their fellow countrymen in Darjeeling and Sikkim areas and were controlled by the monarchical rule of Nepal. Secondly, the simple Lepchas of *Mayal Lyang* particularly Damsang areas could not resist the constant oppression by the Bhutanese from the east. Bhutan occasionally plundered these areas and took away both the assets and women to Bhutan. In search a safe place, a group of peace loving common Lepchas might have migrated towards the west and took shelter in Illam areas, which is far away from Bhutan. Thirdly, traditionally Lepchas used to practice shifting cultivation. In the slash and burn methods they usually cultivate a plot of land for 3-5 years and left it vacate to allow jungle to grow for the next 8-10 years. In the process of shifting from one place to another, a group of Lepchas might have been stayed back and settled permanently in Illam areas of Nepal.

Demographic Profile

Lepchas live in the southern face of the Eastern Himalayas and call their land Mayal Lyaang which later has politically been divided and at present fall in three countries—India, Nepal and Bhutan. Hence the Lepcha population can be found in these three countries. It is so because the land and population, remain the same but they are politically been reshuffled and ruled by different states. In India Lepchas are found in the states of Sikkim and West Bengal. Their main concentration in West Bengal is in the district of Darjeeling. In Darjeeling again they are found more in the subdivision of Kalimpong. In Nepal, Lepchas are found in the eastern part particularly in Illam district. The western part of Bhutan bordering with Kalimpong sub-division particularly the Chamurchi area is the main concentration of Lepchas in Bhutan.

As the Lepchas fall under three independent states, there is no single agency entrusted with the work of collecting demographic details of the Lepchas. Not only the agencies but the method of collection and period of collection are also not matching among these countries. Transparency, accessibility and availability of demographic details in the three countries differ due to their separate political form of government and administration. However an attempt with known limitations, for the first time, has been made to study and examine the Lepcha population in all the three countries.

1. *Lepcha Population in Nepal*

Lepchas are considered as minority indigenous people of

Nepal who have settled from ancient times in the eastern side of Mai Khola in Illam district. Beside Illam Lepchas are also found in small numbers in Dhan Kuta and other districts. The following Table 3.1 shows Lepcha population in Nepal for the decade 1991 – 2001.

Table - 3.1
Lepcha Population in Nepal

Year	*Lepcha population*	*%of total population*	*Change over ten years*
1991	4826	0.03	—
2001	3660	0.02	1166

Source: 1. For 1991 : Niroula 1998, pp. 15-56
2. For 2001: http://en.wikipedia.org/wiki/Demographics_of_Nepal.

Details about Lepcha population in Nepal are not available but a general look reveals two aspects of Lepcha population in Nepal. Firstly, the Lepchas comprise very negligible proportion of the total population of the country. With the decrease in Lepcha population, their proportion to the total population of Nepal has decreased from 0.03 per cent in 1991 to 0.02 per cent in 2001. Secondly, the Lepcha population has decreased by 1166 heads over ten year period of 1991 and 2001. It is difficult to justify and believe such a downsizing Lepcha population over the last ten years. We admit that the sources of data for the two periods are not the same and this may be to some extent responsible for the decrease in Lepcha population. As the present study does not centrally focused on demographic details of the Lepchas we leave this aspect for the time being with a note on its creditability and expect that some one may take up the matter more seriously for further research work.

2. *Lepcha Population in Bhutan*

Much about Lepcha population in Bhutan is not available. They live in the south and south-western part of Bhutan which are mostly adjoining Indian boundary. Lepchas live mostly in the valleys and low hills of the south west Bhutan where there is shortage of good farm land. Lepchas are banned to live in the central inner Himalayan region of Bhutan. They have been granted citizenship of Bhutan. But they suffer tremendous discrimination. It is learnt that Lepchas of Bhutan have mostly adopted the life style of the Nepalese. They use their mother tongue for day to day purposes and prefer Nepali rather than Dzongkha, the state language of Bhutan as their second language. Their economic condition is pathetic and none of them are either in any government service nor are they absorb in any kind of non land activities. Illiteracy is very common and they subsist solely on agriculture. Any way, the following Table 3.2 shows Lepcha population in Bhutan.

Table - 3.2
Lepcha Population in Bhutan

Year	*Lepcha population*	*% of total population*	*Change in ten years*
1990	28,100	1.82	—
1995	30,200	1.84	+2100
2000	34,700	1.88	+4500

Source: http://www.global12ptoject.com/2004/profiles/ _P code cs/341.html.

We cannot instantly verify the demographic profile of Lepchas in Bhutan. But the experts on the Lepchas and the portfolio holders of the Indigenous Lepcha Tribal Association HQ Kalimpong are of the opinion that this figure is ambiguous, confusing and vague and are much on the higher side. As the present study has not much linked with the demographic profile of the Lepchas in Bhutan, we leave this matter here for some one to study it in details.

3. ***Lepcha Population in India***

Lepchas have been identified and recognized as

Scheduled Tribe in three states in India: Sikkim, West Bengal and Tripura. But their main concentration remains in the North district of Sikkim and Darjeeling district of West Bengal. As per Indian Constitution a person is said to belong to ST if he/she belongs to any of the tribes specified in the ST list Modified Order, 1956 of the concern state. Although Lepchas are found in different states of India, may be in lesser number, but they are recognized as ST in the states of Sikkim, West Bengal and Tripura. We prefer to mention the demographic profile of the Lepchas only in these three states where they are identified as Scheduled Tribe.

Lepcha Population in Tripura

Tripura, one of the smallest states in India lies in the eastern part of the country bordering with Bangladesh and Myanmar.in Tripura Lepchas reside in the West Tripura district. In 1961, 71.43 per cent Lepchas in Tripura was Hindu and 28.57 per cent was Buddhist. The 1971 census showed a change in Lepcha religion where the percentage of Hindus decreased to 57.14 and the remaining 42.86 per cent became Christian. Any way, the available population of the Lepchas in Tripura is shown in Table - 3. 3.

Table – 3.3
Lepcha Population in Tripura

Year	*Lepcha Population*	*Ten Years*	*% of state ST population*
1961	07	—	.002
1971	14	7	.003
1981	—	—	—
1991	111	—	.01

Source: a) For 1961 &1971: Census of India
b) For 1991: http://www.neportal.org/north eastfiles/tripura/population/Scheduled Tribe Population 19..........

Lepcha population in Tripura has increased both in absolute number and percentage to state ST population. Lepcha population has doubled over ten years period 1961 to 1971 and become eight times within next twenty years. Lepcha population in Tripura is so negligible that it fails to catch the attention of the scholars on the Lepchas. All scholars on Lepchas focus their study on Sikkim and/or Darjeeling without even mentioning the case of Tripura. But the Lepchas whatever may be the number could attract the attention of the political leaders in enlisting themselves in the category of ST of the state. "It is a known fact that Tripura, due to political and other reasons in most cases follow West Bengal and hence recognized Lepchas as ST without considering much about their demographic details". (D.C. Roy 2005: p. 44).

Lepcha Population in Sikkim

It has traditionally been accepted that the Lepchas are the autochthones of present day Sikkim which they called *Mayal Lyang* . As per their mythology each Lepcha has his/her distinct '*Aagit*', clan; a *Chu*, a mountain deity and a *Daa*, a lake in the mountain and a *Lyep*, door to enter the Mayal Lyang where their ancestors are believed to wait for welcoming them. All the four aspects are linked with Kanchanjunga, located in the state of Sikkim. In all important occasions like birth, marriage, death and any other household customs, Lepcha Mun, priestess and Bongthing, priest invoke Kanchanjunga , their mother deity. Most Lepcha folklore and folktales are linked with Sikkim, their original place of residence. It is believed that *Fodongthing* and *Nazaongnyo*, the first primogenitors of the Lepchas were created out of virgin snow of Kanchanjunga. In a word Sikkim and Kanchanjunga closely related with the life style of the Lepchas. They consider Sikkim as their original homeland. Following Table-3.4 shows Lepcha population in Sikkim.

The growth of Lepcha population in Sikkim is never uniform and follows any specific trend. There are negative growth rates of Lepcha population for the years 1921 and 194 but the social scientists could not give a single reason for such negative growth. It is also difficult to explain the fluctuation in the figure relating to the percentage of Lepcha population to the total population of the state. It is hard to accept such unreasonable and irrational demographic data. As the present purpose does not allow us to collect primary data on Lepcha population nor any alternate source of data is available we are using it with our note of dissatisfaction and reliability on it.

Table – 3.4

Lepcha Population in Sikkim

Year	*Lepcha Population*	*Ten years*	*% of state total population*
1891	5762	-	18.92
1901	7313	+1551	—
1911	9031	+1718	11.29
1921	9021	-10	—
1931	13060	+4039	11.89
1941	12523	-537	10.31
1951	13756	+1233	9.99
1961	-	-	—
1971	22316	+4280	10.63
1981*	23234	+918	7.34
1991	29854	+6620	7.35
2001	40586	+10732	7.51

Source: a) For the period 1891. The Gazetteer of Sikkim by H. Risley, Bengal Government Secretariat Calcutta, 1894.
b). For the period 1901 to 1951, Census of India, West Bengal, 1951.
c). For the period 1971-1991, Government of India, Language Division.

Note: *K.S. Singh (ed.) Peoples of India (1994) p. 689 shows Lepcha population in Sikkim for the year 1981 as 24952 which is 1718 head more than that shown by language division, Govt. of India.

It may be mentioned that the sex ratio of the Lepchas in Sikkim for the year 2001 is 945 female per thousand male. It is much higher than the over all sex ratio of female per thousand male of Sikkim. It may be mentioned that Sikkim recorded the lowest female ratio of 832 in India. The female ratio for the Lepchas (945 per thousand male) is even higher than that of all India ratio of 933for the census year 2001.

Lepcha Population in West Bengal

In West Bengal Lepchas are found in the hilly region of the district of Darjeeling and their main concentration is in Kalimpong sub-division. It was the British who first entered this track and identified the Lepchas as the original inhabitants of the region.

No written documents about the Lepchas are available before the introduction of the British in Darjeeling. In 1835 when British look over the possession of Darjeeling track "there was a collection of 20 huts with a population of 100 souls" (Dozey, 1916: p. 48). It can easily be experienced that Lepchas were the only inhabitants of the entire hill area but within few years due to British policy of immigration Lepchas became minority in their own land. Anyway, following table-3.5 shows the Lepcha population of West Bengal and Darjeeling district.

In the state of West Bengal, Lepchas are concentrated in the district of Darjeeling since the by gone days. But their percentage in their own homeland compared to the total population of the district is not at all notable. Due to large number of immigration, the Lepchas in their own homeland become a negligible fraction of the total population of the district.

Table – 3.5
Lepcha Population in West Bengal and Darjeeling.

LEPCHA POPULATION				
West Bengal			*Darjeeling*	
Year	*Total*	*Ten years*	*Total*	*% Of W.B. Population*
1872	3952	-	3952	100.00
1881	26	-	NA	-
1891	9717	+2882.5	9717	100.00
1901	10052	+335	9972	99.20
1911	9842	-210	9706	98.62
1921	9669	-173	9669	100.00
1931	12719	+3050	12101	95.14
1941	12468	-251	12468	100.00
1951	13430	+962	13168	98.02
1961	15309	+1879	14510	94.78
1971	14568	-741	13536	92.92
1981	23409	+8841	22749	97.18
1991	27888	+4449	26920	96.53
2001	32377	4489	31210	96.39

Source: For the year 1872 to 1951: Census of India West Bengal 1951.P- 115
For the year 1961: census of India West Bengal Part V-A (ii) Special Table on Schedule Tribe 1961.
For 1971, Census of India, West Bengal. Special Table on Scheduled Tribe 1971. P. 268.
For 1981, Census of India, West Bengal. Series – 23 Part IX (IV) Special Tables for Scheduled Tribes. PP. 78-90.
For 1991, Information received over telephone from the Office of Census Operation, Calcutta, West Bengal.
For 2001, Census of West Bengal, CD published by the Directorate of Census of India.

The percentage of Lepcha population to total population of the district of Darjeeling remained very negligible from the beginning of the last century. In percentage term their proportion is also decreasing over the decades. But when the British came in this region, they found that the majority of population was Lepchas.

Census documents on Lepcha population for both West Bengal and Sikkim reveal a sort of erratic behaviour and hence unacceptable. The presence of negative growths (in the decades of 1921 and 1941 both in West Bengal and Sikkim and in 1911 and 1971 in West Bengal) makes the population figure very much doubtful. This erratic behavior needs indebt study, which is beyond the scope of the present study, but some should take up the matter seriously. Surprisingly some scholars [Das, 1978: 28-35; Ghosal. 1990: 23-28] go on narrating such doubtful data without even mentioning any single word about their creditability. It is so much so that some scholars [Thakur, 1988: 62-66, Lepcha, 1979: 162-166], go on finding the causes of such slow growth. The administration for known causes is least bothered and remained silent. The community neither at any individual level nor at Association level ever put any protest against such an unrealistic document. This ignorance can simply be defined as a tribal character of accepting every thing without judging and protesting among the Lepchas. Ignoring every thing we here just note about the insignificant proportion of Lepcha population in their own homeland.

World Lepcha Population

Demographic structure of Lepcha population for the countries like India, Nepal and Bhutan has been collected by different agencies whose purpose, period and method of collection are not the same. Keeping in mind all such conceptual, methodological, practical difficulties and their degree of reliability of data, here we have added Lepcha population in three countries with the sole purpose of getting some idea about the world Lepcha population. The following Table - 3.6 shows world Lepcha population for the period 1991 & 2001.

Table -3.6
World Lepcha Population for the period 1991 & 2001

	INDIA						
Year	*Sikkim*	*West Bengal*	*Tripura*	*Total in India*	*Bhutan**	*Nepal*	*World Total*
1	2	3	4	5	6	7	8
1991	29854	12888	111	42853	28100	4826	75,779
2001	40568	32377	—	72945	34700	3660	1,11,305

* Census figure for Bhutan is available for 1990 & 2000.

** Total figure for 2001 does not include population in Tripura

It should be noted that Lepcha residents of other countries and even Indian citizens residing other than those of West Bengal, Sikkim and Tripura are not available and hence not added in the world Lepcha population figure. So world Lepcha population can no way be less than the figure shown above. The table 3.6 is not a comprehensive statement of Lepcha population in the world but it is self explanatory. The strength and voice of more than one lakh population, if united, can do a lot for themselves and for the cause of humanity. The figure also discard, reject and nullify all such statements of **downfall** (Mainwaring, 1875): **vanishing** (L.A.Waddell, 1899 & A.R.Foning, 1987); **disappearing and dying** (O'Malley, 1905): **verge of extinction** (A.K.Das, 1987) and the like made for the Lepchas from time to time.

4

Study Area: A Brief Profile

Introduction:

It has been stated in the previous chapter that the Lepchas are the aboriginals of the southern face of the Eastern Himalayas. They are the subjects of three countries: India, Nepal and Bhutan. India is their basic homeland and their main concentration is in Darjeeling district of West Bengal and North district of Sikkim. In Darjeeling, Lepchas are found mainly in Kalimpong sub-division.

The present study is based on primary data collected from two different sources: (a) village level and (b) institutional level. Four villages from Kalimpong sub-division have been chosen for investigation. They are: Mane Gumba, Tashiding Busty, Khamdung and Lower Beyong. The main attributes of selecting villages are: location, social set up, economic back ground, religion and political profile. Information collected from the villages is the basis of examining the main contention of the study i.e. identifying the status of women in the Lepcha society. Among the institutions, two colleges located in Kalimpong town have been chosen to collect data in order to substantiate the information collected from the villages. College is the centre of multi- cultural, multi-ethnic, multi-religious, and multi-linguistic gathering of students from different background and region. College is the representation of different village and community. It is assumed that through the students we can know about the village and community they belong to. The two colleges selected for the present study are: Kalimpong College and Cluny Women's College.

Place of Study

Area-wise Kalimpong (1074.81 sq. km.) is the largest among four sub-divisions of the district of Darjeeling (3149.00 sq.km) of West Bengal. The district is located between 27013' and 26031' north latitude and between 88053' and 87059' east longitude. Kalimpong is on 27034' north latitude and 88 029' east longitudes. It is a hilly sub-division and is bounded by Bhutan in the east, Sikkim in the north, Jalpaiguri district in the south and river Teesta on the west. Kurseong and sadar sub-divisions of Darjeeling are on the western bank of river Teesta.

Initially, Mayal Lyaang, the original home land of the Lepchas was spread up to mountain range of Ha Valley in the east which included the whole of present Kalimpong sub-division. In 1700 Bhutan captured the whole of Sikkim and eventually evacuated the portion west of Teesta in 1707 after the request of Dalai Lama. Bhutan retained the whole area east of Teesta under its possession till 1865 when British annexed Kalimpong by military war. Since then it merged with Darjeeling district of West Bengal.

The change of administration over the century has its direct bearing on the composition of population of the sub-division of Kalimpong. The entire region including Kalimpong was inhabited by the Lepchas during their rule over Mayal Lyaang before 1642. During Namgyal rule, Tibetans started residing mostly in the north - eastern part of Sikkim without affecting much the composition of population in Kalimpong area. Bhutan occupied the area for 165 years (1700 to 1865) and their settlement confined along the sides of of Kalimpong - Thimpu road passing through Algarh and Lava. In order to save themselves from Bhutanese attack, oppression and plunder, the Lepchas were cornered and shifted to the far off villages. But their village remains homogeneous in nature. Drastic change in demographic structure of the area has taken place during the British rule (after 1865) when the rulers not only allow but also invited and encouraged,other communities to settle in order to facilitate their administration. The new settlers from Nepal, Bihar, Rajasthan and other parts of Bengal came in such a huge number that Kalimpong become a multi-ethnic region. The proportion of the Lepchas to total population started decreasing and ultimately become negligible and they remained confined in the remote village.

In Kalimpong majority of the Lepchas are found in Kalimpong II and Garubarhan CD block. Area-wise Garubathan (441.9 sq km) is the largest CD block in the district with lowest density (123 per sq. km.) compared to 511 for the district as per 2001 census.

Kalimpong is basically a village based sub-division with agriculture as the primary sector of engagement. The following Table - 4.1 shows the nature of engagement of the population under the different CD blocks of the study area.

In the background of the above let us now discuss the specific details about each of the village of our study area.

Village Study

Information for the present study has been collected from two sources: village level and industrial level. Village level information has been collected from four villages of Kalimpong sub-division. They are: Mane Gumba, Tashiding Busty, Khamdung and Lower-Beyong. Institutional level information has been gathered from two colleges located in Kalimpong town: Kalimpong College and Cluny Women's College.

Table - 4.1

Percentage distribution of worker & non-worker in the study CD block – 2001

CD block / Sub-division	Total workers	Categories of Workers							
		Cultivators Labors	Agr hold	House-workers Workers	Other Workers	Main Workers	Marginal Workers	Non	Total Population.
1	2	3	4	5	6	7	8	9	10
Kalimpong-I	27112 (40.1)	12531 (46.2)	4400 (16.2)	1039 (3.8)	9142 (33.7)	19485 (28.8)	7627 (11.3)	40568 (59.9)	67680
Kalimpong-II	24089 (39.0)	12462 (51.7)	4596 (19.1)	687 (2.9)	6344 (26.3)	16829 (27.0)	7260 (12.0)	36174 (61.0)	60263
Garubathan	22848 (42.1)	7551 (33.0)	3742 (76.4)	2047 (9.0)	9508 (41.6)	15971 (29.4)	6877 (12.7)	31431 (57.9)	54279
Kalimpong (M)	13382 (31.1)	69 (0.5)	129 (1.0)	233 (1.7)	12951 (96.8)	12397 (28.8)	985 (2.3)	29616 (68.9)	42998
Kalimpong Sub-division	87541 (38.8)	32613 (37.3)	12867 (14.7)	4006 (4.6)	37945 (43.4)	64682 (28.7)	22749 (10.1)	137789 (61.2)	225220

Source: *Statistical Hand Book*, Darjeeling - Bureau of Applied Economics and Statistics, Govt of West Bengal, 2003. pp. 28-30.

Basic Information of the Study Village

On the basis of location, religion, distance from town, concentration of Lepcha population etc four villages have been considered suitable and feasible for the present study. Basic information of these villages are:

Village–Mane Gumba

Mane Gumba village comes under Sindibong *Khasmahal* of Kalimpong-I CD Block. It is located at a distance of four km north-east of Kalimpong town. From Jore Bunglow of Darjeeling Sadar sub-division the SH-12 passes through Peshok, Lopchu to meet NH-31A and after crossing Teesta it passes through Kalimpong town towards north to reach Lava and then towards south for Gorubathan and Maynaguri of Jalpaiguri district. Although SH-12 passes through Mane Gumba village from east to west but bulk of the houses lie on the southern slope of the road.

The village received its name after an old Buddhist *Gumba* (monastery) of the locality. It is reported that the monastery was originally located at Dungra Busty where the present 11th mile *Gumba* is located. But during the Bhutan rule (1700 – 1865), the villagers had to shift the monastery to their village due to clash with the Bhutanese monks. But under the patronage and financial help from the Bhutan Raj particularly Bhutan Queen whose house is just bordering the village, the villagers constructed the present monastery. The hearsay also supports that in 19th century one Passang Namgyel Lepcha had been send to Thimpu for Lama training who later joined the *Gumba* as head Lama. The great grand-son of Passang Namgyel Lepcha is the present head lama of the Gumba and is using all landed property of the *Gumba*.

Sindipong or Sindibong is the corrupted form of Lepcha word – *Sying-Li-Pung* (*Sying* means a kind of tree, *Li* means house and *Pung* means a hillock), which literally means a variety of tree, found in the village over the hillock and can be used for construction of houses or furniture. The elderly persons of the village still remember presence of some *Sying* tree during their young days but at present not even a single such tree can found in the village.

The village is surrounded by Upper Sindibong or Tadunchen and SH-12 in the north, Gatte Khola (rivulet) in the east, Ranikhola and Dungra Busty in the west and Relli Road in the south. The village slants sharply from north towards south. The *jhora* or *khola* or rivulet on both east and west boundaries, provide irrigated water for agriculture, run from north towards south. The stony steps passing through the middle of the village connect the two-pacca roads SH-12 in the north and Relli Road in the south. The village got a ridged part at the mid-northern part of the village and which slopes downwards slowly towards east and west while slopes sharply towards south. Thus except the stony ridged middle portion, all the other areas are comparatively flatter and suitable for cultivation. All the essential services like schools, college, hospital, medical centre, post office, market, banks, and other government officials are located within the vicinity of eight kilometer of the village. All the households except one are Buddhist and they worship in the village monastery.

All the households of the village are owned by the Lepchas except one.

Village–Tashiding Busty

Tashiding Busty falls under Kalimpong *Khasmahal* of Kalimpong –I CD block. It is situated at the western boundary of the sub-division. After crossing Teesta and leaving NH-31A, the SH-12 starts climbing uphill through zigzag hilly terrain. The village starts from 3 mile onwards Teesta river towards Kalimpong town and ends where the road again meets the village at 5th mile in the east.

The nomenclature of the village relates its Lepcha origin. *Tashiding* consists of two Lepcha words – *Tashi* and *ding*. *Tashi* is the name of a Lepcha king probably chieftain of Sikkim. The word *ding* means to remain motionless or steady on the feet. Hearsay narrates that once king *Tashi* on his way from Sikkim stood for a while in the village on a flat piece of land / rock to look around with a bit of leisure. Presence of a flat rock known as *Choong – ding – Loong* at the extreme south–western part of the village does support the hearsay. *Chaong* in Lepcha means south and *Loong* means leisure. The eastern bordering village Ngasey has derived from the Lepcha word *ngaa-so* means refreshing or taking rest after exerting labor. As per the same hearsay king Tashi had a temporary halt in the village for rest. Names of the villages, their Lepcha inhabitants and the hearsay support the characteristics of typical traditional Lepcha villages of the region.

There were six typical Lepcha houses, *Doo-kye-moolee* or in short *Ronglee* in the village. *Rong* means Lepcha and *Lee* means house. All the *Ronglees* got their typical Lepcha names. They were: (i) *Cholongbong* – (orange orchard), (ii) *Ding* – (flat land), (iii) *Kankibong* – (variety of tree), (iv) *Salbong* – (variety of tree), (v) *Siking* – (beside), (vi) 5th mile – as per the location of the house.

The typical Lepcha name of the houses, name of the village and their inhabitants unequivocally support the hearsay and establish the Lepcha origin of the village.

The village is bounded by Ngasey on the east, Dara Gaon and Tanek on the north, Tashiding forest land on the west and 5th mile *jhora* (rivulet) on the south whose other sides is forest land and villages like Bhamse, Poshier and Shiba Church Mission compound areas.

The village slopes from east towards west to meet either SH-12 or Tashiding forest. Beside 5th mile *jhora*, the village also drained by four small rivulet which are watering during monsoon periods. They also help in channeling water through traditional method for irrigation purposes in the neighbouring lands. As almost entire eastern and northern part of the village is bounded by zigzag SH-12, the village is well communicated. All the three markets, Teesta Bazar on the west, Kalimpong Bazar on the east and Malli Bazar on the north are within 8 km. and well communicated by pucca road. All other essential services like schools, college, medical centre, banks, govt. offices are available within the radius of eight kilometre of the village. The only school Tashiding Junior Basic School has established on a plot of land donated by one Lepcha inhabitant, caters the need of primary education in the locality. Most of the Lepchas of the village are Christians but the village is without any public place of worship. The nearest Church for the Protestants is one hour walking distance while the Roman Catholic Church is located at three kilometer east on SH-12.

It is a Lepcha village where 95 per cent households are owned by the Lepchas.

Village: Khamdung

Khamdung is located at the western border of the sub-division with its boundary with Sikkim. It is one and a half km walking distance from Melli, the junction between Sikkim and West Bengal. The village is bounded by forest in the north, Pethong village in the east, Bhalukhop village in the west and Digo village in the south. Lepchas of Khamdung used to go to the extreme north in the forest areas for casual hunting and collecting fire woods and fodder for their cattle. They also reach Teesta river to catch fish for their household consumption. The village falls under Kalimpong-II CD block with Algarh as its block headquarter.

Khamdung can be reached from Tirpai, four Km from Kalimpong town or from Deolo down to the south on foot. It is two and a half hour walking distance from Rangpoo, the township at the boarder between Sikkim and West Bengal. From the village one has to walk about two km on a rough hilly terrain upto Tripai and then can avail hired taxi for Kalimpong town. Lepchas of Khamdung prefer to visit Kalimpong on all occasions than to go to Rongpoo or Malli on the Sikkim side.

All the households of the village belong to the Lepchas.

Village–Lower Beyong

Lower Beyong is located at the eastern side of Kalimpong town. It is the largest among our study villages and falls under Git Dubling Khasmahal of Kalimpong-II CD block. SH-12 passes through Kalimpong town towards north to reach Lava and then towards south for Garubathas and Maynaguri. Before reaching Lava, the road meets a forest controlled pucca road which via Budhabare reaches Kafer, an important tourist spot of the region. Lower Beyong is just below the Budhabare market.

Budhabare is the main trading centre of the locality. Although the aerial distance is only 15 km from Kalimpong town but one has to cover nearly 45 km through hilly track to reach there. Beside one bus service some jeeps also ply between Kalimpong and Budhabare. It is the only market place for selling agricultural produce and buying daily consumables. Wednesday is the weekly market day when temporary shops from nearby places gather for selling variety of commodities. One can get groceries from a few permanent shops and few tea stalls remain open throughout the week. During the harvest of cardamom and ginger, dealers from outside setup their temporary tent to buy the cash crop from the villagers.

Most households of the village belong to the Lepchas.

Basic Statistics of Study Area

Basic statistics of the study area containing number of household, population, religion, distance from subdivision HQ, school, college etc are plotted in Table- 4.2.

Table-4.2 reveals that out of the four villages under the study area two each are from Kalimpong-I and Kalimpong-II CD block. Village Mane Gumba and Tashiding are from Kalimpong-I CD block while Khamdung and Lower Beyong are from Kalimpong-II CD block. As the sub-divisional head quarter is located in Kalimpong-I CD block, it is nearer to the first two villages belonging to Kalimpong-I CD block than the other two villages from the other CD block. Lower Beyong is the remotest of the four villages under the present study

Villages have been chosen on the basis of their distinct features of religion and location. Mane Gumba is located in the north of Kalimpong town and is the nearest to the town. This village is dominated by the Buddhist (70.80 per cent). It is the only village where 23.36 per cert population recorded as nature worshipper. Earlier all of them were Buddhists but very recently they have returned to their original religion of nature worshipper. Tashiding is located in the western side of the town and is dominated by the Christian (87.36 per cent) of both the denomination—Roman Catholics and Protestants.

Although Khamdung falls under Kalimpong-II CD block but it is very near to Kalimpong town and is located in the eastern boundary of the state bordering with Sikkim. The percentage of Buddhist (80.77) is more than that of the Christian (19.23). Lower Beyong is the remotest of the four villages under study and is a mixed village with 59.93 per cent Buddhist and 41.07 per cent Christian.

Lower Beyong is the largest village in respect of both population and household. It comprises of 45.96 per cent of

Table 4.2
Basic Statistics of the study area

Name of village	Name of CD Block	No of Households	Sub Div	Distance From (in km) Pucca Road	Market	Pry School	Sec School	College	Lepcha Population Male	Female	Total	Femal per 1000 male No.	Religion Buddhist	Christian	Others
1	2	3	4	5	6	7	8	9	10	11	12	13	14	15	16
Mane															
Gumba	Kpg-I	28	04	—	4	—	2	5	64	73	137	1141	97	8	32
													(76.80)	(5.84)	(23.33)
Tashiding													22	152	—
Busty	Kpg-I	35	07	—	7	—	5	7	88	86	174	977	(12.64)	(87.36)	
Khamdung													105	25	—
	Kpg-II	26	10	5	10	—	8	10	72	58	130	806	(80.77)	(19.23)	
Lower													221	154	—
Beyaog	Kpg-II	65	45	2	2	—	3	45	190	185	475	974	58.930)	(41.07)	
													445	339	32
TOTAL		154	—	—	—	—	—	—	414	402	816	971	(54.53)	(41.54)	(3.93)

Source: Field Survey.

total population and 42.21 per cent of total household of the study area. This substantiates our proposition that during the foreign rule (Tibetan and British) Lepchas have slowly but steadily cornered themselves in the remote areas.

Sex Compostion

The sex composition of population in the study area is 971 female per thousand male. This figure is less than that of total Lepcha population in the state which is 981 female per thousand male.

Mane Gumba is dominated by the Buddhist Lepchas and is located nearest to the town has more female than males (1141 females per thousand males). Presence of good number of unmarried girls may be one of the causes behind the high rate of female population. Khamdung, the other Buddhist dominated village recorded 806 females per thousand males which is the lowest among the study area. The sex ratio of the other two Christian dominated villages is almost the same and is nearer to the average ratio for the study area. Sex ratio and religion are uncorrelated and independent to each other.

Literacy Rate

The average literacy rate of the study is 82.35 per cent. It has been observed that literacy rate is the highest (87.93 per cent) in Tashiding Busty which is dominated by the Christians (87.36 per cent). The second highest literacy rate is found in Khamdung (85.38 per cent) where sex ratio is the lowest (806). The literacy rate is moderate and average in Manė Gumba (83.21 per cent) which is dominated by the Buddhist (70.80 per cent) but has highest sex ratio (1140). No correlation between literacy rate and sex ratio could be established from the data available in our study area.

Women education is the backbone of any society. Both status and empowerment of women are directly related with the in educational attainment. Literacy rate of population of our study area is shown in Table—3.3.

Table - 4.3 shows that the average literacy rate in the Lepcha villages of our study area (82.35 per cent) is satisfactory and it is above the all India average rate (65.38 per cent.). Literacy rate among the Lepcha males (87.44 %) and females (77.11%) are higher than their corresponding figures for all India level (75.85 % and 54.16 % respectively). Lepcha females are more literate than the females in all India level but they are less literate than the male members within their own community. Christians Lepchas, both male and females, are more literate than the Buddhist Lepchas. Literacy rate is the highest in Tashiding village (87.93 per cent) which is dominated by Christians. It has been noted that religion, proximity to town and existence of educational institutional are some of the factors which are positively related with the level of literacy rate.

A perusal of Table- 4.3 reveals that there are more illiterates among the females (22.59) than among the males (12.56 per cent). The highest percentage of illiteracy among the females is found in Khamdung (24.14 per cent) and Lower Beyong (25.40 per cent). Both the villages are under Kalimpong-II CD block and are located in remote areas. Compared to very negligible illiteracy rate among the males (6.94 per cent) of Khamdung, there is high illiteracy rate among the female (24.13 per cent). The same for Tashiding Busty is 7.95 per cent for the males and 16.82 for the females. Proportionately higher rate of illiteracy rate among the females in all the villages of the study area is a matter of great concern.

Table 4.4 shows that among the literates higher percentage of Lepchas are found to fall under the category of secondary education (50.59 per cent) followed by primary

Table 4.3
Literacy and illiteracy Rate in the Study Area

	LITERATE			*ILLITERATE*			*TOTAL POPULATION*		
	M	*F*	*Total*	*M*	*F*	*Total*	*M*	*F*	*Total*
1	*2*	*3*	*4*	*5*	*6*	*7*	*8*	*9*	*10*
Mane Gumba	58 (90.63)	56 (78.71)	114 (83.21)	6 (9.37)	17 (23.29)	23 (16.79)	64 (100.00)	73 (100.00)	137 (100.00)
Tashiding Busty	81 (92.05)	72 (83.72)	153 (87.93)	7 (7.95)	14 (16.28)	21 (12.07)	88 (100.00)	86 (100.00)	174 (100.00)
Khamdung	67 (93.06)	44 (75.86)	111 (85.38)	5 (6.94)	14 (24.14)	19 (14.62)	72 (100.00)	58 (100.00)	130 (100.00)
Lower Beyaog	156 (82.11)	138 (74.59)	294 (78.40)	34 (17.89)	47 (25.40)	81 (21.60)	190 (100.00)	185 (100.00)	375 (100.00)
TOTAL	362 (87.44)	310 (77.11)	672 (82.35)	52 (12.56)	92 (22.69)	144 (17.65)	414 (100.00)	402 (100.00)	816 (100.00)

Source: Field Survey.

Table – 4.4
Type of Education by Sex Among the Lepchas of the Study Area

Name of Village	*Primary Education*			*Secondary Education*			*Degree and Above*			*Technical & Other*		
	M	*F*	*Total*	*M*	*F*	*Total*	*M*	*F*	*Total*	*M*	*F*	*Total*
1	*2*	*3*	*4*	*5*	*6*	*7*	*8*	*9*	*10*	*11*	*12*	*13*
Mane Gumba	18 (31.03)	19 (33.93)	37 (32.46)	32 (55.17)	30 (53.57)	62 (54.39)	7 (12.07)	7 (12.50)	14 (12.28)	1 (1.72)	—	1 (0.88)
Tashiding Busty	11 (13.58)	24 (33.33)	35 (22.88)	54 (66.67)	37 (51.39)	91 (59.48)	14 (17.28)	11 (15.28)	25 (16.34)	2 (2.47)	—	2 (1.31)
Kham-dung	34 (58.75)	23 (52.27)	57 (51.35)	28 (41.79)	21 (47.72)	49 .(44.14)	5 (7.46)	—	5 (4.50)	—	—	—
Lower Beyaog	81 (51.92)	-69 (50.00)	150 (51.02)	72 (46.15)	66 (47.83)	138 (46.94)	2 (1.28)	3 (2.12)	5 (1.70)	1 (0.64)	—	1 (0.34)
TOTAL	144 (39.78)	135 (43.55)	279 (41.52)	186 (51.38)	154 (49.68)	340 (50.59)	28 (7.74)	21 (6.77)	49 (7.29)	4 (1.11)	—	4 (0.59)

Source: Field Survey.

education (41.52 per cent) and degree education (7.29 per cent) is very negligible. It has been noted carefully that in all the categories the percentages of females are less than the males. Nearly half of the Lepchas (50.59 per cent) completed their secondary education. The proportion of population completed degree (7.29 %) and technical education (0.59%) are not at all satisfactory. The negligible proportion of Lepchas attaining higher education is a matter of great concern. No females attain any sort of technical education. The highest level of education among the females is graduation from both humanities and commerce stream. Non availability of technical institution in the locality may be responsible for not getting any sort of technical education by the females.

Table-4.5 shows sex wise enrolment of students in different categories of educational standards. Nearly 1/3rd of the Lepcha population of the study are the students. It has been noted that no child of age group 5—10 remain confined within the house without going to the school. It is appreciable that all irrespective of sex and village send their children to the school. But the fact which matters much is high percentage of students in the category of primary standard (54.08 %) and secondary standard (42.06 %) and very negligible percentage in the categories of degree level (3.43 % and technical education (0.43 %).This indicates very high level of drop outs among the Lepchas. The percentage of population whose highest education is primary standard is 41.52 and only 50.59 per cent of population could reach up to secondary level. The rest i.e 7.89 per cent could avail the opportunity of higher education. It may be observed that only 13.85 per cent literates possess at least one public examination certificate. The high dropout case is a matter of great concern and the same is more among the females. It should be dealt with carefully for further development of the Lepchas. Time, purpose and resources are not sufficient to deal this matter for the present study.

Table - 4.5
Enrolment of students by sex in different types of educational standards in the Study Area

Name of Village	Total Students			Primary Education			Secondary Education			Degree and Above			Technical & Other		
	M	F	Total	M	F	Total	M	F	Total	M	F	Total			
1	2	3	4	5	6	7	8	9	10	11	12	13	14	15	16
Mane Gumba	13 (100.00)	16 (100.00)	29 (100.00)	6 (46.15)	3 (18.76)	9 (31.03)	5 (38.46)	9 (56.25)	14 (48.28)	1 (7.69)	4 (25.00)	5 (17.24)	1 (7.69)	—	1 (3.45)
Tashiding Busty	14 (100.00)	17 (100.00)	31 (100.00)	4 (28.57)	8 (47.06)	12 (38.71)	8 (57.14)	9 (52,94)	17 (54.84)	1 (7.14)	1 (5.88)	2 (6.45)	—	—	—
Khamdung	29 (100.00)	20 (100.00)	49 (100.00)	19 (65.52)	10 (50.00)	29 (59.18)	9 (31.03)	10 (50.55)	10 (38.78)	1 (3.44)	—	1 (2.04)	—	—	—
Lower Beyaog	61 (100.00)	63 (100.00)	124 (100.00)	37 (60.66)	39 (61.91)	76 (61.29)	25 (40.98)	23 (36.51)	48 (38.71)	—	—	—	—	—	
TOTAL	117 (100.00)	116 (100.00)	233 (100)	66 (56.41)	60 (51.72)	126 (54.08)	47 (40.14)	51 (43..96))	98 (42.06)	3 (2.56)	5 (4.31)	8 (3.43)	1 (0.85)	—	1 (0.43)

Source: Field Survey.

Family Size

It has been noted that Lepcha family is basically medium sized with 4 to 6 members. The percentage of family with maximum six member is as high as 71. 89 out of which 37.27 per cent dominated by female members and 38.18 per cent are balanced family.

Table - 4.6 reveals that all even sized families (e.g. with members 2, 4, 6 and 8) are more balanced between the male and female members. All the families with two members are identified as balanced. These families are those who after marriage have started their new family life by separating themselves from their parental establishment but they are without any issue. It has been noted that the large sized families are more dominated by the males while small and medium sized families are more dominated by the females.

The percentage of family dominated by the male and female members is the same in case of three member family. The number of Lepcha family with their lone child as male or female child is the same. These families are identified as balanced family in respect of sex composition.

The five member family size is more dominated by the females. Females in this category dominate in all the villages of our study area. Out of 22 such families in this category, the percentage of female dominated families are 59.39 while that of the male dominated families are only 40.91 per cent.

The large sized family with more than eight members comprises only 7.19 per cent of the total family in our study area. It is interesting to note that as high 90.91 per cent family in this category are dominated by the females and a very negligible 9.09 per cent are male dominated. It may be noted that presence of good number of unmarried girl child and widows are the two determining factors of female dominance in these category.

Table – 4.6
Sexwise Distribution of Family Size in the Study Area

Family Size	*MANI GUMBA*				*TASHIDING BUSTY*				*KILAMDUNG*				*LOWER BEYONG*				*TOTAL*			
	M	*F*	*B*	*T*	*M*	*F*	*B*	*T*	*M*	*F*	*B*	*T*	*M*	*F*	*B*	*T*	*M*	*F*	*B*	*T*
2	—	—	3	3	—	—	3	3	—	—	1	1	—	—	2	2	—	—	9	9
			33.3	(33.33)			33.3	(33.33)			11.1	(11.11)			22.2	(22.22)			100	(100.0)
3	4	—	—	4	3	2	—	5	1	4	—	5	—	2	—	2	8	8	—	16
	50.0			(25.00)	37.5	25.0		(31.25)	12.5	50.0		(31.25)		25.0		(12.5)	100.	100.		(100.0)
4	—	—	4	4	2	2	7	11	—	5	1	6	4	6	10	20	6	13	22	41
			18.1	(9.75)	33.3	15.4	31.8	(26.83)		38.5	4.55	(14.63)	66.7	46.2	45.5	(48.79)	100.	100.	100.	(100.0)
5	2	5	—	7	1	2	—	3	1	3	—	4	5	3	—	8	9	13	—	22
	22.2	38.4		(31.82)	11.1	15.4		(13.64)	11.1	23.1		(18.18)	55.6	23.1		(36.36)	100.	100.		(100.0)
6	—	2	3	5	1	—	1	2	1	2	2	5	2	3	5	10	4	7	11	22
		28.5	27.2	(22.73)	25.0	0.1		(9.09)	25.0	28.6	18.2	(22'73)	50.0	42.9	45.5	(45.45)	100.	100.	100	(100.0)
7	1	2	—	3	3	—	—	3	2	1	—	3	6	4	—	10	12	7	—	19
	8.33	28.5		(15.79)	25.0			(15.79)	16.7	14.3		(15.70)	50.0	57.1		(52.63)	100.	100.		(100.0)
8	—	—	—	—	2	2	1	5	1	—	—	1	1	3	3	7	4	5	4	13
					50.0	40.0	25.0	(38.46)	25.0			(7.69)	25.0	60.0	75.0	(53.85)	100.	100.	100.	(100.0)
Above	1	1	—	2	—	2	—	2	—	1	—	1	—	6	—	6	1	10	—	1
8	100.	10.0		(18.19)		20.0		(18.18)		10.0		(9.09)		60.0		(54.55)	100.	100.		(100.0)
Total	8	10	10	28	12	10	12	34	6	16	4	26	18	27	20	65	44	63	46	153
	(18.18)	(15.87)	(21.74)	(18.31)	(27.27	(15.87)	(26.09)	(22.22)	(13.64)	(25.40)	(8.69)	(16.99)	(40.91)	(42.86)	(43.48)	(42.48)	(100.00)	(100.00)	(100.00)	(100.00)

Note: M = Male; F = Female; B = Balanced population; T = Total Population

Source: Field Survey. The seven member Lepcha family constituting 12.87 per cent of the total families under the study are is dominated more by the males (63.16 per cent) and only 36.84 per cent are dominated by the females. Males in this category are dominated in all the villages irrespective of their location and economic status.

Table-4.6 carries some significance over the issue of female dominance in Lepcha society. The families dominated by the female member ranks first constituting as high as 41.18 per cent of the total family of the study area. The second ranking family is the balanced family where the number of members of both the male and female are the same. They constitute 30.06 per cent of the total families of the study area. The percentage of family dominated by the male member ranks third and constitutes only 28.76 per cent of the total family under the study area.

Institutional Study

Lepcha girls studying in two colleges located in Kalimpong sub-division have been identified as the second source of collecting information for the present study. In the town there are only two colleges which cater the degree education to the students not only from within the sub-division but also from the neighbouring areas of Bhutan, Sikkim and Jalpaiguri district of West Bengal. It may be noted that all these areas are the strong holds of Lepcha inhabitants. Students are considered as the representative of different families and villages with different socio-economic backgrounds. Information collected from the students not only substantiate our information collected on the Lepchas from the village level study but was expected to add some extra information which would enrich our knowledge on examining the status of women in the Lepcha society.

Kalimpong College

Kalimpong College, a co-educational institute established in 1962, is not only a pioneering institution but till 1998 was the only institution in the vast sub-division in extending degree education to the large number of students of the local areas. It extends humanities, commerce and science (both pure and bio) in pass and honours courses. Students are admitted on the basis of merit but a separate list is prepared for the SC/ST students. The college has no hostel facilities and out stationed students are to arrange their private accommodation of their own. There is one Lepcha Boys Hostel nearby under the management of Indigenous Lepcha Tribal Association, Kalimpong where Lepcha boys from far off villages stay and study in different schools and college. All Lepcha students because of their inclusion under SC category receive scholarships from the government. Kalimpong College is affiliated under North Bengal University and is recognized by the University Grants Commission. Very recently the college has started a centre of distance education to extend masters degree facilities among the students of the locality. The fees and other charges of the college are very minimum and are determined as per the university norm. The college plays an important role in imparting higher education not only among the Lepchas but among all the students in the local areas.

Cluny Women's College

Established in 1998, Cluny Women's College extends collegiate education for the girl students of the local areas. It offers both pass and honours courses in humanities group only. Beside regular collegiate degree, it also has the facilities of extending vocational education and diploma course in Communicative English and Computer Application. The college has shifted to its personal building but due to new infrastructure it accepts comparatively less number of students. It is affiliated under North Bengal University and is recognized by the University Grants Commission.

Students Profile

The basic statistics of the two colleges for the academic year 2006 —2007 has been shown in the following paragraphs.

Kalimpong College

Year-wise enrolment of students of Kalimpong College has been shown in the following Table – 4.7.

Table-4.7 shows the students profile of Kalimpong College after classifying them on the basis of year, stream and different categories like general, SC and ST. A perusal of the table reveals that ST category of students ranks seconds (34.79 per cent) marginally next to the general category of students (36.69 per cent). There are 919 girl students which comprises 46.05 per cent of the total student strength of the college. It is more interesting to note that percentage of girl student (52.73 %) in the general category for all the streams taken together exceeds than that of the male student (47.27 %). It can further be noted that the number of girl students in third year class is more than the boys. This indicates that pass percentage of girl students is more than the boys at the University examination.

Cluny Women's College

Table- 4.8 shows students profile of Cluny Women's College. The ST category student ranks second (29.24 percent) which is next to the general category (55.93 per cent). It is to note that the ST category of students in both the Colleges dominates over the SC category of students.

Table- 4.9 shows some basic information about Lepcha students studying in both the colleges: Kalimpong College and Cluny Women's College.

Table-4.9 shows sex-wise statements of Lepcha student vis-a-vis ST student in both the colleges of Kalimpong sub-division. As Cluny Women's College is a girl's College and offers only humanities to the students, a number of columns and rows remain blank.

There is a general tendency among the Lepchas to study humanities and interest to study either commerce or science stream is very negligible. Lepchas comprises 19.27 per cent of total ST students of the two colleges. The percentage figure for the Lepcha girls (23.83%) is higher than the boys (15.00%).

Table – 4.7
Students Profile of Kalimpong College for the year 2006 – 07

Stream & Year	GENERAL			SC			ST			OBC			TOTAL		
	Boys	Girls	Total	Boys	Girls	Total	Boys	Girls	Total	Boys	Girls	Total	Boys	Girls	Total
1	2	3	4	5	6	7	8	9	10	11	12	13	14	15	16
BA-I	147	45	192	28	22	50	175	128	303	35	73	108	385	268	653
	(39.18)	(16.79)	(29.40)	(7.27)	(8.21)	(7.66)	(45.46)	(47.76)	(46.40)	(9.09)	(27.24)	(16.54)	(100.00)	(100.00)	(100.00)
—II	70	80	150	14	20	34	80	74	154	90	37	127	254	211	465
	(27.56)	(37.91)	(32.76)	(5.51)	(9.47)	(7.31)	(31.50)	(35.07)	(33.12)	(35.43)	(17.55)	(27.31)	(100.00)	(100.00)	(100.00)
—III	6	134	140	18	14	32	99	67	166	80	21	101	203	236	439
	(2.96)	(56.78)	(31.89)	(8.89)	(5.93)	(7.29)	(48.76)	(28.39)	(37.81)	(39.41)	(8.89)	(23.01)	(100.00)	(100.00)	(100.00)
BCom															
—I	50	40	90	8	3	11	12	11	23	17	11	29	87	65	152
	(51.47)	(61.54)	(59.21)	(9.19)	(4.62)	(7.24)	(13.79)	(16.92)	(15.13)	(19.55)	(16.92)	(18.42)	(100.00)	(100.00)	(100.00)
—II	3	13	16	2	1	3	8	3	11	6	6	12	19	23	42
	(15.79)	(56.53)	(38.09)	(10.53)	(4.340	(7.14)	(42,10)	(13.05)	(26.19)	(31.58)	(26.08)	(28.58)	(100.00)	(100.00)	(100.00)
—III	16	17	33	1	1	2	5	2	7	2	6	8	24	26	50
	(66.67)	(65.38)	(66.00)	(4.17)	(3.85)	(4.00)	(20.83)	(7.69)	(14.00)	(8.33)	(23.08)	(16.00)	(100.00)	(100.00)	(100.00)
B.Sc (Bio)-I	22	6	28	2	1	3	8	3	11	6	6	12	38	16	54
	(57.89)	(37.50)	(51.85)	(5.26)	(6.25)	(5.56)	(21.06)	(18,75)	(20.37)	(15.79)	(37.50)	(22.22)	(100.00)	(100.00)	(100.00)
—II	10	17	27	2	1	3	3	1	4	4	4	8	19	23	42
	(52.63)	(73.91)	(64.29)	(10.53)	(4.35)	(7.14)	(15.79)	(4.35)	(9.52)	(21.05)	(17.39)	(19.05)	(100.00)	(100.00)	(100.00)
—III	12	19	31	1	1	2	5	2	7	6	4	10	24	26	50
	(50.00)	(73.08)	(62.00)	(4.17)	(3.85)	(4.00)	(20.83)	(9.69)	(14.00)	(25.00)	(15.38)	(20.00)	(100.00)	(100.00)	(100.00)
BSc (Pure)-I	3	5	8	3	—	3	1	2	3	3	2	5	10	9	19
	(30.00)	(55.56)	(42.10)	(30.00)		(15.79)	(10.00)	(22.22)	(15.79)	(30.00)	(22.22)	(26.32)	(100.00)	(100.00)	(100.00)
—II	2	4	6	1	—	1	1	2	3	2	1	3	6	7	13
	(33.33)	4(57.14)	(46.15)	(16.67)		(7.69)	(16.67)	(28.57)	(23.08)	(33.33)	(14.29)	(23.08)	(100.00)	(100.00)	(100.00)
—III	5	6	11	—	—	—	1	1	2	1	2	3	7	9	16
	(71.42)	(66.67)	(68.75)	—	—	—	(14.29)	(11.11)	(12.50)	(14.29)	(22.22)	(18.75)	(100.00)	(100.00)	(100.00)
Total	346	386	732	80	64	144	398	296	694	252	173	425	1076	919	1995
	(32.16)	(42.01)	(36.69)	(7.43)	(6.96)	(7.22)	(36.99)	(32.21)	(34.79)	(23.42)	(18.82)	(21.30)	(100.00)	(100.00)	(100.00)

As a whole there are at present 87 Lepcha girls students studying in different streams of two colleges in Kalimpong; while the number for the boys is only 60. It has also been noted that the number of Lepcha girls in second and third year classes are more than the corresponding figures for the boys. This shows that the girls have crossed at least one University Examination. A complete picture could have been obtained by examining a batch for three consecutive years but time, manpower and resources restrict us to do so. Thus the percentage of Lepcha girls taking higher education is more than the boys. But their total strength in the colleges is not appreciable compared to the total female population in the region.

Table – 4.8
Students Profile of Cluny Women's College for the year 2006 – 07

Stream	*Year*	*CATEGORY*				
		General	*SC*	*ST*	*OBC*	*Total*
BA	I	64 (54.70)	3 (2.56)	35 (29.91)	15 (12.83)	117 (100.00)
	II	31 (59.61)	2 (3.85)	16 (30.77)	3 (5.77)	52 (100.00)
	III	37 (55.22)	5 (7.46)	18 (26.86)	7 (10.46)	67 (100.00)
TOTAL		132 (55.93)	10 (4.24)	69 (29.24)	25 (10.59)	235 (100.00)

A set of questionnaire has been supplied to all the Lepcha girls studying in both the Colleges. But the response is very disappointing. Most of them, in spite of several reminders and request, could not turn up with the questionnaire and a good number of the returned the same without filling most of the entries.

Table – 4.9
Sex wise Lepcha and ST Students Profile of Kalimpong College and Cluny Women's College for the year 2006 – 07

Stream Year	Kalimpong College				Cluny Women's College		TOTAL			
	ST		Lepcha		ST	Lepcha	ST		Lepcha	
	Boys	Girls	Boys	Girls	Girls	Girls	Boys	Girls	Boys	Girls
1	2	3	4	5	6	7	8	9	10	11
BA-I	175 (100.00)	128 (100.00)	29 (16.57)	14 (10.94)	35 (100.00)	6 (17.14)	175 (100,00)	163 (100.00)	29 (16.57)	20 (12.27)
—II	80 (100.00)	74 (100.00)	11 (13.75)	15 (20.27)	16 (100.00)	10 (62.50)	80 (100.00)	90 (100.00)	11 (13.75)	25 (27.78)
—III	99 (100.00)	67 (100.00)	15 (15.15)	22 (32.84)	18 (100.00)	12 (66.67)	99 (100.00)	85 (100.00)	15 (15.16)	34 (36.65)
BCom—I	12 (100.00)	11 (100.00)	—	3 (27,27)	—	—	12 (100.00)	11 (100.00)	—	3 (27.27)
—II	8 (100.00)	3 (100.00)	—	3 (100.00)	—	—	8 (100.00)	3 (100.00)	—	3 (100.00
—III	5 (100.00)	2 (100.00)	—	—	—	—	5 (100.00)	2 (100.00)	—	—
B.Sc (Bio)—I	8 (100.00)	3 (100.00)	2 (100.00)	—	—	—	8 (100.00)	3 (100.00)	2 (25.00)	—
II	3 (100.00)	1 (100.00)	—	—	—	—	3 (100.00)	1 (100.00)	—	—
III	5 (100.00)	2 (100.00)	1 (20.00)	—	—	—	5 (100.00)	2 (100.00)	1 (20..00)	—
BSc(PURE)—I	1 (100.00)	2 (100.00)	—	—	—	—	1 (100.00)	2 (100.00)	—	—
—II	1 (100.00)	2 (100.00)	1 (100.00)	2 (100.00)	—	—	1 (100.00)	2 (100.00)	1 (100.00)	2 (100.00)
—III	1 (100.00)	1 (100.00)	1 (100.00)	—	—	—	1 (100.00)	1 (100.00)	1 (100.00)	—
Total	398 (100.00)	296 (100.00)	60 (15.07)	59 (19.93)	69 (100.00)	28 (40.58)	398 (100.00)	365 (100.00)	60 (15.08)	87 (23.83)

Table – 4.10
Details of Questionnaire issued and received to students of Kalimpong College and Cluny Women's College for the year 2006 – 07

			No of Questionnaire		*Questionnaire returned with studentpercentage of completed information*			
Name of College	*Total Lepcha girls*	*Issued*	*Not Returned*	*Blank*	*20%*	*50%*	*75%*	*100%*
1	*2*	*3*	*4*	*5*	*6*	*7*	*8*	*9*
Kalimpong College	59	48	34	10	—	—	3	1
Cluny Women's College	28	19	1	2	8	3	2	3
Total	87	67	35	12	8	3	5	4

Table- 4.10 shows details of questionnaire issued and received from the students of the two Colleges.

In the event of above dismal picture it was decided not to analyze such incomplete information but the information which are necessary and relevant for the present study have been recorded and acknowledged at the proper place.

5

Religion and the Status of Women as Mun

Introduction:

Originally Lepchas are nature worshippers. Kanchenjunga is their divine deity and heavenly mountain and most religious activities correspond to this mountain. Lepchas believe that God Himself has created them out of pure and virgin snow of the wonderful mountain. They'worship spirits, mountains, rivers, trees, forests, and all other natural objects surrounding themselves. They believe in the existence of God whom they call Rum and offer their prayer and thanksgivings to Him on all religious occasions. Lepchas are agriculturists and the first fruit of any season is offered to God before it is either consumed or marketed. About Lepcha religion Mainwaring wrote: "Their religion was particularly simple; they believed in one good spirit, and in innumerable evil spirits; to the former they conceived their worship was due, and to Him they offered their prayers and thanksgivings; the latter they considered prowled about, and hunted every spot; to them they attributed whatever sickness or misfortune befell, therefore deemed it requisite to propitiate them, which they did by offerings of rice, & c".

Lepcha religion is known as Bongthimism or Munism

according to the important role played by Bongthing, the Lepcha priest and the Mun, their priestess or the priest. From birth till the soul reach to heaven, the role of Bongthing and Mun is so important and inevitable that their religion is known as per them.

While describing Lepcha religion, G Gorer made a detailed description about Mun. He wrote: " As opposed to Lamaism carries with it no social organization; the Mun and their parallel priests are simply individuals who, through their possession by a spirit, have certain gifts and duties ; unlike the lamas and the civil officers their position carries with it no sort of title in ordinary life. Besides the Mun three other types of priesthood by possession are recognized; these are the Padem, the Yaba, and the Pau. The Mun spirit is a female spirit, the other three are male. They are attached to family lines and are roughly hereditary; they often descend from grandfather to grandson or from grandmother to granddaughter; but there is no regularity about this and a man may inherit a possessing spirit from a woman, and vice versa" (1938 ;p- 215).

Traditionally there was no concept of hell in Lepcha religion and there was only heaven which they call Rum Lyaang. K.P.Tamsang mentioned: "since the advent of Lamaism into Sikkim and Darjeeling district, they now believe in more mythical world besides their own ancestral belief of Rum Lyang. Now they believe in Rum Lyang (heaven), Nyolang (hell), Numsyim - Nyolyang (human world), Moong Lyang (evil spirit world), Thamchyang Lyang (animal world) and Muknyam Lyang (spirit world). (K.P.Tamsang, 1983, P-55).

Origin Of Mun And Bongthing :

As per Lepcha tradition, Itbumoo, the great Mother Creator created Fodongthing, the male and Nazaongnyo, the female out of pure and virgin snow of *Kingtsoomzaomboo Choo*, i.e. Mount Kanchanjunga. They are the primogenitors of the Lepchas and they are claimed to be the first human being in the world. Lepchas call themselves as *Rong-Kup Rum-Kup*, the son of snowy peak and the son of God. After the creation of *Fodongthing* and *Nazaongnyo* the Mother Creator asked them to live separately in Naho and Nathor Lake located below Kanchanjunga and lived like brother and sister. But when they grew young, they forgot the words of God and started living like husband and wife. As a result of disobedience *Nazaongnyo* gave birth to various *Mungs*, the evil spirits. These *Mungs* started giving various troubles to the mankind. According to Lepcha tradition *Laso Mung* was the most ferocious and went on doing brutal and vile activities. Lepchas became fade up with wicked activities of the *Laso Mung* and prayed to *Itbumoo* for its solution. To destroy *Laso Mung*, and "in order to rejuvenate their moral strength, Lord Tamsangthing wished to give the supernatural powers to a chaste man and to chaste woman and made them to bring back the lost moral philosophy of the Lepchas. Thus the first consecrated Bongthing was Thikoong Azaor Boongthing and the first consecrated Mun was Nyookoong Nyoolik Mun." (K.P.Tamsang; 1983; p. 47). Thus *Nyookoong Nyoolik* was the first Mun and *Thi-Koong Azaor* was the first Bongthing in the Lepcha society. *Thi-Koong Tek*, one of the signatories on the Lepcha side with *Khy-Bumsa* on the Tibetan side in the famous Blood Treaty in the thirteenth century which paved the long lasting Tibetan suzerainty in Mayal Lyaang, was the 32nd direct descendent of *Thi- Koong Azaor* Bongthing. Thus in Lepcha religion, both Mun and Bongthing were the direct creation of God but Mun was created first and was given more power than Bongthing. Even today Mun is more powerful and respected than Bongthing in the Lepcha society. G. Gorer wrote: "Padem are weaker than Mun and capable of exorcising far fewer devils; they can not prophesy nor perform the death ceremony. For many men Padem is the first step to becoming Mun" (1938: p. 215).

A.R.Foning gave a detailed description of the origin of Bongthing and Mun. According to him Mungs, the evil spirits, the devils and demons were created when Nazong Nyu started giving birth illegal sons. These "mungs, started to pester and trouble mankind. When the Great Good Mother saw this, she had compassion on us humans, her favourite creation, and created a bongthing who she sent down to us. He was commissioned not only to control these trouble-making mungs, but was also to do everything for our welfare. Accordingly, the bongthing came down to earth and summoned these mungs to a conference. There he agreed to a certain proposal and had a covenant with them. According to the agreement, the bongthing promised to offer animal and bird sacrifice to them, and they in turn, promised to leave human beings unmolested after receiving the same.... No sooner the agreement was arrived at between the bongthing and the mungs, then, true to their nature, these mungs started giving more nad more trouble. For the bongthing this meant that more and more time required for the offering of the sacrifice; it became full time work for him. So, when the bongthing found that he could hardly find time to attend to looking after human welfare, which he was expected to do, he picked up a female from among the mortals, and with due ceremony, delegated his other functions, that of welfare work to her. He confined himself to the work of appeasement of the mungs for which he had been particularly sent, and took on only some of the work relating to welfare. He assigned the work on the incorporeal and spiritual side wholly to the female, who, lateron, came to be known as 'mun'. The bongthing we consider and acknowledge to be the accredited agents of Itbu-moo, the creator, and on account of the delegation of spiritual and divine power from above, the female or the mun ordained by him we also consider to be divinely placed among us" (1987: pp. 60-61).

The term Bongthing has been derived from two words – *Abong* and *Athing*. *Abong* in Lepcha means 'the trunk', 'the main' or 'the original' and *Athing* means 'honourable and highly respected one'. *Abong – Athing* later becomes Bongthing which literally means the original and highly respected person. Bongthing also means 'Master of Mouth'. There is no written form of *Mantras* and all are oral and connected with the Lepcha traditional culture, custom and beliefs. He can also perform the task of *Peeboo,* the go between in Lepcha marriage.

Mun can neither be hereditary nor can be learnt by practice but it is purely gifted by God's grace. It is believed that in most cases the power of the Mun comes hereditarily may be even after the gap of several generations. The soul of the ancestral Mun may come either from the maternal or paternal side. A.R.Foning wrote: "anybody and everybody cannot aspire to be a mun and bongthing. The 'spirit' will manifest itself. It has been found to 'possess' only those of certain families who have mun and bongthing right down the generations. It is set, invariable pattern, may be sometimes in the succeeding generation, as from father to son, mother to daughter. Sometimes, the 'spirit' might even manifest itself after a lapse of three or four generations. The signs and manifestations are unmistakable" (p. 72). But it is being learnt that a bongthing may be trained and need not be an incarnated always but the mun should invariably be incarnated and under no circumstances be trained. Anyway, the incarnated person has to pass through both physical and mental hazards for several days during the time of entry of the soul in the new body. Dorjee Tshering Lepcha of Mane Gumba narrated how his niece (elder sister's daughter) Passing Kit Lepcha became Mun at the age of 14 when she was a student of class eight. Dorjee said, "When Passang Kit was a student of class eighth she could neither speak nor understand Lepcha and was not well acquainted with Lepcha traditional culture and custom. But after becoming Mun she is now so fluent in Lepcha language and culture that outsiders could not believe it. The process through which Passang Kit has to pass for becoming a Mun is very tough and painful. Initially she had fever and as a normal course we consulted the doctor in the local hospital but no medicine could respond to her fever. Gradually she developed some peculiar symptoms which the doctors could neither explain in their medical knowledge nor prescribe any appropriate medicine for them. We were frustrated and at last as per the advice of some of our neighbors we consulted the Mun who appraise us about the state of becoming a Mun and advised us to keep patient observation on her movements. She had vomiting, could not take meal, spent several sleepless nights, remain mum for days together, and many other abnormalities in her behaviour. We were puzzled, confused and at a complete loss but the only ray of hope was the Mun's predictions which Passang Kit was following like an obedient girl. Surprising all after a fortnight Passang Kit become normal but she became a completely new girl she received the Mun soul of her great great grand mother who was a Mun during her time".

Areas of Activities of Mun–Bongthing

Mun and Bongthing are the mediators between the Lepchas and the spirit world, both good and bad. Anyone who is well versed in Lepcha language and well aware about their culture and custom can act as Bongthing. Only a male member among the Lepchas can be the Bongthing which may be ordained hereditarily or can be learned or acquired by training. Mun can be both male and female. A.K.Das stated that "in Darjeeling Mun are found to be women and Bongthing men" (1978: p. 193). But in our study area we could find both male and female working as Mun but Bongthings are only the males. G. Gorer also wrote "both men and women can be Mun, but only men can be Padem (or bongthing)" (1938: p. 215). He/ She is divinely ordained person and gifted the power to perform religious activities of the Lepchas and can even talk with the spirits. It is the duty of the Mun to bring back the soul of the departed person to Kanchanjunga from where they originate. It is believed that Kanchanjunga is the original home land of the Lepchas and each clan or Moo has its own Chu, Daa and Lyep. After death the souls of the Lepchas need to return to Kanchanjunga where their ancestors are waiting to receive them. It is only Mun who can catch the souls of the departed person and directs them the way towards Kanchanjunga to meet with their ancestors. It is strongly believed that the Mun can catch souls moving haphazardly in the world and direct them to their ultimate destination for eternal rest. While writing the functions of mun A. R. Foning mentioned that "among the various functions of the mun, the most important and the most impressive one, I find, is the transportation of the soul of the departed into Rum-Lyang, the place of the gods, where we meet souls of our ancestors, when we ourselves are dead and gone from this world. This is an exclusive undertaking of the mun" (1987: p. 64). In another occasion the author describes the functions of bongthing as "between the mun and bongthing, the bongthing is very much more in demand and in circulation. The simple reason for this is that, in all families, there is always, and invariably, some sort of sickness occurring and, according to us, these are the works of some malignant mungs or evil spirits and devils; and it is the bongthing who has been commissioned by Itbumoo herself to tackle them for us. Further, they are not called in for sickness alone; they are called to attend in our day-to-day lives also. The demand for them is great" (1987: p. 79). Very recently while conducting her research on the Lepchas Jenny Bently also found the importance of mun than bongthing among the Lepchas in Dzongu, North Sikkim. She wrote: "some Lepchas consider the mun more powerful than the bongthing. Most rituals specialists themselves though state that the mun and bongthing are both just as powerful, but have different duties. They use different items during sacrifice. A bongthing from Dzongu describes that the padhim or bongthing uses the bark and the leaves of a banana tree. bamboo and chi. The mun uses a plant called phusur and chi as well as animal sacrifice. Their ceremonies also start at a different point in Lepcha mythology. The mun starts the incantation at the beginning of existence, whereas the bongthing starts at the origin of the clan. The mun and the bongthing have their own guardian deities they have to conduct rituals to twice a year. They are responsible for the incantation of different deities (see Siiger 1967: 162-166). Most ceremonies can though be done by both (such as the agricultural ceremonies, see Foning 1987: 61), except guiding the soul (a pil) of a dead person. This can only be done by a mun (Siiger 1967: 163, Gorer 1984: 215)" (2007: p. XVI).

Lepchas believe that human diseases are caused by sinister eye of the Mung and they need to be praised by appropriate offerings. Mun knows which spirit is responsible for what type of diseases and how they can bring under control by offering different articles. In the first instance the Mun identifies the diseases and then connects the devil responsible for the particular diseases and then prescribes appropriate offerings to satisfy the Mung. In many cases the Mun is also the bare footed healer in the village who prescribes the herbal medicine for the Lepchas before they go to the doctor for modern allopathic treatment.C.D.Beauvoir Stocks mentioned the role of Mun as a medicine person in the village. She wrote: "when a child is very ill, a Mun is called in to sacrifice to the demons. When the child recovers it is said she has cured it." (1925: p. 463). G Gorer also observed the same types of functions of Mun. He said "the chief function of the Mun is to ward off the misfortunes and illnesses caused by devils, which is done, partly by sacrifices, especially animal sacrifices, and partly by direct communing with the super naturals. On certain occasions the Mun become possessed by their guardian spirit and prophesy: at death ceremonies they summon the soul of the dead man to speak his last wishes through their mouth, and then conduct it into the rum lyang – the place of the Gods – where it is reborn as an infant, and grows up to an eternal life similar to the life here on earth" (1938: p. 182). In another occasion he wrote: "the services of the Mun are continuously necessary in the life of every Lepcha. They must always be present at birth, at marriage they are the only essential priests, and at death of laymen their role is of more emotional importance than the lamas. Throughout life they are necessary for cleansing from supernatural danger, for blessing and solemnizing different undertakings, and, above all, for expelling devils" (1938: p. 230).

Types of Spirits

Lepchas have strong belief in the existence of spirit. In their religious world spirits are closely connected in almost all types of their day to day activities. All happenings, good or bad, are due to the blessings or curse of the concerned spirit. The Lepcha spirit world consists of two types of spirits; good spirit and bad spirit. Good or benevolent spirits are responsible for all good things for the Lepchas and they call them Rum. Some spirits are bad or malevolent and cause harm to the Lepchas and they call them Mung. Rum, the good spirits look after the house, property, cattle, crop and orchards and are responsible for all sorts of wellbeing of human society. The Mungs, bad spirits are responsible for causing enmity, jealousy, diseases, illness, death, epidemics, loss of property, loss of crop etc. Rums are worshipped and offered thanks for all the blessings which make Lepcha life smooth and prosperous. Mungs are to be praised with appropriate offerings to get rid of their sinister eye. Rums are worshipped regularly and there is a routine time and manner of their offerings. Mungs are praised only when they are required to do so and there is no specific time for their worship.

A. Rum or Good Spirits

In the followings list some good spirits and their offerings and worshiping in the Lepcha religious world are furnished:

1. *Li - Rum*: *Li-Rum* is the household deity or God who protects the house, property, animal, crop and over all wellbeing of the Lepchas. In Lepcha, *Faat* means offering. *Li - Rum Faat* is like offerings to Goddess Laxmi of the Hindus and all Lepchas offer their household deity once a year in the month of *Tafa* (April – May) on any day except Sunday. Besides the scheduled yearly offering, Lepchas on all important occasions like destruction or construction of house, setting for any outside trip, or starting anything new, prefer to take the blessings of their household deity. It is an individual offering and there is no fixed time for such salute to the household deity in their house.

2. *Lyaang - Rum*: In Lepcha *Lyaang* means 'land'. Lepchas worship *Lyaang Rum*, the God of land so that they can get good rain in time for the field. It is told that in the afternoon of each offering Lepchas receive at least one shower of rain every year. It is a common offering and is generally organized at the village level. All the villagers assemble near a hill top to offer Chi, hen, egg, rice, fish, fruits etc to the benevolent spirit for their betterment. Nowadays the *Faat* is being organized in a large scale at the *Poom Shezoom* level and at the Association level. The day is celebrated as a picnic day when all take meal from the *Faat* location through individual contribution and subscription.

3. *Muk - Zik - Rum*: In Lepcha *Muk* means greenery that pervades nature around us, *Zik* means sprouting of grass i.e. vegetation and Rum is the benevolent spirit. It is an offering to Mother Nature for her favor in balancing the ecology. It is conducted jointly at the village level in the month of February each year. The Lepcha Association fixed 20th February as the

day for the *Faat*. In this offering Bongthing on behalf of the village thanks the benevolent spirit for timely supply of all natural gifts like, mist, cloud, sunshine, clear air, water etc All such things are essential to make the soil and earth fertile so that plants and human habitation and life can continue in the planet.

4. *Tendong / Tungraong Lho Rum*: Offering to *Tendong / Tungraong Lho Rum* is observed on 7th and 8th of August each year in Sikkim by the state government and on 26th August in Kalimpong by the ILTA. *Tendong or Tungraong Lho* is the holy and sacred mountain that saved the Lepchas from drowning during the great flood which occurred in the prehistoric days when Lepchas were the only inhabitants in this region. *Tengrong* in Lepcha means ladder and the name is given as per the shape of the mountain which is located in the North district of Sikkim. As per Lepcha folktale the flood was caused due to the river Rangeet which suddenly turned back towards its origin out of frustration and disappointment of not reaching the meeting place with his beloved Teesta river as promised by him. Each year Lepchas of Sikkim offer prayer and worship the mountain for its blessing with the request that such deluge should not repeat further in this part of the world.

5. *Chu - Rum*: In Lepcha *Chu* means the Himalayan peak with snow and *Rum* means God. It is the prayer for the Mount Kanchanjunga, the guardian Deity of the Lepchas. They believe that their primogenitors, *Fodongthing* and *Nazaongnyo*, were created by *Itbumoo*, the Mother Creator out of the pure and virgin snow of Mount Kanchanjunga. Each Moo, Lepcha clan, has its own *Chu* (peak), *Daa* (lake) and *Lyep* (entry point) in the foot hills of Mount

Kanchanjunga. Lepchas believe that their souls return to their respective *Chu* to meet and take eternal rest with their ancestors. In all occasions Lepchas worship and offer their thanksgivings to Kanchanjunga for protecting them from all evils, troubles and misfortunes.

6. *Mut –Rum or Pong Rum*: This is the offerings to the jungle spirit. *Mut Rum* is the name of the jungle spirit and the Lepchas in traditional days worshipped him both before and after hunting. Only the male members are allowed to attend in the offerings. It is believed that this particular "God cannot stand the sight of women. This is the reason why this worship always takes place away from the house of a remote place where, even by chance, females do not appear. Besides, they themselves know this and thus scrupulously avoid coming anywhere near the place. Where this worship is going on." (A. R. Foning; p. 236). Lepchas thank the jungle God for providing with all sorts of fruits and animals throughout the year for human survival. They need to surrender all the weapons used in hunting before the deity at the time of offering. Lepchas enjoy the day with songs and jungle dance. After hunting, the animal first needs to offer to the God. The spirit is also believed to protect and save the cultivable land from rats, insects and animals.

7. *Tung - Baong - Rum*: *Tung -Baong -Rum* is a female spirit who is also known as *Nangler Rum* and is the benevolent spirit who looks after the new born baby. She is worshipped after the birth of the new born baby. On reaching three nights and four days of birth, Lepchas perform this *Faat* in order to purify both the mother and the child. The Bongthing thanks *Kathaong Fee* and *Nanglyen Nyoo*, the guardian

deities of birth and also confer *Aagit, Chu, Daa,* and *Lyep* to the newly born baby. A male baby receives his fathers *Aagit, Chu, Daa* and *Lyep* while the female child receives those of her mother. After offerings to *Tung Baong* spirit the child become the member of the Lepcha society and also establish his/ her right on Lepcha land, property and are liable to maintain and guided by the Lepcha customary laws.

8. *Sugi - Rum*: It is the *Faat* connected with ovation and thanks giving to their respective teachers. All the Bongthings and Muns assemble in one place to offer their respect, admiration and reverence to *Thikoong Azaor*, first Bongthing and *Nyookoong Nyoolik,* the first Mun and also to their respective teachers who taught them the skill of doing the religious activities. They ask for their continuous help and blessings in this regard so that they can help the community in their development. Once a year in the month of October, Bongthing and Mun of any locality assemble to offer their thanks-giving. All the medicinal plants are to be placed in front of the prayer for retaining their herbal power for the benefit of the human being.

B. Mung or Bad Spirits

Whenever there is any misfortune of any degree, Lepchas believe it to be due to the sinister eye of the evil spirit whom they call Mung. There is no routine time and pattern of their worship but are offered as and when they are required to do so. To please these Mungs, Lepchas offer hen compulsorily along with Chi, fruits, rice, fish etc.

1. *Laso - Mung*: He is an ogre i.e. man-eating monster who used to kill and eat the Lepchas whenever they entered the forest in the earlier days. The ogre Mung lived disguised and camouflaged himself in the form

of different animals. But the Mung was killed in a war by ten brave Lepchas who cut into pieces the different parts of its body. The different Moos in the Lepcha society had been originated as per the type and nature of involvement of the individual in the war. Even today the last week of each year is celebrated by dancing, singing and burning the effigy of the Mung. Lepcha calendar year is named as per the shape of the animal which the devil took in order to hide him during the war. There are twelve such shapes of animals in the Lepcha calendar.

Beside *Laso Mung*, Lepchas believe that all diseases and misfortunes are due to the evil eye of the concerned spirit and there are good numbers of such bad spirits. Some of them are as follows:

2. *Arot - Mung*: He is the devil responsible for causing accidents and committing suicide among the Lepchas and if not pleased the same thing may repeat in the family.

3. *Midyup-Mung*: He is not that dangerous but is responsible for cough and cold.

4. *Shor - Mung* : He is responsible for creating enmity among the Lepchas. He is very cruel and provocate the Lepchas to quarrel over the land issue. He is responsible for miscarriage and need to be satisfied with two chickens in the 7th and 8th month of pregnancy.

5. *Sungrong or Sumu - Mung*: He is very dreadful devil and lives in high altitude above 18000 feet.

6. *Apal - Mung*: He is the devil responsible for frightening the children.

7. *Khung - Mung* : He is the devil causing unauthorized

sexual relations among the Lepcha boys and girls before marriage.

8. *Soomu - Mung*: She is extremely ugly and dirty female Mung who harasses the travellers at night by changing the shape.

Both Bongthing and Mun are used as mediators between the Lepchas and the spirit world. There is no specific choice between the Bongthing and Mun for the offerings of any particular type of Rum or Mung and whoever is available locally are called for the offerings.

Types of Mun

Mun is the gift of Almighty and has been bestowed with divinely adorned power of super human capacity. But it has been admitted that the present Lepcha Muns do not possess super natural powers, knowledge and wisdom like those of the earlier days. Mun was created to protect the Lepchas from troubles created by the devils. Different types of extra ordinary powers were needed to control different deadly and terrific devils.

According to the types of power conferred to them and the nature of activities performed by them, there are different types of Mun in the Lepcha religious world. K.P.Tamsang has classified Mun in seven different categories: "(a) *Avor Mun,* (b) *Pildon Mun,* (c) *Angan Mun,* (d) *Tungli Mun,* (e) *Munjyum Mun,* (f) *Mun Mook Mun* and (g) *Lyang – Eet Mun.*

(a) *Avor Mun : Avor Mun* possess the equal supernatural power as that of the ancient *Nyoolik Mun,* but sometimes, these *Avor Muns* for attaining their own selfish ends, they misuse their power by destroying whatever they wish. As for example, as *Avor Mun* named Domit had by her supernatural power made it fall lightening and thunderbolt on a precipitous rock called *Simumdrop Sugaor* of river Reli at Kalimpong and reduced it into pieces, is a real fact, which is still narrated even to this day by the aged Lepchas of the nearby villages of the place where the fact had occurred...

(b) *Pildon Mun: Pildon Mun* performs from the ordinary ceremonies to the delivering up of the soul of a dead person to heaven. By her supernatural power, she finds out the wondering soul of the dead person who is believed to be wondering in the atmosphere for forty nine days and then take him/her back to heaven, that is why, this class of Mun is called *Pildon Mun*. In Lepcha *Pildon Mun* means a Mun who finds out the soul. And she has the power to call back the spirit of the dead person on her own body and speaks out in the voice of the dead person and tells the good and bad happenings of the future of the family members and bids goodbye to all saying not to be grieved for now he or she is going to his or her heavenly home......

The rest Muns perform rituals, ceremonies, forecasts, make predictions and act as medicine women for the Lepchas but they can not deliver the souls of the dead persons to heaven." (1983: pp. 48-49).

G. Gorer found two groups of Mun in Dzongu: the good group i.e Tang-li Mun the bad group i.e Mun-mook Mun. To quote Gorer: "it is believed that there are two sorts of Mun, a good group called Tang-li Mun and a bad group called Mun-mook Mun; the difference is similar to the traditional difference between white and black magicians. 'Mun-mook Mun like thieves : they think and do evil and are possessed by devils which they employ for their own selfish ends; they alone can send devils (the term used for sorcery).' They are believed to have an influence like the evil eye. On the other hand 'When Tang-li Mun sacrifice they do so with benevolence in their heart towards the people and houses to which they are summoned'' (1938: p. 216-217).

Jenny Bentley could find six types of Mun in Sikkim which are to some extent different from those in Darjeeling areas. She wrote:

"In Dzongu I recorded six different kinds of mun:

1. ***Niulick nysong mun:*** This mun is, together with the *thenli tnsong mun* considered the most powerful. This mun has the ability to guide the *a pil* of the dead person away from the domains of the living into the area design for the dead people. *Niulick nysong mun* can also perform animal sacrifice. This mun is also known in Kalimpong. It is the name of the first mun that arrived on earth and sometimes also generally used to describe any mun.

2. ***Thenli tnsong mun:*** This mun is considered just as powerful as the niulick neusong mun. They though do not use animal sacrifice. Their main ability is to show and preserve how the creation really is. In Kalimpong I was also told about a *tungli tungsong mun*. It is said that this mun does not perform any ceremony, but just finds out what has happened and for which reason a person is sick. The mun will chant for hours and find the mung or the circumstance causing the illness and give directions to how it can be cured. The bongthing will then come and perform the ritual. This type of mun is also noticed by Gorer. He puts all mun that are not engaged in evil activities in this category.

3. ***Abhar mun:*** Abhar means middle. This indicates that the mun is of middle power and cannot guide the soul of the dead. Foning describes a type of mun he calls avore. This mun spirit will appear in a group of people at different times, but is a rare phenomenon (Foning 1987: 80,81). Tamsang also names the avor mun in his list of different mun types. He states that the avor mun has the same power as the first mun, nyulick, but can become misguided (Tamsang 1983: p. 47).

4. ***Mun muk***: This mun also only has medium powers, but uses them for evil means. *Mun muk* does not show his or her real face to the outside, but conducts the ceremonies in secret. They are said to do their rituals in the dark, during night time. Instead of warding of the mung they direct them at a specific person, causing illness, misfortune or even death. The mun muk is also known in Kalimpong (Foning 1987: 79), but was not mentioned by my main informant in Kalimpong. Siiger and Gorer both refer to "black magic" performed by evil mun (Siiger 1987: 166, Gorer 1984: 216).

5. ***Angang mun:*** The *angang mun* does all his ceremonies in the sitting position. This mun is also known of in Kalimpong (see Siiger (1967: 166) for description of the equipment).

6. ***Pildong mun:*** The name of this mun derives from the Lepcha word *a pil* (soul) and doñg (bring back). When a person falls ill, one reason can be that he or she has lost a pil, the soul. This mun has the ability to go and search for the lost *a pil* and bring it back into the body of the person. If this is successful, the person will recover again. The *pildong mun* is also known in Kalimpong. Foning calls these types of mun the most powerful, because they can lead the souls into the land of death. (Foning 1987: 77, See also Tamsang 1983 : 48).

   My informant from Kalimpong names three kinds of mun that I did not hear of in Dzongu:

7. ***Rabchu rabdem mun:*** This mun can also guide the *a pil* of the dead, but the chants that he or she use in the rituals are different from the *nuilick nyong mun*.

8. ***Phyong chok phyong flee mun:*** This mun is considered to have a lot of power. The main activity

of this mun is when two parties are engaged in a dispute over land or other things. The mun will make one quarrelling party ill, by inviting a mung into chi and throwing it into the air. And then afterwards the same will be done to the other side. Then both parties will be ailing and seek a compromise. I am not sure how this mun relates to the mun muk, because the activities are also harming a person, even if, in the end it is for the benefit of all.

9. ***Sokuk sochok mun:*** This mun can influence the atmosphere and the wind. He or she can chant and bring or stop rain. This ability is something I only heard associated to lamas in Sikkim.

Foning and Tamsang name a mun, I did not hear in Kalimpong or in Dzongu: the mun *jyum mun*. Tamsang lists another mun, the *lyang eet mun*. These mun can do any rituals except leading the *a pil* of the soul to *rum lyang* (Foning 1987: 80; Tamsang 1983: 47,49)". (p. Appendix xvii - xix).

Religious Conversion and the Role of Mun

Over the different phases of political rule in the Lepcha land, the Lepchas got influenced by the ruler's religion and in the process got converted first into Buddhism and then into Christianity. The role and position of the Mun also changed with the changed circumstances.

Buddhism and Mun

On his way to (B.S.K.Grover) or on his way back (R.Temple) from Tibet Guru Padmasambhaba propagated Buddhism in the Eastern face of Eastern Himalayas in 8th century. But actual conversion of nature worshipper Lepchas into Buddhism took place with the colonization of Sikkim by the Tibetan rulers during 17th century. With the support of the Chogyel, the lamas worked hard for the spread of

Buddhism among the Lepchas of Sikkim. They made an admixture of Buddhism and Nature worshipper so that it can be accepted to the Lepchas easily. Mahayana form of Buddhism had special bent of imbibing Munism or Bongthimism in the Buddhism. Even then the task of conversion was not that easy. "The Chronicle of the Kings asserts that fourteen Lepcha priests and priestesses plotted to kill the king with the aid of Black Magic. Their wicked plan miscarried. (R.V. Nebesky. 1956. p. 121).

The old manuscripts of the Lepchas were burnt into ashes by the order of the King. Many religious scripts including *Tashi Namthar* were translated into Lepcha language. Matrimonial alliances were another method of religious conversion. Both Chogyel and some elites of the society married Lepcha girls. The alliance helped the rulers to administrate and there was open access for the Lepchas to become elites. These Lepchas turned elites took advantages of Royal relations and accelerated the process of conversion of the Lepchas into Buddhism in Sikkim.

Another important aspect of Buddhism is the prayer flag. Till the other day, the Buddhist Lepchas used to display prayer flags written in Tibetan language in the open air. As there is no similarity between the Tibetan script with Lepcha script, most of the Lepchas do not understand what is written in the prayer flag and also details of the activities carried out by the Lama. But recently prayer flags are available in Lepcha language which they can read and understand. Lepchas are using two types of prayer flays *(Toor)*: one during death and the other during all other occasions. As it is written in Lepcha language Mun and Bongthing become legal authority in hoisting the prayer flags. Although prayer flag has nothing to do with the nature worshipper Lepchas but the Mun and Bongthing got an additional work of raising prayer flag in the Buddhist culture.

Christianity and Mun

Conversion of the Lepchas into Christianity dates back to the mid 19th century. After the annexation of Darjeeling track by the East India Company, Christian Missionaries started functioning in this area and the process of conversion into Christianity started.

The first phase of conversion started in 1841 with the arrival of Rev. William Start and ended in 1865 at the death of Rev. W. Niebel. Both of them worked hard in the translation and printing the Gospel into Lepcha language which is the first printed material in Lepcha language. In the second phase, Rev. J.C.Page started working among the Lepchas since 1868. Rev. W. Macfarlane started the third phase of Missionary work in Darjeeling since 1870 and in Kalimpong from 1872. He was very enthusiastic with the Lepchas and found that "the Lepchas seem to be very hopeful people for us in the hills." (Perry L.C., 1997: p. 42). Rev Namthak Ronggong and Rev. Dyonshi Sada were the first Lepcha Pastors who were the main instruments of Rev. Macfarlane to bring the large number of the Lepchas under Christianity. Beside the Protestants, the Roman Catholics became more powerful and started their Mission at Pedong in 1891.

The impact of these Missionaries was so rapid that large number of Lepchas converted into Christianity within very short period of time. It was found that during 1901 –1911, all the Lepchas were Buddhists. But in 1831, there were 10,099 Buddhists: 1,950 Christians and 670 animists. In 1941, the number of Christian Lepchas increased to 2,559 while those of Buddhists decreased to 9,911.

During this period, Mun and Bongthing started loosing their position and power in the Lepcha society. Christians left nothing to be done by the Mun and Bongthing and everything is carried out by the Pastor or Father in the Church. Christianity is Church oriented activity and both Mun and Bongthing became idle spectator.

It is reported that the Protestant Christians are rigid in their religious belief and do not allow the rituals performed by the Mun and Bongthing in any occasion. Church is the only place where the rituals are to be performed and that too as per the guidance and instruction of the Pastor of the Church. But the Catholic Christians are more liberal and in many occasions the Father of the Church allows the Lepchas, although such cases are very limited, to perform their rituals as per their traditional customs and beliefs and where the Mun and Bongthing play some role. It may be noted that Mun Northen Lepcha of Lower Menchu, Kalimpong himself was a Catholic Christian before he acquired the power of Mun. He reconverted into Buddhism after be became a full fledged Mun and now a days one of the most powerful Mun in the region.

Jyuktenmoo and the Mun

Jyuktenmoo is a peculiar blending between the nature worshipper and the Buddhist or the Christian Lepchas. In this type of mixture, the Bongthing and the Mun not only act as agent between the common Lepchas and the Rum, the good spirit and the Mung, the evil spirit but they perform more difficult task of performing their activities along with the Lama and the Pastor/Church Father. The role and position of Mun, Bongthing, Lama and Pastor are different under different types of religious activities. In some cases like house constructions, death rituals etc., the Mun and Bongthing play dominant role while the Lama and the Pastor act as subsidiary role. But in case of Mane, Chu Chu function which are Gumba oriented activity, the role of Lama is more than that of Mun and Bongthing. In all such functions, the Mun and Bongthing work under the guidance and directions of the Lama. When the religious activities are performed at the house of the Lepchas, Mun and Bongthing play dominant role over those of Lama and the Pastor/ Church Father. But in case the religious functions take place in the Gumba or in the Church, the Mun and Bongthing have to work as per the direction of the Lama and the Pastor or Church Father. Here the role and position of the Mun and Bongthing become secondary and subsidiary. It may be noted that Jyuktnmoo is in practice between the Mun/Bongthing with Lama and not with Pastor or Church father. Church plays the vital role in all types of religious activities and the role of Mun/ Bongthing is almost nil. So Jyuktenmoo is practised by the Buddhist Lepchas and not by the Christian Lepchas.

General Information of Some Mun and Bongthing

There is a common saying, both among the Lepchas and outsiders, that the Lepchas are a dying and vanishing tribe. The popular and well circulated book *'Lepcha: My Vanishing Tribe'*, written by A.R. Foning, a Lepcha scholar, carries the impression in the outside world that the tribe is on the verse of extinction. It is true that the indigenous tribe with their rich culture, custom and tradition had to pass through different difficult phases. They were over run both politically and culturally by dominant communities in the recent past. The major blow remained their religious conversion which is responsible in eating up their rich culture. In the process the Mun and Bongthing had lost their original and prestigious strong position in their society. But the present decade may be termed as 'Lepcha Cultural Revival Decade' when the Indigenous Lepcha Tribal Association has taken a number of positive steps in rejuvenating their traditional culture. The Mun and Bongthing have, to some extent, regained their lost status and started participating in different cultural and religious activities. Existence of good number of Mun and Bongthing in the locality is self explanatory and is the evidence of their high position in the Lepcha society.

The following Tables -5.1 and 5.2 show details of some of the Mun and Bongthing as found in the local areas:

Tables - 5.1 and 5.2 show that Mun and Bongthing are still present in and around Kalimpong. It is true that Mun has become rare and their number is much less than Bongthing but there are Mun and they are always ready to go even far of places to serve the community. The Indigenous Lepcha Tribal Association organized training programme for increasing the number of Bongthing but no such training can be done for the Mun which is purely God gifted.

Table – 5.1
Details of Some Lepcha Mun in and Around Kalimpong

Sl No	*Name*	*Sex*	*Address*
1	Mun Northen Lepcha	Male	Lower Menchu, Pedong. Kpg Daj
2	Munue Mong mit Lepcha	Female	Do
3	Munue Mongali Lepcha	Female	Do
4	Mun Ong Tsh Lepcha	Male	Peyong, Dalapchand. Kpg, Darj.
5	Munue Jer mit Lepcha	Female	Mirik, Darj.
6	Munue You mit Lepcha	Female	Sukhia pokri, Darj.
7	Mun Mangal Sing Lepcha	Male	Upper Pembling Kpg Darj.
8	Mun Nima Tsh. Lepcha	Male	Nimbong, Kpg Darj.
9	Munue Narim Lepcha	Female	20th Mile Pedong Kpg. Darj.
10	Munue Taso Lepcha	Female	15th Mile, Payong Kpg, Darj.
11	Munue Duk mit Lepcha	Female	Mane Gumba, Kpg, Darj.
12	Munue Passang kit Lepcha	Female	Do
13	Munue Imit Lepcha	Female	Ruchuk Busty 12thMile Kpg Darj.
14	Munue Bura mit Lepcha	Female	Lyangay Busty. Kpg Darj.
15	Munue PhurKit Rongmit Lepcha	Female	Sakyong Pendong Dzongu Sikkim.

Source: Field Survey

Table – 5.2
Details of Some Lepcha Bongthing in and Around Kalimpong

Sl No	*Name*	*Sex*	*Address*
1	Bongthing Ambar Sing Lepcha	Male	Middle Pembling, Kpg,Darj
2	Bongthing Laxman Lepcha	Male	Lower Pembling, Kpg, Darj.
3	Bongthing Prem TshLepcha	Male	Sukhiapokri, Darj.
4	Bongthing Som Tshering Lepcha	Male	Mirik, Darj.
5	Bongthing Sancha Bhr Lepcha	Male	Do
6	Bongthing Gayboo Lepcha	Male	6th Mile, Kpg, Darj.
7	Bongthing P.T.Simikmoo Lepcha	Male	Do
8	Bongthing Sherap Lepcha	Male	Dukka Pedong, Kpg, Darj.
9	Bongthing Choden Lepcha	Male	8th Mile Kpg. Darj.
10	Bongthing Passang Tsh Lepcha	Male	Pulung Busty, Sukhia, Darj.
11	Bongthing Kessang Tsh Lepcha	Male	Do
12	Bongthing Wangdi Lepcha	Male	Noak Dara, Kpg, Darj
13	Bongthing Palden Tsh Lepcha	Male	Do
14	Bongthing Tshering D. Lepcha	Male	Lower Beong, Kpg Darj.
15	Bongthing Nim Tendu Lepcha	Male	Do
16	Bongthing Zoang Sing Lepcha	Male	Do
17	Bongthing Noku Lepcha	Male	5th Mile Kpg, Darj.
18	Bongthing Sanu Lepcha	Male	Bong Busty, Kpg, Darj.
19	Bongthing Kalachu Lepcha	Male	Do
20	Bongthing Aching lepcha	Male	Do
21	Bongthing O.T. Namchu	Male	Mane Gumba, Kpg Darj.
22	Bongthing O. T. Goulookmoo	Male	Do
23	Bongthing Dorjee Lepcha	Male	Do
24	Bongthing Temba Lepcha	Male	Ririk, 12th Mile Kpg, Darj.
25	Bongthing Ram Sing Lepcha	Male	Reon, Kpg. Darj.
26	Bongthing Budha Sing Lepcha	Male	Sindipong, Kpg. Darj.
27	Bongthing Bahadur Lepcha	Male	Pashyor, Kpg Darj.
28	Bongthing Prem Tsh Lepcha	Male	Khamdung, Kpg, Darj
29	Bongthing Tshering Lepcha	Male	Do

Source: Field Survey.

Epilogue

The status of women in Lepcha religious world got changed over the different phases of religious conversions. The Mun, the mediator between the common Lepchas and the spirit world, used to occupy not only a prestigious and commendable position but was inevitable in the Lepcha religion. In course of time, the position of Mun has first been taken by Lama and then by Pastor and Church Father. In Jyuktenmoo, the Mun and Bongthing, to some extent, have regained their lost status and started working simultaneously with the Lama. There is a sharp line of religious division between the activities of the Mun and Lama. Jyuktenmoo is the blending of Munism and Bongthimism with Lamaism. The Gumba oriented activities are performed under the leadership of the Lama while all domestic rituals are performed under the leadership of the Mun and Bongthing. The Christian Lepchas prefer to go to the Church in all religious occasions and thereby Mun lost all her significance and prestigious position in the Lepcha society. Recently the Indigenous Lepcha Tribal Association in all its socio- cultural and religious activities invites the Mun and Bongthing to inaugurate the function with Chi Faat as per pure Lepcha tradition. Lepchas are passing through a revival phase where they, mostly the Buddhists, have started using the service of Mun to a large extent in most religious activities.

Anyway, the existence of Mun, the female mediator between the Lepchas and the spirits is a unique feature among the Lepchas who are basically the nature worshippers. The society by respecting the Mun respects the females. Females occupy a prestigious position and status in the Lepcha society due to the important role and power of the Mun. After the arrival of the Tibetans and the Europeans in this part of the country, Mun started loosing her earlier position. Even then they continued to hold prestigious position in the Lepcha society. They are more required and used by the Buddhists Lepchas than by the Christians. The Indigenous Lepcha Tribal Association has been playing an important role in reviving the lost status of the Mun in their society in recent years. In brief we can say that:

(a). Mun plays a very important role from cradle to grave in the Lepcha society. In recent years she started regaining her lost status due to the interference of the Indigenous Lepcha Tribal Association.

(b). The selection of Mun never follow any hereditary rules; divinely ordained power of Mun is not always hereditable nor can it be acquired through training. But in many cases the power is inherited by the ancestors and the power passes to the posteriors.

(c). Mun never claims any special status in the society but people with respect regard her as a gifted personality in the society.

(d). Mun performs spiritual acts which are of high religious values to the Lepchas.

(e). Mun performs as the mental healer and the bare footed doctor of the village. She possesses enough knowledge about the herbal medicine.

(f). Mun represents a highly strong personality protecting the whole body of the Lepcha religious beliefs and rituals against all odds.

(g). Mun has never been considered as a profession but is a sort of voluntary service for the betterment of the fellow community.

(h). Mun preserves the old and rich tradition, culture and custom of the Lepchas.

(i). Mun becomes rare and as a result their presence in any village is not only enrich the position of the village but the community knows the village by the name of the Mun.

(j). The tune of most Lepcha songs are derived from the chanting tune of the Mun.

(k). It is no other person but only a Mun who can collect the haphazardly floating *a pil*, soul of the dead person and guide him / her to reach the Chu where the ancestors are waiting to receive eternal rest.

(l). Mun has no gender bias. A Mun can be either a man or a woman.

6

Bride Price and The Status of Women

Introduction

Lepchas still maintain their day's old system of bride price (*Taya - Kup - Afaar* or *Nyom-sa-afar* or *Myaok Panol*). It symbolizes both the utility of women to men and the compensation to the parents for giving the girl in marriage. Each Lepcha family welcomes the girl child and the society celebrates at the birth of a girl child in the village. The parents take lot of pain in bringing up the girl child and they should be rewarded at the time of marriage. It is also a shift of working hand in both the farm and household activities from the parent's house to in-law's house and should be compensated by one time payment.

E.T. Dalton as early as 1872 observed bride price among the Lepchas and considered it as the cause of late marriage among the tribe. Bride price is indispensable and called it 'credit' where the groom needs to repay it even by selling his labour in his in-law's house. Dalton wrote that "they do not marry young, as they often find it difficult to make up the necessary sum demanded by the parents of the girl, but the marriage is sometimes allowed to take place on credit, the girl remaining in her father's house and her husband living with her there till he can pay or has earned money which entitles him to take her home" (1872: p. 100). H.H. Risley in 1891 observed the same to those of Dalton. He also noted bride price as the cause of late marriage for the boys among the Lepchas but found that "girls usually marry between the ages of sixteen and eighteen" (p. 8). He also noted bride price so compulsory that the poor man "is often allowed to marry, as it were, on credit, but the bride does not leave her father's house, and the husband goes to live with her and work for his father- law until the full amount has been made up" (1891: p. 8, 9). The intensiveness of bride price has reduced and is no more considered as a 'credit' for the boy but the bride price still exists in some other form.

In earlier days Lepcha marriage (*Bri)* was considered to be a service marriage where the groom had to render physical service in the house of his would be in-law. Customarily a boy had to pass through several hard stages before qualified himself as groom for the marriage. There were seven stages in the Lepcha marriage and it needed seven long years to complete it. In many cases a Lepcha boy had served even seven long years before marriage in bride's house. The groom generally extended physical labor in agricultural field and thereby compensated in advance the loss of the girl's labor in the field after marriage. But in course of time this system has faded away mainly due to non availability of sufficient agricultural land. The service marriage has gradually been changed to marriage by purchase where the groom has to pay, in terms of both cash and kind, to his in-laws and thereby compensates in advance the absence of the girl in the family whom they brought up with so much of care.

A. Campbell, the then superintendent of Darjeeling could find the presence of bride price in Lepcha society in 1840's. He wrote: "Marriage among the Lepchas are not contracted in childhood, as among the Hindoos, nor do the men generally marry young. This arises mainly from the difficulty of procuring means of paying the parents of the bride the expected douceur on giving the suitor his daughter to wife; this sum varies from 40 rupees to 400, or 500, according to the rank of the parties. It is not customary to allow the bride to leave her parents' home for that of her husband until the sum agreed on has been paid in full; hence, as the consummation of the marriage is permitted while the female is still under her father's roof, it is by no means uncommon to find the husband the temporary bondsman of his father-in-law, who exacts, Jewish fashion, labour from his son, in lieu of money, until he shall have fairly won his bride" (1840: p. 384).

C.D.Beauvoir Stocks in 1925 also noticed bride-price among the Lepchas. He wrote: "As the bride-price the boy works in the girl's father's fields for one or two years, and unless he can pay the full amount they ask for their daughter then, and present them with a large brass pot, he must work for another year.

In a case I investigated personally, the son had to pay Rs. 300 for his bride, and yet had to work for three years for his father-in-law. The man is allowed to cohabit with the girl; sometimes children are born before the man brings his wife home" (1925: p. 466).

The bride price (*Taya - Kup - Afaar or Nyom-sa-afar*) still prevails in the Lepcha society but its amount and magnitude has reduced to such an extent that it has now just become a symbol of girl's position in the society. Beside some cash, the groom needs to present *Chi, Aamoo Dum - Dyem* (mother's dress), silver coin, front leg of bull, hind right leg of bull, liquor, dress and jewellery of the bride etc. The bride price is considered as security of the girl child in her in-laws house. Under any circumstances if the bride returns to her parent's house, the bride price need to be returned to the groom. The bride price is to be preserved and may be used by the groom as interest free loan to meet the emergent financial crisis.

Items of Bride Price

The Lepcha Customary Law published by the Indigenous Lepcha Tribal Association mentioned a detailed list of items of Lepcha bride price:

The bride price or marriage price paid to the bride's parents and relatives shall include the followings:

"a. ***Nyaom Aasek Gyu*** — Engagement price.

- i) Chi, fermented beverage — One bundle basket.
- ii) Garland (*Phogo Rip Lyaak*) — One
- iii) 6 (six) Rupees silver coins.

b. ***Myaok Panol*** — Groom's customary, official presents to the Bride's parents and relatives in the marriage ceremony:

- i) *Aamoo Dum - dyem*:

  (mother'dress) — One set
- ii) Father's Guardian Spirit — 1 (one) Lepcha hat, of longevity and Life — 3 (three) Silver coins Only.

  —1(one) garland (*Phogo Rip Lyaak*)
- iii) *Aamoo Kaomjung* — Rs 101.00 (One hundred & one)only *(Sungdrong*)
- iv) *Bikgoo Nin - Chyer* —Rs. 35.00 (Thirty Five) only. *(Pomo Pakyong)*
- v) Parental uncle and —1 (one) garland and Rs 5 (five). Aunt (2) Silver coin/ coins each only.
- vi) Maternal Uncle and — 1 (one) garland and Rs 5 (five).

Aunt (2) Silver Coin/ coins each only

vii) *Faaming* (brother) (one) —1 (one) garland and Rs 5 (five) silver coin/coins only.

viii) *Piboo,* Go-between — (one) garland and Rs 5(five) from Bride side silver coin/coins only.
1 (one) basket of Chi with 1(one) garland and Rs 5 (five) silver coin/coins on top of it only.

ix) *Laom -- sut.* It is also called — 1 (one) front left leg of a bull

Myaok Mungkoong — 1 (one) hind right leg of a bull

c. ***Nyaom Lee Haon*** – Bride's entrance to the new house. The items shall be arranged , provided, and taken to the Groom's parents.

i. 1 (one) basket of Chi, fermented beverage.

ii. Two bottles of liquor.

iii. Front leg of a bull.

d. ***Nyaom Mungkong Zo-gool.***—a complete dressed cock.

The above item, *Nyaom Mungkong Zo-gool,* shall be taken by the Bride's party consisting of Bride's paternal, and maternal uncles and aunts, on completion of the marriage ceremony at the Groom's house, to the Bride's parents as a token of respect and donating and indicating that their daughter has been handed over to the lap of the Bride Groom's parents.

e. **Bride's dress and jewelry.** Although it is not mandatory and compulsory, the following dress and jewelry may be provider by the Groom's parents for the Bride:

i) *Dum – dyem* (dress) —'1 set

ii) *Jyoordaong Tago* (black gawn) — one

iii) *Takvil Lyaak* (neckless) — made of cane splits

iv) *Kakel* (bangle) — made of cane splits

v) *Aanyaor Kong* (ear rings) — made of cane splits

vi) *Ka – Chhyaop or Chhyaap* — made of silver

Chhyaap with *Saret – Aajet* design

vii) *Panthop* (badge) — made of silver

viii) *Sambraang Baor* — made of silver"

(Lepcha Customary Law, ILTA. 2003. P - 6,7).

A.R.Foning make a list of presents to be given by the groom at marriage to the bride's party:

i) "Two full baskets of chee.

ii) One fore and one hind legs of a bull with the tail attached. These legs must retain the hooves, complete with unshaven skin all around, up to about six inches above them.

iii) 'Amu Dum-dyam', wearing apparel for the mother.

iv) 'Abo Ayong-lu', a body wrapping shawl for the father.

v) 'Panol', or presents, for 'Mu-zyong', the maternal uncle.

vi) 'Panol', or presents, for 'Bo-ku', the paternal uncle.

vii) 'Panol', or presents, for 'Phaming', the brother.

viii) 'Panol', or presents, for 'Mu-nyu', the maturnal aunt.

ix) 'Panol', or presents, for 'Bo-nyu', the paternal aunt.

Panol may be offered to other brothers, uncles and aunts; but it is not obligatory" (1987: p. 206).

Late marriage and no marriage in the society are due to the non availability of bride price for the poor Lepchas. Gaeboo Lepcha, a bachelor of 45 years lamented 'where from could I manage the bride price so as to marry a beautiful Lepcha girl of my choice.' This initiates love marriage and exogamous marriage among the Lepchas. In case of marriage by elopement, the groom needs to pay *Choridanda,* (sort of penalty) which even today is much less than the bride price. The large number of Lepchas crossing their normal marital age and larger number of exogamous marriage are due to the existence of bride price in the Lepcha society. Even in the modern age of fast change all around, Lepchas still continue to preserve their traditional system of bride price which can be explained as the higher position and status of women in the Lepcha society compared to their male counterpart.

The system of bride price and the position of women can better be understood from different features of marriage associated in Lepcha society. Following paragraphs contain different aspects of Lepcha marriage as experienced from our field study.

Origin of Lepcha Marriage

Conceptually marriage is a social contact for the satisfaction of physical, biological, psychological and spiritual needs of male and female. It helps in procreation of new generations which is inevitable for the continuation of human civilization. Marriage can be regarded as one of the central features of any society. It correlates different types of socio-economic relations among the individuals in the society. For the Lepchas, marriage (*Bri*) is not only the union of two souls but involves the integration of two clans, two families, two Moos, two groups and two villages. It is one of the powerful binding forces which helps in keeping the Lepcha society united and homogenous.

Like those of most the tribes, Lepchas have their own legends and mythologies regarding the origin of their marriage. Sonam Wangdi Lepcha narrates:

"*Tarbongmu*, the youngest son of *Itbumu*, the supreme Goddess of creation, lived happily with his mother at the foot of Kanchanjunga. On his attaining the maturity he expressed before his mother his desire to see the world, and obtaining her due permission he set out on an excursion. While he returned, as was obvious his mother asked him as to what he could see and perceive. He narrated his experience and told how beautiful birds he could see over *'Palit Samper Koong'*. *Itbumu* advised *Tarbongmu* to put snares and catch those birds for her. So the following day he brought many birds and presented to her mother who become pleased. But the next day when he reached that *Koong* he found that his snares were removed by someone else. He returned home with empty hands. On the third day as was advised by his mother, he ambushed by the side of bushes and was able to detect who the wrong doer was. A beautiful girl *Naripnom* by name was the remover of the snares. Charmed by the beauty of the girl he forgot her mischievous act and he fell in love with her and wanted to possess her but she did not like it. Very much disappointed, he told his mother of his unfulfilled desire. She advised him to contact his elder brother *Kosmi-Thing* who lives at *Rungzing Patham*. *Komsi- Thing* whole heartedly helped his brother. On his advice, *Tarbongmu* collected a pig, an ox, a copper vessel, new cloth and rug. Then millet from Mayal was brought and Chi was prepared.

After the Chi was prepared, the mother, *Itbomu* supplied the butter. *Komsi- Thing* sent the presents to *Naripnom* and she agreed to get married to *Tarbong*. A lot of people assembled for the ceremony, where the Gods were supplied with Chi and butter and sacrifice.

Thus *Tarbong and Naripnom* were married and the custom of marriage originated from that day." (1979: pp. 181 - 183).

Lyansong Tamsang, President of Indigenous Lepcha Tribal Association gives a detailed account of the origin of Lepcha marriage in a slightly different way. He wrote:

"Thousands of years ago, a young, robust and powerful Lepcha named Tarbongthing after journeying and exploring Mayel Lyang for many months arrived at a place called 'Pari Pagyen'. Very tired, fatigued, and hungry, Tarbongthing looked for a shelter for the night but no village or human settlement was in sight. He saw a fruit tree nearby with hundreds of birds on it. His one thought was to satisfy his hunger and, therefore, he set Radoo Ramyang, a bamboo trap, to catch birds on the fruit tree. He caught a few birds and satisfied his hunger.

"The next day Tarbongthing set Radoo Ramyang once again on the same fruit tree and went away to look for the village. When he returned to his shelter in the afternoon, Tarbongthing found, to his annoyance, there were only dry twigs and leaves hanging on the trap instead of birds. Tarbongthing was puzzled, angry as well as curious to find out the person who was perpetrating a mischievous deed on him. The next day once again, he very carefully set Radoo Ramyang on the same fruit tree and hid himself under the bushes and watched.

"In the afternoon, Tarbongthing saw a young beautiful girl coming out from the wood towards the trap and freeing the birds one after another from the trap and putting dry twigs and leaves on it instead.

"On seeing this, Tarbongthing sneaked behind her and caught her very firmly. The young and beautiful girl. although surprised, fought back to free herself from Tarbongthing but Tarbongthing, somehow, overpowered and subdued her at the end.

"Tarbongthing asked her, 'Why did you free the birds from the traps? The young girl replied that she was the guardian, preserver and champion of the birds and asked him, 'What harm did these birds do to You? She further said that she freed the birds from the trap because they have an equal right to live in this beautiful Mayel Lyang.

"Both of them were young, beautiful and handsome. They were attracted to each other, in fact, it was love at first sight.

"When she wanted to go home because it was getting very late, Tarbongthing barring her way asked her name and place of residence. The girl answered that her name was, 'Narip Naom' and she came from 'Sakyong'. Tarbongthing again asked her if she would run away with him to start a new family life of their own. Hearing his appeal, Narip Naom replied, 'If you really want my hand in marriage, you must ask my mother's and uncle's permissions. My mother's name is Taee-Tanye Moo-Nyoo. Having said this, she hurriedly left and disappeared into the woods.

"Tarbongthing returned to his mother, Numkoot Amoo Nyoo and narrated his stories including his meeting with the young and beautiful girl, Narip Naom. He expressed his desire to marry Narip Naom to his mother because he was in love with Narip Naom. Numkoot Amoo Nyoo, Tarbongthing's mother, summoned her brothers and sent them to 'Sakyong' to ask Narip Naom's hands in marriage to Tarbongthing.

Narip Naom's mother and uncles were also very happy indeed and welcomed the proposal of a marriage between Narip Naom and Tarbongthing, however, Narip Naom's mother and uncles said that Tarbongthing, the groom his uncles must adhere to and fulfill the marriage conditions.

"A meeting of the Lepchas was convened at 'Rungjyeng Purtam' to finalize the Lepcha Marriage Customary Law and the necessary items to be provided and presented as a bride's price during the wedding of the bride's party. Tarbongthing and his uncles agreed to all the conditions of the Lepcha Customary Law and the bride price. At the end of the meeting, a bamboo was planted to commemorate the occasion. The sacred bamboo grove of the Lepchas called 'Chimoo Aeyong moo pobong' still stands in Zaongoo, North Sikkim.

"Tarbongthing and his uncles were able to collect the bride price and placed them in front of the bride's mother, uncles, aunts and relatives during the wedding. And thus the first Lepcha marriage ceremony was solemnised between Narip Naom and Tarbongthing and the first Lepcha Customary Law originated in Mayel Lyang. The die hard Lepchas continue to practise their ancient Lepcha Marriage Customery Law even today. The Lepcha women continue to receive the respect, dignity, and honour they so deserve from their Lepcha men even today.

"During a Lepcha marriage ceremony, Peeboo or Bekboo, ago between, or a Boongthing/Mun, or elders, while blessing the newly wedded couple, always narrate the story of Tarbongthing and Narip Naom and how the Lepcha marriage system originated in the Lepcha world." (2008: pp. 11-13).

Types of Lepcha Marriage

We could notice eight different types of marriage in Lepcha society. They are:

i) *Arranged Marriage:* In this type of marriage the boy after attaining the marriageable age, seeks the hand of the girl through *Peeboo*, the go between or match maker of the Lepcha society. This is the oldest and true Lepcha method of marriage and is still practiced by most of the Buddhist Lepchas. The Christians, on the other hand, in most cases just follow the first stage of approaching the girl's hand but rest of the procedures are performed in the Church as per the Christian tradition. Details of the true Lepcha arranged marriage has been discussed later in this chapter under the sub-heading 'Procedure of Lepcha Marriage'.

ii) *Marriage by Test:* It is like Hindu '*Sayamvar* Marriage' where the groom is selected on the basis of bravery, courage, strength, capacity etc. In Ramayana *Rama (Haradhanu Bhanga)* and in *Mahabharata Arjuna (Lakshaveda)* have been tested their bravery before going for their marriage. This type of marriage is rarely found among the Lepchas in the present day. K.P. Tamsang narrates one such story in one of his unpublished manuscripts. He wrote: "about a century ago a rich Lepcha named C.R.Gay lived with his wife Pemo and his daughter Lakit in Samalbong village of Kalimpong sub division. Lakit was very beautiful and homely type of girl. A fame for her beauty spread like wild fire far and wide. Lepcha boys from far came to seek her hand in marriage. The girls parents were in trouble and worried. If they say yes to one, the rest would be annoyed and thereby may cause quarrel and enmity and they were afraid of witchery caused by the jealous antagonists. One day the girls mother thought of a scheme and accordingly the girl's father proclaim to all the candidates seeking her daughter's hand in marriage to assemble themselves at Khani river just on the foot of Samalbong village at a particular date and time. Hundreds of aspiring candidates assemble at Khani river at fixed appointed date and time. From Khani river upward Samalbong village there is a steep hill. The girl's father pointed to the hill says to all the candidates – look the steep hill is more than a mile in length and distance. It is just as steep as the sharp edge of a *Baan*, the Lepcha knife. All the candidates by pulling out their knife and holding it in their mouth placing the sharp edge inwards must run up the steep hills without taking out the knife from mouth and rest anywhere on the ran must reach up at the top hill. After reaching, they should take out the knife from mouth and cut a branch of the *Taknil*, variety of wood and placing it on the ground must sit down on its cross leg. The candidate who can do this will be married with Lakit. (Unpublished Manuscript of K.P.Tamsang available with his son L.S.Tamsang).

iii) *Junior Levirate:* It is a preferential type of marriage which has two components: Sororate and levirate. In the former the man marries the unmarried sister of his wife after her death while in the later the younger brother marries the wife of his elder brother if she becomes a widow. The system is known as *Aangaop* in Lepcha which is rarely practice in recent days. The system was made compulsory in earlier days perhaps to restrict the properties particularly land to go in the hands of outsiders. It is permitted by the society and made obligatory on the part of in-laws of the bereaved widow or widower to supply the bride or groom to the younger brother or sister of the deceased. But senior levirate was restricted where the widower could not marry elder brother or sister of the deceased spouse. In the absence of any unmarried brother junior cousin of the deceased husband is preferred for levirate marriage. In case of no unmarried male member, the widow was ceremonially returned to her parent's house along with a milch cow. Later on the widow could be married with outsider by returning the bride price etc. This was applied to the widower also. In sororate marriage, in the absence of younger sister of deceased wife, younger member of his wife's family was preferred for marriage. But both levirate and sororate are the system of the past and in our study area only one such case was noted in Lower Beyong village. Both the families and the society decided the junior levirate marriage of Laden Lepcha with Ongmit Lepcha, the widow of his elder brother. Even after ten years of conjugal life and giving birth five children the couple got separated and Laden preferred for an exogamous marriage with Sumitra Rai, a non-Lepcha girl at the age of nearly forty years.

The Lepcha Customary Law published by the Indigenous Lepcha Tribal Association wrote about two types of *Aangaop* and substantiate with the basic reasons for such marriage. It states:

"*Aangaop* shall take under the following circumstances only:

a. On the untimely death of a husband, a young widow, if she wishes, after one year, she shall be betrothed and married to one of the following relations, if he is willing and happy, in that order of priority, in consultation with the family members, elders and village Lepcha Association from both sides:

   i) Dead husband's single younger brother.

   ii) Dead husband's single nephew.

b. On the untimely death of a wife, a younger widower, if he wishes, after one year, he shall be betrothed and married to one of the following relations if she is willing and happy, in that order of priority, in consultation with the family members, elders and village Lepcha Association from both sides:

i) Dead wife's single younger sister..

ii) Dead wife's single niece.

Under this unique marriage system of *Aangaop*, the child/children, if any from the previous marriage shall continue to receive the same love, affection, and care from the new step-father or step-mother. A child/children shall remain happy and above all in safe hands.

In case of no issue, younger sister of the wife, if she is willing and happy, shall also be given in *Aangaop*.

This way, the same harmony, balance, understanding, relationship, and unity shall prevail in the house and between the two families, class and villages."

iv) *Marriage by Service:* In this type of marriage the groom stayed in bride's house and extend physical labor basically in the agricultural field. It is said that Lepcha marriage has seven stages and it takes seven years to complete it. During his stay in the bride's house, he needs to satisfy all members of the bride's family, particularly her parents. If they dissatisfy the candidature is cancelled and give the chance to another person. In some cases, the groom need to pay both cash and kind in place of physical labor. In Lepcha agriculture human labor is considered most important non-land input, the females are playing a vital role in extending not only helping hand but in some cases their service is indispensable in the cultivation. Dawa Tshering Lepcha, 77 years old of Mane Gumba had to stay three years in his in-laws house in order to satisfy them and qualify himself suitable for the marriage. It is told that Late Kam Dorjee Lepcha, who expired in 2000 at the age of 78 had to spent seven years in his in-laws house before marriage. Late Atta Tshring Lepcha who expired in 2006 at the age of 85 stayed and learn farming during his four years stay in his in-laws house. Similarly late Ongu Tshering Lepcha became an expert carpenter during his three and half years stay in his in-laws house. This system of marriage is also known as probationary marriage. The final solemnization of the marriage depends upon the satisfaction of all members of the bride's family during the probation period. Naturally the groom used to devote all his energy, time and mind in satisfying the members of the would be bride's family. If unsuccessful, the boy needs to return empty handed without marrying the girl. But in most cases the marriage has been materialized. But this type of marriage is the story of the past and in course of time the hard physical labour of the groom in bride's house has now been replaced by a token bride price.

v) *Marriage by Mutual Consent and Elopement:* In Lepcha this type of marriage is known as *Titbunong Fhyum*. Under such marriage the girl elopes with the boy on her own and should not return so long her parents give consent for their marriage. Normally within three days of such elopement, the boys side should approach the parents of the girl and after paying some penalty as decided by the society marriage is solemnized. The fine is popularly known as *Choridanda* in Nepali and *Tukmu- Thyum* in Lepcha. In case of exogamous marriage, elopement is widely practiced and is considered as the easiest method of getting the consent of both the sides.

Sumit Ghosal observed that "even elopement of widow is permitted which otherwise is almost difficult for remarry except junior levirate. A widow can not perform marriage ritual but she is allowed to get a husband by elopement. In such a case the Lepchas perform a ceremony called *Kha Daw - Thik - Shet* i.e. offering of scarf by the relatives of the widow to the man." (1990: p. 160). Marriage by elopement is widely practiced in the Lepcha society and is the most common form of mate selection in this region. All sorts of problems regarding social marriage can very easily and quickly be solved by the process of elopement. Marriage in such cases are mostly exogamous in nature where either of the side is a non-Lepcha. Details of such marriage have been discussed later in this chapter.

vi) *Love Marriage:* It is the most popular type of marriage of the today. It is one of the gifts of the modern civilization and the Lepchas are very much influenced by the modern media like TV, cinema and above all by the neighboring communities. It may both be endogamous and exogamous. In both the cases the boy and the girl choose their life partner themselves and thereafter their parents are informed for consent. The parents fall under obligation and have no other option but to accept and allow the marriage. In case of endogamous marriage after the primary selection, the rest of the procedure are performed as per the Lepcha tradition. In case of exogamous marriage, no such marriage rituals are generally performed and the Lepchas follow the procedure of marriage by elopement. Even love marriage between two Lepcha families turned to the marriage by elopement if the two sides are from two different religious faiths or from the same clan. Very recently the Youth Wing of the Lepcha Association is trying hard to reduce such marriage and the Association also restricts in recommending such cases for the issue of ST certificate by the government.

vii) *Widow Marriage:* If there is no remarriage within the family i.e. junior levirate marriage is not permitted and if the widow possesses no children , she may return to her parent's house. In such cases, the widow may be remarried without charging any sort of bride price and without maintaining all the procedures of Lepcha marriage. A.K. Das wrote: "The Bongthing and the Lama solemnize their marriage within a few hours after praying to God and chanting hymns. A widow may marry after one year of her husband's death when it is believed that the soul of the deceased has gone to the other world." (1978: p. 136) The same procedure is followed in case of the divorced person. But such cases are very rare among the Lepchas. Only one case of divorce has been noted in our study area. Phulmit Lepcha of Lower Beyong village has divorced her husband on the ground of his too much addiction to alcohol.

viii) *Marriage by Exchange:* A.K. Das has observed that "it is quite common for two siblings of one family to marry two siblings of another whether it is two brothers marrying two sisters or an exchange of sisters, each brother the sister of the other. Gorer also observed similar types of exchange among the Lepchas of Sikkim". (1978: p. 137). But not a single such case has been identified in our study areas. In case the couple possesses no male child, they prefer to find a son- in-law who is willing to stay in their house permanently and take the responsibility of both property and human beings of the household. Three such cases have been noted in Mane Gumba where Ramit Lepcha, Aimit Lepcha and Marmit Lepcha are the heads of the households and their husbands S.T. Lepcha, Y.T. Lepcha and Pari Lepcha respectively stay in their in-laws house. Same is the case with Taku Tshering Lepcha of Tashiding Busty where Runchi Lepcha inherits her patent's property. Those boys who willingly stay with their in – laws house are known as *Komok Myok* in Lepcha.

Among the above eight types of marriage, marriage by test, junior levirate, marriage by exchange, widow marriage, and marriage by service are the types of the past and are rarely practiced in the present day. The types of marriage which are commonly practiced are – arranged marriage, marriage by elopement and love marriage. Arranged marriage is widely practiced by the Buddhists and is most common in the village areas. The Christians who mostly live in the town areas undergo with the other two types of marriage. Love marriage and marriage by elopement are mostly exogamous in nature and create a lot of identity crisis in the Lepcha society. The slow growth rate of population in the Lepcha society may be due to the increasing number of exogamous marriage where a Lepcha girl looses her capacity of transmitting her mother's Moo among the future generations. This is a matter of great concern for the Lepchas and deserve special attention by the appropriate authority.

C.D. Beauvoir Stocks made an account of relation between brothers and wives in a family. "It is the youngest brother who has the monopoly of his wife, though it is hard to understand if this has any claim to ultimo geniture, inheritance of 'nasti' and fields being divided amongst all the brothers who live together. Thus though a man may live with his brother's wives, should the brothers be older than himself, he could not cohabit with the younger brother's wife, who is called a nyom meaning bride" (P- 468). But we could find not a single case of such relation. Now a days families are nuclear and each brother is staying with his wife and children. If any such relations exist between the brothers and the wives , it is treated an illegal and punishable in the society.

Restrictions and Taboos in Lepcha Marriage

There are some taboos and restriction connected with marriage in the Lepcha society. Lepcha marriage is Moo exogamous in nature. Exogamy is defined as a "social rule that prohibit a person from marrying within a defined social group of which he is a member" (E.A. Hoebel quoted by Vatsyayan ;1997; 192). Lepchas by custom can not marry within their own Moo. Restrictions have also been imposed to marry within both father's and mother's Moo. To be more specific, no Lepcha boy can marry a girl whose father belongs to his own Moo. And at the same time the girl should not be from his mother's Moo. In case they fall within the same Moo, either from father's or mother's side, Lepchas generally avoid four generations gap in selecting their life partner.

Gorer quoted nine generations back on the father's side and at least four generations on the mother's side. He stated that "in theory people of the same *ptso* are allowed to marry if they are separated by nine generations from the common ancestors, and to indicate that a person of the same *ptso* is very far removed a Lepcha will always say 'we can marry'; but in point of fact I did not come upon nor hear of a single instance of two people of the same *ptso* marrying. It is generally stated that though such a marriage was permissive, people would feel shame in it" (1938: p. 148). A.K. Das wrote "marriage is generally forbidden with cross or parallel cousins and any other types of cousins" (1978: p. 137). Sumit Ghosal also found restrictions in Lepcha marriage within the near relatives. "Lepcha exogamy is of a special kind for it does not permit a man to marry relative of his father provided the relationship is removed by five (but some say seven) generations. Such a marriage is of course only possible with a person descended through the father's or more possibly grand father's sisters since she being married, belongs to a different clan. In the case of a marriage between the descendants of two sisters a separation of only three generation is demanded. The Lepcha count descent five generations back on the father's side and at least three on the mother's. in actual practice all this means is that any two related people who do not belong to the same clan, may marry provided the relationship between them is sufficiently distant as to have been forgotten for all practical purposes" (1990: p. 145). C.D.Beauvoir Stocks not only mentioned restrictions but noticed severe punishment in case of violation of the law in Lepcha marriage custom. "Only the law of not marrying blood relations is strictly adhered to, and severe punishment is meted out to those who break this rule. In the cases of known incest, the man and woman are sent away from the village never to return. In this connection it is interesting to note that the mother's relations are considered to be much nearer kin than the father's. The Lapcha believe it to be only the father who transmits bone to his offspring, while from the mother they obtain their flesh and blood" (1925: p. 465).

While narrating the function of moo in Lepcha society P.T. Simikmoo of Ngasay village has repeatedly stressed on the restrictions of marriage within the same Moo. During selection of life partner the first thing to enquire is the family Moo of both the parents. Gorer also stated that except as an exogamic classification the *Ptso* (clan) is functionless. During our field survey it has also been noted that Moo is very much functional in marriage which confirms that Lepcha society is Moo exogamous by character. Not a single case has been identified where the Moo of either the daughter-in-law and the mother-in-law or the son-in-law and the father- in- law is the same. It is to note that the Lepcha male Moo is different from those of the females.

Lepchas can not dare to marry their sisters. They believe that their ancestors, Fudongthing and Nazong-Nyu did mistake by behaving as husband and wife. Mother Nature created them as brother and sister and due to their mistake they gave birth to the demons, devils and evil spirits.

The Lepcha Customary Law published by the Indigenous Lepcha Tribal Association, Kalimpong mentioned the followings on Lepcha marriage:

Lepcha Marriage

"No Lepcha marriage shall take place within the same *Aagit* , clan, in accordance with the ancient Lepcha Customary Law. No Lepcha shall marry within his or her closely related family members either. If, in case, it happens, it should be termed as *Naamtaok* or *Thaam Nyaot* in Lepcha meaning ill–omened, ill-starred, taboo, and evil. If such marriage, unfortunately, shall take place, then the man and woman involve in such illegal, forbidden, illicit, prohibited liaison shall be banished, expelled, exiled, separated, never to return, from the village and community for good because the same DNA and bone structure shall be found in the members of the same clan resulting in genetic defects. A Lepcha with genetic defects shall never be fully developed and healthy, physically and mentally. The illicit offspring shall not be accepted and entitled to the ancestral land and property.

The following very important points, aspects, features,, and particulars shall also be looked into, enquired, examined before the matrimony:

a. Family or clan effected with '*Daom*', leprosy, and other dangerous hereditary diseases and illness..

b. *Sthong - Daot* - Member of the family or clan attacked, injured, or killed by a tiger.

c. A family or clan which has a history, tendency, and inclination towards suicide and murder.

d. A family or clan involved in fighting and killing over land and water disputes.

No marriage shall take place with such family or clan if the above factors, cases from (a to (d) are found to be true.

Only after 4 (four) generations on the mother side and clan, after the death of the great grand mother, a Lepcha man shall be allowed to marry from his mother's clan, *Aagit,* again.

Marriage outside the Lepcha community

Lepcha Man– No law or rule exist concerning a marriage outside the Lepcha community: however, in case of a love marriage with a woman outside the community, the parents of the Lepcha son shall act as follows:

a) In consultations with the village elders and Lepcha Village Association they shall bestow, confer, grant a suitable, appropriate female Lepcha 'Aagit', clan, to the newly wedded non-Lepcha bride with due Lepcha traditional ceremony called Aali Oom by a Bongthing/ Mun (priest/priestess) or a competent Lepcha elder in order to safeguard the interest of their future offspring, especially, girls.

b) A non-Lepcha bride/wife with newly acquired female Lepcha *Aagit,* clan, however shall not be entitled to her husband's ancestral land and property.

Lepcha Women

a. If a Lepcha girl shall marry outside her community with a non-Lepcha, she, automatically, shall forfeit her claim and right as a Lepcha, ancestral and, and property. She shall become a non-Lepcha. Her off-spring either male or female shall become non-Lepcha.

b. An illicit off-spring, bastard, fathered by non- Lepcha shall not be entitled to the Lepcha ancestral land and property." (Lepcha Customary Law. ILTA. pp. 4-6).

Forms of Lepcha Marriage

In general Lepcha society follows 'monogamous marriage' i.e. union of one man with another women. Plural marriage or polygamous union is not the usual practice among them. Anthropologically polygamy has been classified into polygyny and polyandry. In polygyny, a male marries several females at the same time. In polyandry, a female marries several males at the same time. The following table – 6.1 has been prepared to show the types of monogamy, polygyny and polyandry in our study area:

Table 6.1 has been prepared on the basis of data collected from those couples whose at least one member survives during the survey period. It is evident that as much as 95.92 per cent couples are practicing monogamy while the percentage of polygyny and polyandry are as low as 4.57 and 0.51per cent respectively. It can thus safely be inferred that Lepcha society is monogamous in nature. The exceptional cases of polygyny and polyandry are individualistic in character and got no resemblance to the society

Table – 6.1
Forms of Marriage among the Lepchas in the study Area

Sl	*Forms of Lepcha Marriage*				
No	*Name of Village*	*Monogamy*	*Polygyny*	*Polyandry*	*TOTAL*
1	*2*	*3*	*4*	*5*	*6*
1	Mane Gumba	33(91.67)	3(8.33)	—	36(100.00)
2	Tashiding Busty	51(98.08)	1(1.92)	—	52(100.00)
3	Khamdung	27(90.00)	3(10.00)	—	30(100.00)
4	Lower Beyong	76(96.20)	2(2.53)	1(1.27)	79(100.00)
5	Total	187(95.92)	9(4.57)	1(0.51)	197(100.00)

Source: Field Survey.

The existing literature on the Lepchas also observed that monogamous form of union is normally practiced by the Lepchas. Hooker observed that "Lepcha is in moral superior to his Tibet and Bhutan neighbours and polyandry is unknown and polygyny rare" (1855: p. 89). Waddles observation on Sikkimese Lepcha is different to those of Hooker. Waddle state that the prevalence of paternal polyandry in Sikkim where the elder brother's wife become the joint wife of all the brothers but if the second brother marries, then his wife is common to the second and younger brothers, and not to the elder. (1899: p. 197). Morris opines oppositely and states that Lepchas do not practice polyandry, except in rare cases. He narrates that their customs permit, but in actual practice two brothers only share a wife when one is continuously absent from home when polyandry does occur it is always as in Tibet, what is technically known as adelphic polyandry (co-husbands are always brothers). Morris believes that polyandry, such as it is in Zongu, has arisen entirely as a result of contact with the Tibetans. He concludes that it is unusual for a Lepcha girl to be actually married to more than one man. It is common for her occasionally to have connections with younger brothers, though not married to the, unlike polyandry where they are legal husbands. (1938: p. 225).

Our study confirms that polyandry is unknown among the Lepchas while polygyny is rare and the Lepchas are following monogamous union. Barring a few cases which are purely exceptional, Lepcha society is monogamous in its form.

Procedure of Lepcha Marriage

Marriage is divinely gifted aspect to the Lepchas and they belief that it should be performed with sanctity and purity. Traditionally it took as much as seven long years to complete all the seven stages. The seven stages are:

The first stage of Lepcha marriage is known as *Nyom - Vyat*. The literary meaning of *Nyom - Vyat* is 'ask for bride's hand.' In a closed circuit community of the villages, it is easy for a *Peeboo* to identify a girl or a boy with all the suitability of their marriage concerning their individual Moo, family status, economic conditions etc. *Peeboo* places the proposal before the boy's family. Then the paternal and maternal uncles of the groom go to the bride's place with the proposal accompanied by the *Peeboo*. The parents of the bride take the help of the *Pamiboo* to take account of the groom's position.

The second and third stages are *Nyom - Panol* and *Nyom-Khyomoo*. The guardians of the boy visit the girl's place and offer presents usually jewelry to the girl. If the girl accepts the presents, it would mean the family of the girl agrees the proposal. The procedure of marriage can not continue in case the girl rejects the presents offered by the groom's parents.

The fourth stage is *Nyom - Tungbong*, a performance of rituals related to fertility. In all these four stages, *Peeboo* and *Pamiboo* guide both the families according to the typical Lepcha tradition. The date of marriage is fixed after the calculation of the planetary position by the match maker of the two sides.

Customarily the Lepcha bride and her family always enjoy an upper hand over the groom and his family. Marriage is costly to the groom's family. They are to arrange all the presents including the *Chi*, *Phogo Rip Lyaak* (garland), *Pultams* (hind legs of ox), *Aamoo Dum - dyem* (mother's dress), *Zher – Kaat* (token money for the nearest relatives), *Khadas* (holy scarf) etc. Arranging all these in pure Lepcha tradition and displaying them on the venue of the wedding ceremony, the *Byekboo* offer Chi and rice to the Creator, *Fudong - Thing* and *Nazong Nyu*. He also offers Chi and asks for blessing from *Tarbong* and *Naripnom*, *the* first couple in the Lepcha world.

As soon as the groom's party reaches the bride's house, the bridal party takes hold of all sorts of interactions to be followed between the two families. Rigorous checking of behavioral pattern of groom's band concerning marriage rules is carried out by the bridal side. Any fault detected on the part of the groom in any side is liable to be punished usually by paying a fine as told by the person of the bride side. Even a slight delay on arrival may call for a fine, an unconditional apology, and even some physical punishment; otherwise the entry point may be blocked for the groom. Although in all such cases both *Pamiboo* and *Peeboo* lead their respective parties, *Peeboo* follows the advice and instructions of the *Pamiboo.*

Now, *A - Sek* (linking stage) and *Rum Faat* (prayer to *Tarbong* and *Naripnom*), the two important and final stages of Lepcha marriage starts after short refreshment break. Matchmakers of both the sides supervise the whole thing including the proper arrangement of necessary articles of marriage, instructions of in- laws of both sides, presenting gifts to close in - laws etc. It is the unique way of showing respects to the elders of the family and the neighbors. At this stage the *Pamiboo* and *Peeboo* are the priests, the mediator between the couple and the God, narrator of Lepcha tradition, conserver of Lepcha culture, and the final coordinator on whom both the sides keep trust and faith for their wellbeing. *Pamiboo* narrates the interesting story of *Tarbong* and *Naripnom, the* first couple of the Lepcha society. This is one of the highly sacred and holy story told and retold to communize the fellow beings. Both the makers must know the pros and corns of the story; any fault detected on their part is tantamount to grave disqualification and liable to be punished with penalty.

In some instances, an interesting debate takes place between the mediators at this stage. It is not only interesting but also exhibits the power and potentiality of Lepcha language as a whole. A mere connubial function becomes an academic session of the linguistics. Because the understanding of Lepcha myth and culture terns to be the yardsticks of judging the Lepchaness of the boy's side. So the debate begins with the typical question of Lepcha marriage puts forth by the *Pamiboo* to *Peeboo* in order to judge the expertise of the later. It also involves the socio- anthropological characteristics of the community. Nothing is asked in a direct manner, rather number of rhetoric, puns and symbolisms are used in monosyllabic style.

Although Lepcha society at present is not overly matriarchal, higher status of bride is a socially recognized phenomena. The position of the bride makes the position of the *Peeboo* more vulnerable than a *Pamiboo.* A *Peeboo* has to take out the bride from the family for the groom he represents. It requires refined knowledge, tact, diplomacy, instantaneous strategy, patients perseverance. *Pamiboo* on the other side holds an advantageous position as part of the socially recognized gender of the higher position – the bride. He tries to trap the *Peeboo* by his strategy.

The last stage is the *Li - Hrone* means the entrance of the hitherto unknown house as the most important dutiful member. The bride must enter into the hearth first in her in-laws house with some fire wood for the cooking *chulla.* It symbolizes the primary duty of the bride as the caretaker of the house and the kitchen. In Lepcha society hearth is the hub of policy making and policy execution.

The role of matchmaker upholds the position of the bride in the Lepcha society. The *Pamiboo* is respected and is placed next to Bongthing, the Lepcha priest. The same person may act as *Peeboo* in another occasion. But his/her position in the marriage will be determined as per the side he/she is representing. Representing bride is always more prestigious, respectable, impressive and highly esteemed than that of the spoke person of the groom.

To be a *Peeboo* one must fulfill certain essential criteria. He or she must be able to an expert of the Lepcha language, especially in oratory skill and rhythmic style typical of its own. Expertise is also required in Lepcha tradition and custom of marriage which ranges from thorough knowledge of history and origin to the assemblage of necessary paraphernalia of marriage.

Peeboo is a genetic term – the other terms that are often used are Byekboo and *Pamiboo.* In practice a *Peeboo* may link a bride and a groom by giving information of a mate. His/her role ends there. In other case, he/she is an informant and performs all necessary duties, rites and rituals to link two persons for life. In both these cases, he/she is to be called either *Peeboo or Byekboo.* The *Peeboo* is the match maker of the bride side. He /she deserve great respect as leader of the bride party and determine and lead the whole process of marriage. Conceptually the act of *Peeboo, Byekboo, Pamiboo* may be performed by both the males and females. But females are rarely found to perform this role and it is the domain of the male members only. The Bongthing and the Mun fulfills all the criteria to act as *Peeboo* but only some Bongthing are found to perform the same and no Mun is found to involve in the function. Women played a crucial role in Lepcha society as Mun but not at all as *Peeboo.*

The procedure of Lepcha marriage is performed differently by different religious groups. After choosing their iife partners the Christians normally handed over the matter to their parents who with the help of *Peeboo*, the match maker finalizes the matter as per their custom. The marriage is normally performed at the Church as per popular common Christian procedure of exchange of ring, offering prayer and giving tea party or lunch party either in the Church or at home. As a matter of identity a gate is constructed in front of both the houses in the typical Lepcha style and both the bride and the groom wear their typical Lepcha dress, Dum- bun *or*

Dum- Dyem *and* Dum- praa but the dress instead of typical Lepcha color is normally white in color and prepared especially for the day to be used in the Church. As the dress is costly and very ceremonial, few Lepchas go for making new dress and some how manage for the day.

C.D.Beauvoir Stocks narrated the role of go between in completing the procedure of Lepcha marriage. "In the Rong-tribe in order that a marriage may be arranged, two go betweens are required, one acting for each family. They introduce the subject first of all by visiting the girl's parents and presenting them with a brass water-vessel. Should the parents accept this gift, the purpose of the visit is disclosed. and a day is fixed when they will come with the boy to introduce him. On the appointed day, the two go betweens arrive with the boy, who brings with him a pig and a roll of white cloth from Assam. They also place several rupees before the parents, which is eventually deducted from the bride-price, and which varies according to the wealth of the boy. They bring a big copper pot to cook the food in, and a brass pot to boil 'chi'. The drink is then made and a great feast is given to which all the villagers are invited. The young man brings a cock with him which he and the bride eat. A year passes and then it is the turn of the boy's parents to give a feast. The go betweens come with the boy to fetch the girl from her home. The parents do not follow her as it is considered unlucky were they to go with their daughter. This time it is the girl who brings a pig with her and a basket of 'chi'. The boy's family kill two bullocks, one pig and seven fowls, and before eating offerings of food and drink are made to the Rum.

"The lamas and the village headman drink the health of the bride and bridegroom and are witnesses to the marriage, this being the only legal proceeding that is taken. At these feasts the girl sits between a 'nyom-mu' and a 'nyom-byng'. These are two sisters, generally of the mother – handmaidens they could be termed – the 'nyom-mu' must, however, be married. They receive the remains of the bride-price which they give to the parents. That night, the visitors sing and dance till the day breaks, stamping their feet on the floor" (1925: p. 466-467).

The Buddhists on the other hand, are still solemnizing their marriage as per Lepcha tradition and style. But the rites have been softened and the procedures are amended, loosed and curtailed as per the demand of the modern day. For example, in traditional it took seven long years to complete the marriage ceremony but now it has been reduced to end within a day or two. *Peeboo* still remains the key person in Lepcha marriage. *Peeboo* is well versed in Lepcha language and knows the Lepcha tradition, culture and custom. *Peeboo* has no gender fixed role but a skilled woman with her mastery over the language, knowledge on Lepcha culture, custom and good oratory skill can perform the duty of a *Peeboo*.

Empirical Findings

Traditionally Lepcha marriage is Moo exogamous and race endogamous. It means the Lepchas prefer to marry within their own race but they avoid any sort of matrimonial relation within their same *Aagit* or Moo. This marriage within the same tribe may also be defined as 'Divisional or tribal Endogamy'. During the early Tibetan rule, the aliens tried to rule and established their supremacy by marrying the indigenous Lepcha girls. The newly established marital relation helped the Tibetan rulers to acquire sympathy and loyalty from among the Lepchas. In Sikkim the intermarriage between the Lepchas and the Tibetans is so common and spread in such a way that a new ethnic group 'Sikkimise Bhutia' has emerged in the state. Although the rulers have changed in Sikkim but the trend of intermarriage continues even today. The situation is comparatively better in the Darjeeling district of West Bengal. Even then the multi colored, multi ethnic and multi- lingual society Lepcha girls started preferring inter tribal marriage. Ranjana Lepcha, 28 years old young and smart graduate of Tashiding Busty could not restrain herself in expressing her desire in preferring inter tribal marriage. She argued; "Lepcha boys are less educated, un-smart, and not placed comfortably in their life. I can not find any reason to be that conservative in restricting myself within the Lepcha community only rather we should accept what God desires us to do". The following Table -6.2. Table- 6.3 and Table – 6.4 shows the Lepcha exogamous and endogamous marriage in the study area. All the tables are prepared on the basis of data collected from those couples whose at least one spouse is surviving during the survey period.

Out of 227 cases of married couples recorded in our study area, 41.41 per cent have been recorded as race exogamous and 58.59 percent as race endogamous. The higher percentage of race exogamous marriage in the Lepcha society is a matter of great concern.

The race exogamous marriage is of two types: a) Lepcha boys marrying non-Lepcha girls and b) Lepcha girls marrying non-Lepcha boys. The percentage of Lepcha boys marrying non-Lepcha girls is as high as 65.96 while 34.04 per cent exogamous marriage has been recorded where the Lepcha girls are marrying non-Lepcha boys. In the first case the bride enters the Lepcha family from different culture and as the society is patriarchal she needs to accommodate and acculturated herself with the Lepcha culture. The society has to face some problems like transferring of female Moo in case of new born girl child etc. There is a system of Lepchanisation of non-Lepcha bride by Bongthing or Mun who confers and grants any appropriate female Moo to the newly wedded non-Lepcha bride through a celebration known as *Aali Oom*. For this there should be one motherly Lepcha female who should be ready to transfer her own Moo to the new comer and thereby ready to adopt her in her mother's lineage. But in

Table – 6.2
Lepcha Race Exogamous Marriage: Lepcha Girls Marrying Non-Lepcha boys

Sl No	Name of Village	Nepali	Rai Sherpa	Tibetan/ Bhutan	Others	Total Buddhist/ nature worshipper	Total Christian	Total
1	2	3	4	5	6	7	8	9
1	Mane Gumba	5(83.33)	1(16.67)	—	—	5(83.33)	1(16.67)	6(100.00)
2	Tashiding Busty	8(72.73)	2(18.18)	—	1(9.09)	I(9.09)	10(90.91)	11(100.00)
3	Khamdung	3(60.00)	2(40.00)	—	—	2 (40.00)	3(60.00)	5(100.00)
4	Lower Beyong	6(60.00)	4(40.00)	—	—	6(60.00)	4(40.00)	10(100.00)
5	Total	22(68.75)	9(28.13)	—	1(3.12)	14(43.75)	18(56.25)	32(100.00)

Table – 6.3
Lepcha Race Exogamous Marriage: Lepcha Boys Marrying Non-Lepcha girls

Sl No	Name of Village	Nepali	Rai Sherpa	Tibetan/ Bhutan	Others	Buddhist/ nature worshipper	Total Christian	Total
1	2	3	4	5	6	7	8	9
1	Mane Gumba	5(55.56)	4(44.44)	—	—	9(100.00)	—	9(100.00)
2	Tashiding Busty	17(65.38)	5(19.23)	4(15.38)	—	3(11.54)	23(88.46)	26(100.00)
3	Khamdung	6(46.15)	4(30.77)	3(23.08)	—	11 (84.62)	2(15.38)	13(100.00)
4	Lower Beyong	4(28.58)	9(64.28)	1(7.14)	—	7(50.00)	7(50.00)	14(100.00)
5	Total	32(51.61)	22(35.48)	8(12.90)	—	30(48.39)	32(51.61)	62(100.00)

Table - 6.4
Lepcha Race Endogamous Marriage: Lepcha Girls Marrying Non-Lepcha Boys & Lepcha Boys Marrying Non Lepcha Girls

Sl No	*Name of the Village*	*Lepcha Girls marrying Lepcha boys*			*Lepcha Boys marrying Lepcha girls.*		
		Buddhist/ Nature worshipper	*Christian*	*TOTAL*	*Buddhist/ nature worshipper*	*Christian*	*Total*
1	*2*	*3*	*4*	*5*	*6*	*7*	*8*
1	Mane Gumba	11(68.75)	5(31.25)	16(100.00)	29(96.67)	1(3.33)	30(100.00)
2	Tashiding Busty	—	8(100.00)	8(100.00)	1(5.00)	19(95.00)	20(100.00)
3	Khamdung	9(81.82)	2(18.18)	11(100.00)	15(78.95)	4(21.05)	19(100.00)
4	Lower Beyong	16(69.56)	7(30.44)	23(100.00)	37(57.81)	27(42.19)	64(100.00)
5	Total	36(63.16)	22(37.93)	58(100.00)	82(61.65)	51(38.35)	133(100.00)

Source: Field Survey.

case of second type of exogamous marriage, the girls are altogether leaving the Lepcha society by marrying the non-Lepcha boys. As the Lepcha girls are marrying in patriarchal society, they need to leave their original Lepcha culture and need to acclimatize and accustom themselves with the new culture of their in-laws. This is the other name of loss of Lepcha girl in the Lepcha world. This has a long term negative impact on the growth of Lepcha population in the district. G.Gorer as early as 1938 observed that Lepcha girls are being taken away by non-Lepcha boys. To justify this he could find the reasons. "The Lepcha woman is esteemed for her physical appearance and her mild and yielding character" (1938: p. 38).

Out of recent Lepcha girl's marriage, 35.36 per cent has been recorded as race exogamous marriage and 64.44 per cent for the race endogenous marriage. Although in percentage term the case of Lepcha girl's endogamous marriage is higher than that of their exogamous marriage but the matter is alarming and should be dealt with carefully and seriously. A comparison between the exogamous marriage (31.79) and endogamous marriage (68.21) for the Lepcha boys marrying non - Lepcha girls reveals that their contribution is slightly better than the girl's case from the view point of retaining and preserving Lepcha culture, custom and tradition. But both the cases need indebt study and should be dealt with seriously.

Among the good number of factors responsible for Lepcha exogamous marriage, we could identify three dominant factors: i) location of the village, ii) religious faith and iii) educational standard. Village wise Tashiding Busty (39.36%) recorded highest percentage of race exogamous marriage followed by Lower Beyong (25.53 %), Khamdung (19.15 %) and Mane Gumba (15.96 %). The percentage of exogamous marriage is more among the Christians (54.53) than among the Buddhists (45.65). The following table-6.5 has been prepared to show village wise details of exogamous marriage as a percentage to population, number of households, literacy rate etc

Table - 6.5 shows village-wise details of exogamous marriage as percentage to the population, number of household, literacy rate and distance from the sub divisional town. It has been seen that among the factors responsible for exogenous marriage religion, literacy rate, nearness to the town are highly positively correlated. Village-wise data shows that all the three indicators contribute positively in acquiring highest percentage of exogenous marriage for Tashiding Busty. Lower Beyong which is located in remotest areas with low rate of literacy and comparatively more Buddhist faith got fourth and last rank in respect of percentage of exogamous marriage.

Table - 6.5 shows that the percentage figure of exogamous marriage in all the villages is more for the category of Lepcha boys marrying non- Lepcha girls than the category of Lepcha girls marrying non - Lepcha boys. Exogamous marriage as a percentage to total population in our study area is 11.52; and it is as high as 21.26 percent in Tashiding Busty and as low as 6.40 in Lower Beyong Busty. This high percentage of exogamous marriage is a matter of great concern from the view point of preserving Lepcha culture, custom and tradition. Exogamous marriage as a percentage of number of household for the study area is 61.04. The rate is as high as 105.71 in Tashiding Busty and as low as 36.92 in lower Beyong Busty. On an average every alternate house is an example of exogamous marriage. The system becomes a matter of regular routine feature in Lepcha society. It affects adversely the Lepcha culture, custom and traditional values.

Chie Nakane (1966) observed intermarriage between Lepcha- Bhutia and Lepcha- Nepali communities is responsible to make Sikkim a plural character. He observed

Table – 6.5

Exogamous Marriage as percentage to Population, Household, Literacy Rate

Sl. No. Name of Village	Exogamous Marriage			Exogamous marriage as % to			Distance from Sub Divisional Town (In Km)
	Lepcha Boys marrying Non Lepcha girls	Lepcha Girls marrying Non Lepcha Boys	Total	Population	Household	Literacy Rate	
1	2	3	4	5	6	7	8
Mane Gumba	9(60.00)	6(40.00)	15(100.00)	10.95	53.57	13.16	4
Tashiding Busty	26(70.00)	11(30.00)	37(100.00)	21.26	105.71	24.18	7
Khamdung	13(72.00)	5(28.00)	18(100.00)	13.85	69.23	16.22	10
Lower Beyong	14(58.00)	10(42.00)	24(100.00)	6.40	36.92	8.16	45
Total	62(66.00)	32(34.00)	94(100.00)	11.52	61.04	13.99	—

Source: Field Survey.

more Lepcha man marring Bhutia woman and not the other way round. Bride price plays an important role in this case. "Arich Lepcha man may have a Bhutia wife, because he can afford to pay a high bride price to enable him to have a Bhutia wife instead of a Lepcha wife. They say, further, that Lepcha girls often want to marry Bhutia men, but usually they are unsuccessful because Bhutia men look down on the Lepcha" (1966: p. 247). The descendants, in both the cases, claim and recognized themselves as Bhutia not the Lepchas. This has a strong negative bearing on the Lepcha culture and custom.

Another aspect of Lepcha marriage is the presence of good number of both boys and girls crossing their marital age. The unmarried girls in the study area blame that the traditional system of approaching the girl's hand by the boy's side is responsible for their bachelorship while the bachelor boys are the victims of high bride price. "I was waiting, waiting and waiting for a Peeboo to come and seek my hand form my parents for a Lepcha boy and in the process I become aged and crossed my age in marriage" says Jamit Lepcha, 57 years old unmarried woman of Mane Gumba. The Lepcha girls who married non -Lepcha boys frankly admit that they cannot just wait to remain unmarried just because the boys are not approaching with the bride price. It has also been commonly said that the Lepcha boys are mostly introvert and feel shy in approaching the girls but in between the beautiful Lepcha girls fall in love with the non-Lepcha boys and decide to marry him. The following Table - 6.6 shows a comprehensive statement of both Lepcha boys and girls above their normal marital age of 20 years.

A perusal of Table - 6.6 shows that as high as 18.75 per cent of population of both the sexes of the study area is lying above the normal marital age. The percentage of boys (56.86) crossing marital age is higher than that of the girls (43.14). The raw data reveals that most of the persons are comparatively uneducated and are engaged in agricultural activities. Agriculture is labor intensive and the Lepchas do

Table- 6.6
Boys and Girls Crossing Normal Marital Age in the Study Areas

Sl No	Name of Village	Girls crossed Normal Marital Age: Buddhist	Girls crossed Normal Marital Age: Christian	Girls crossed Normal Marital Age: Total	Boys Crossed Normal Marital Age: Buddhist	Boys Crossed Normal Marital Age: Christian	Boys Crossed Normal Marital Age: Total	Total
1	2	3	4	5	6	7	8	9
1	Mane Gumba	11(91.97)	1(8.33)	12(100.00)	15(100.00)	—	9(100.00)	27
2	Tashiding Busty	1(5.56)	17(94.44)	18(100.00)	1(4.00)	24(96.00)	26(100.00)	43
3	Khamdung	2(100.00)	—	2(100.00)	4(50.00)	4(50.00)	13(100.00)	10
4	Lower Beyong	16(47.06)	18(52.94)	34(100.00)	23(58.97)	16(41.03)	14(100.00)	73
5	Total	30(45.45)	36(54.55)	66(100.00)	43(49.43)	44(50.57)	62(100.00)	153

Source: **Field Survey.**

not want to loose labor by marrying their girl child. Although most un-married girls are staying with their parents but a considerable number of them are also staying with their brothers. Existence of nearly 20 per cent of population above normal marital age may also be considered as one of the causes of low growth rate of population among the Lepchas.

A comparison between Lepcha race exogamous, endogamous and the percentage of population crossing normal marital age reveals the following:

1. The proportion of Lepcha race endogamous marriage (58.59) is more than that of their exogamous marriage (41.41) but the high proportion of exogamous marriage (from both the boys and girls side) is very alarming particularly for a small community like the Lepchas.
2. The percentage of race exogamous marriage is the highest in Tashiding Busty (39.36) which locates near the town areas, comparatively educated, and are mostly Christians. The factors like education, religion, urbanization etc are the positive factors responsible for raising the rate of exogamous marriage.
3. In race exogamous marriage, a clear trend in all the villages has been marked among the Lepcha boys to marry non-Lepcha girls than the Lepcha girls marrying non Lepcha girls. This is more so among comparatively less educated boys and girls who stay outside in connection to their job or other engagements.
4. Comparatively more educated girls have been found to prefer non-Lepcha boys for their marriage. It has been noted that the standard of education among the girls is higher than that among the boys and hence girls do not prefer less educated Lepcha boys.

5. Race endogamous marriage is higher in all the villages than exogamous marriage except in Tashiding village which records higher exogamous marriage (57.00%) than endogamous marriage (43.00 %). It is a serious matter.

6). Race endogamous marriage is higher among the boys than among the girls who generally leave our study area after marriage.

7. The proportion of Lepcha race endogamous marriage is the highest in Lower Beyong which is located far off the town which is located far off the town and is mostly Christians.

8. A comparison between exogamous marriage with Lepcha boys and girls crossing marital age expresses pathetic results. In all the villages the number of boys and girls crossing marital age exceeds the number of exogamous marriage for both the boys and the girls. These number of boys and girls could otherwise been married with their Lepcha counterpart and thereby could preserve traditional Lepcha values.

9. The society has given due respect to the women and placed them highly but the girls by exogamous marriage and crossing their marital age are not performing their duties to the society.

Folk Tale

The system of marriage and the position of girls in the Lepcha society can not be completed without mentioning the popular folk tale regarding the love story of two important rivers of the region. Lyansong Tamsang narrated the story as:

"The rivers Rangnyoo and rangeet were lovers and used to meet secretly, but when their love was known and exposed.

they decided to leave the place and go down to the plains of India. As they did not know their way, they decided to take guides to lead them. River Rangeet, the male, was guided by a bird, 'Tut Fo', and river Rangnyoo, the female, was guided by a snake, 'Paril Bu'. Their guides agreed to take two lovers to an appointed place at 'Panzaok' meaning dense forest in Lepcha, but now it is incorrectly called 'Pashok' or 'Peshok' near Teesta Bazaar.

"As river Rangeet was led by a bird, it traveled through circuitous routes in search of food; therefore, he arrived at the appointed place, 'Panzaok', late. If you observe this river carefully, it zig-zags, twists and turns and flows slowly up to Peshok. The female river, Rangnyoo, led by a snake, traveled straight to the appointed place on time and waited for her lover, Rangeet. Rangnyoo flows straight like a snake running fast with its head held high. When river Rangeet finally arrived at the appointed place, he was very, very surprised and shocked to see his lover, Rangnyoo, already there waiting for him. In anger he uttered out 'Thi-as tha!' meaning, 'when did you arrive!' Unable to pronounce this monosyllabic Lepcha word, 'Thi-sa-tha' properly, the non-Lepchas, today, call it 'Teesta'; therefore, Rangnyoo is also known by the name of Teesta today. River Rangeet was very, very angry, disappointed, upset and ashamed because, being a male, he should have arrived first at the appointed place. He decides to return to his original place, Himalaya. As a result, a great deluge occurred in the land of the Lepchas, Mayel Lyang, the present day Sikkim and the Darjeeling District" (2008: pp. 20-21).

The love story between the two important rivers of the region is very popular and both the Bongthing and the Mun utter the same in any marriage as reference and witness. It also placed the females at a comparatively higher position than those of the males.

A song composed by Sonam Tshering Lepcha and Hildamit Lepcha is very popular among the Lepchas. It has been translated by Lyangsong Tamsang as:

Farewell to the Himalayas (A Duet song)

Rangnyoo, the female:

Oh ! Rnageet, my ; love,
Please don't grieve and get up set.
On your strength, Sa ra ra ...Sa ra ra ...
My below
You above
Let us go together with love, Sa ra ra ... Sa ra ra ...
You are my eternal love,
A friend in need, in this world,
Please don't grieve and get up set, Rangeet,
Let us go together with love Sa ra ra ... Sa ra ra ...

Rangeet, the male :

Rangnyoo, Rangeet,
You and I,
Our union at 'Panzaok"
A place to remember by, Sa ra ra... Sa ra ra...

You are mine, I'm yours,
This world is ours.
This story will remain forever,
Of Rangnyoo and Rangeet, Sa ra ra... Sa ra ra ...
Even if you had arrived earlier,
You brought a song of colour,
My question, 'Thi-sa-tha?'
Will remain for ever. Sa ra ra ... Sa ra ra ...

Fadaong, Tukryook birds from the Himalayas
Carrying 'Kursaong and Punten flowers,
Will tell the tale of ours union,
To remind of us forever. Sa ra ra ...Sa ra ra ....

Farewell ! Himalayas ! Farewell !

We are leaving this land today. Farewell to you all. Sa ra ra ...Sa ra ra....

(2008: pp. 85- 86).

Epilogue

The traditional pattern of marriage and the existence of bride price placed the Lepcha women highly in their society. A. Campbell went to the extent by saying that the husbands were the temporary bondsmen of their father-in-laws where the groom needed to give their physical labour in lieu of cash already agreed for the marriage. This days old system of 'marriage by service' later turned to bride price and shows the position of women in the society. Buddhist Lepchas still follow the Lepcha customary law of marriage and appoint Peeboo for performing the procedure of marriage. It is true that the bride price has lost its earlier glamour in terms of amount, volume and variety but its very existence placed the women highly even today. Even in case of popular and modern system of marriage by elopement, the groom party needs to approach the bride's parents for the girl's hand. They are to pay a penalty, *Choridanda*, as decided by the society to the bride. It is also practiced even by the Christians in case of race exogamous marriage. Higher rate of race exogamous marriage has changed the social structure by converting bride price into *Choridanda* but keeps the higher position of the women in the society. Nearly 12.00 per cent marriage in the study area is exogamous marriage which has been found to be initiated by religious conversion, educational attainment, urbanization etc. The practice of inter-marriage with neighbouring communities had been noted by A. Campbell as early as the first half of the nineteenth century. He wrote that "the Lepchas intermarry with the Limboos and Bhotiahs, and the offspring of such unions become members of the father's tribe, without any disqualification whatever" (1940: p. 384).

Although the Lepcha women have lost their earlier higher position but still they maintain comparative higher position in the society than their male counterpart. Among the women again the Buddhists are still preserving their traditional customs by employing Peeboo and other necessary relevant customary laws. Naturally the women are enjoying comparatively higher position among the Buddhists Lepchas than among the Christians. Be whatever may be the degree of highness, but the Lepcha women, even today, are enjoying comparatively higher social status and position in the Lepcha society.

7

Moo and the Status of Women in the Lepcha Society

Introduction

Lepchas call their clan as Pu - tso or Agith but it is popularly known as Moo. Lepcha society is casteless society. There are no upper or lower castes among the Lepchas and all are equal. Except Karvo Moo there is no caste wise division in the Lepcha society and all can perform any kind of profession in their day to day life. But Risley could find "two thars, Barhurgpuso and Alinpuso, rank higher than the other eight, and do not permit intermarriage with them". He also found the cause behind that. "The distinction is said to arise from the fact that the officials of Sikkim state are invariably chosen from these two thars, and they probably are the descendants of the Khamba clans men who followed the chief from Tibet" (1891: p. 8). Anyway, there is no bar in marriage among the different Moos. The clan or Moo is an important component in the Lepcha social organization. Lepcha Moo is an extensive form of lineage constituted of blood relations. There are some unilineal types of small groups who are the relatives and linked in terms of blood.

Moo is dyadic relations between person and person. In Lepcha society male Moo differs from female Moo and the genealogical relations among the Lepchas can better be shown with the help of Moo. Each Moo relates with particular ancestor and hence persons belonging to same Moo have some sort of relation among themselves, may be of very distance type. The same blood is running in the veins of the same Moo. Unlike the Hindu *Gotra*, the Lepcha Moo can not be changed even after marriage. Moo is obtained by birth and under no circumstances it can be changed. The girls carry the mother's lineage while the boys carry their father's lineage. Although Lepcha society is patriarchal but in case of Moo there is a peculiar blending of both patrilineal and matrilineal.

But in recent times Lepchas are not following the customs of using father's and mother's moo by the son and daughter separately. A.K. Das has also noted the sort of discrepancy in using male and female moo. "Now a days, in most of the areas of Darjeeling District, the members of an Agit acknowledge a traditional bond of common descent in the paternal line. Here the sons and daughters are both associated with father's Agit i.e. Agit name descends from father to sons and daughters.

"But in some interior village of Kurseong on the other hand a daughter gets her mother's Agit and a son his father's. In other words it may be stated that the descent of Agit here is unilineal in nature but sex-linked in character" (1978: pp. 103-104).

Large number of intermarriage with non-Lepchas and non-use of Moo due to religious conversion are responsible for breaking the custom of inheriting Moo by the son and daughter separately from their father and mother respectably.

Origin and Types of Lepcha Moo

As per Lepcha folktale Moo is connected with Kanchanjunga, the guardian deity of the Lepchas. It is believed that Lepchas originate from the snow of mount Kanchanjunga. Each Moo originates from separate peak in the range and after death their soul returns to their original peak for rest. Each Moo is named after the name of the mountain peak (Chu) where there is also a lake (Daa) just below the Chu. The number of Moo among the Lepchas is in proportion to the number of Chu and Daa in Kanchanjunga range. On enquiry, however, it has been found that most of the Lepchas do not know their Daa connected with their Moo. It has been claimed that all the peaks on the Kanchanjunga range have their Lepchas names which even the Geological Survey of India could not name them and identify them as per numerical number. Name of Lepcha Moo and the peak in Kanchanjunga range give a sense of territorial belongings of the Lepchas in the region and confirm their aboriginality in this region.

Using Siiger, Jenny Bently opines that "the parrilineage originate from a supernatural or a legendary ancestor and is therefore stands in the relation to father-mountain and mother lake. Every male clan is linked to a sacred peak (chu) and every female clan has its origin in a lake (da) (Siiger 1967: 114; Steinmann 1996). The Lepcha clans are thus tightly attached to each of the 108 peaks of the Sikkimese Himalayas through the legendary stories (Tamsang 1983 : 64, 65). The reference to these mountain peaks is important in ritual life of every individual. The corresponding mountain peaks and lakes are recited during the marriage ceremony whilst linking the clans of the bride and the groom. After death the mountain peaks and lakes function as entry point of the spirits into the realm of the death (Steinman 1996). Today many young Lepchas do not know the peaks and lakes their clan took its origin at, but the notion that the Kanchanjunga and the surrounding landscape are keepers of their ancestral lineages is embedded in their hearts and beliefs. When naming mountain the Lepchas add the suffix

– thing or – athing (lord) to express respect (Steinman)" (2007 : 90).

The Lepcha Moo has another mythological origin. Sumit Ghosal writes:

"According to *nuliknasong,* the history of the Lepcha tribe. there was a demon or monster called rosumung. The monster was perpetually engaged in one sort of perverse activity or another – destruction, thieving, defying authority, playing magical tricks. In sort, this character was a sociopath of the first order. So the Lepchas had killed him in a battle. The early ancestors of the present day Lepchas participated in that war and according to the role performed by them all the descendents of them have been given the clan names as follows:

a). Lukshongmu – The man who plucked all the teeth of the demon is called by the above clan name thereafter.

b). Simikmu – The man who pierced the eye of the monster.

c). Suthumgmu – The man who cut the body of the monster into pieces.

d). Sadamgmu – the man who threw dust at the eyes of the monster during the battle.

e). Korvomu – The man who prepared the swords for the war.

f). Brimu — The man who made the string of the bow.

g). Ademmu – The man who made the necessary sitting arrangements for the fighters during the war.

h). Jaribu – The man who prepared food for the soldiers.

i). Mallamu – The man who prayed to God day and night for the welfare of the Lepchas during the war.

j). Fenthatimu – The man who made the bow and arrow."

(1990: pp. 146-147).

In Lepcha Moo means 'dwellers of' and hence the clan names are from the localities or region where they originally come from. Using Lepcha folk tales, Lyangsong Tamsang gives a detailed account of the origin of ten Lepcha Moos which are not the same to those of Ghosal. Tamsang writes:

"When the devil, Laso Mung Pano, was finally slained, the Lepchas and Tamsangthing moved to a place called 'Tarkaol Tam-E-Tam', meaning the valley of deliverance, and Tamsangthing bestowed upon the Lepchas the following clans:

1. The Lepchas who prayed, remembered Itboo_Deboo, the Creator, and requested Him to deliver the Lepchas from the clutches of the devil, Laso Mung Pano, were given the title of 'Munlaommoo'.
2. Those Lepchas who made and prepared weapons like swords, Banmaok etc to fight against the devil, they were called 'Karvomoo'.
3. Those Lepchas who served Tamsangthing, Nyolik Nyosong Mun, Azaor Boongthing, and Lepcha leaders during the battle against the devil were given the title of 'Adenmoo'.
4. Those Lepchas who helped to make bows and arrows to fight Laso Mung Pano were called 'Phyoong Talimmoo'.
5. Water, rations and food suppliers were given the title of 'Joriboo'.
6. Those Lepchas who constructed and made bridges, roads, ropes and bow-strings were called 'Brimoo'.

7. The Lepchas who dared to check if Laso Mung Pano's heart was beating and was breathing was given the title of 'Lutsaom moo'. In Lepcha 'Alut' means heart and 'Asaom' means breath and if you remove the two common prefixes 'A', it becomes 'Lutsaom'.

8. The person who broke the eyes and blinded the devil was called 'Seemickmoo'.

9. The Lepcha who separated Laso Mung Pano's head and legs with his 'Banmoak' was called 'Sungngootmoo'.

10. The Lepcha who beat up, crushed the body of Laso Mung Pano into dust and blown them into thin air from a hill top was given the title of 'Sungdyangmoo" (2008: pp. 9,10).

Using the same folk tale of Laso Mung Pano, A.R. Foning gave slightly different titles for their involvement in killing the demon and the origin of Lepcha Moo. He wrote:

"In this victory celebration those who had prominently taken part in the fray were given honours and titles. The one who ventured first to go and feel the body to find out if it was breathing or not, was called 'Luck-som' because asom or som, means breathing. The one who punctured the eye balls was called 'Samik' ; amik or mik means eyes. The one who cut off the limbs was called 'Sangut' ; ngut means to cut. The one who pounded the bones was called 'Sang-dyang' ; dyang means to pound. The one who made the weapons, - swards, arrows, and spears – was called 'Karvo'. Karvo means blacksmith. Those who fed the hunters or fighters were called 'Zo-reebu' ; Zo means rice, and reebu means distributor. The ones who prepared the seats for the celebration were called 'Aden', den means a carpet seat. Lastly, the one who offered thanks to the Almighty on behalf of the hunters who succeeded in the enterprise was called 'Manlom-moo', manlom means thanks" (1987: p. 126).

J.R. Subba while discussing the family pattern among the Lepchas noted different types of moo. He writes that "the Lepchas have no caste distinctions but they are divided into groups by birth and marriage. The Lepcha family is patrilocal or exogamous putse/ptso, which is believed to have originated from some supernatural or legendary ancestor. The descent is reckoned through the male. Some of the putse are *sangdenmoo, lingsingmoo, karyokmoo, heemoo, karyakmoo, thyungmen-solongmoo* etc. ... Each putse is under the guardianship of a certain supernatural being whom all the male members of the putse worship" (2008: p. 253). The author fails to note the female moo and its importance in the Lepcha society.

Lepcha clan plays a crucial role in their cultural domain. It is so important that W.W. Hunter in his Statistical Account of Darjeeling mentioned nine types of clan. "The Lepchas have no caste distinction, but they speak of themselves as belonging to one of the following nine septs or clans, namely – Barphung phucho, Adeng phucho, Tharjoph phucho, Singiang, Singut, Tingel, Luksom, Tirem, and Sangmi" (1876: p. 47).

Beside the above mythological origin of Moo Lepchas classify Moo on the basis of geographical division over the Himalayan range where the Lepchas reside. At present Lepchas are the residents of three countries: India, Nepal and Bhutan. On the basis of geographical area there are four different Moos found in the Lepcha society – (i) Renzong Moo, the Lepcha inhabitants of Darjeeling, Kurseong, Siliguri and Sikkim: (ii) Damsang Moo, the Lepcha inhabitants of Kalimpong area : (iii) Illam Moo – those Lepchas living in Illam district of Nepal and (iv) Pro Moo, those Lepchas living in the western border of Bhutan. A.R.Foning identified three Moos as per the geographical division of the areas over which Lepchas are residing. "Among ourselves, we have evolved certain recognized groups, classified regionally. The

'Renjyong-mu', for those within the present state of Sikkim, and also including those of the present Darjeeling and Kurseong subdivisions of the district of Darjeeling in the state of West Bengal in India. Then, we have the 'Ilam-mu', the ones of Ilam, the easternmost district of Nepal. This region happened to be a part of the Lepcha country once. Lastly, we have the 'Tamsang-mu' and the 'Dalim-mu' of the south east, inhabiting the lands which lie to the east of river Rong-Nyu or Teesta. As the names indicate, the groupings have been done and named according to the old-time administrative jurisdictions under Sikkim kings" (1987: p. 123).

These regional identification markers are used only among the Lepchas for their intra-regional belongings. But nobody use them for their personal identity or as title or as Moo. It is like the fact that all citizens of one country are identified as per the name cf that particular country eg citizens of India are Indians. Another difficulty with the region based moo is that Lepcha moo is sex linked and females possessed separate moo than those of males. In case of region specific moo, separation of moo on the basis of sex is not possible. The region specific moo is of little practical use in day to day life except in large gathering when two Lepchas introduce themselves they use it initially for identifying their place of origin.

Importance of Lepcha Moo

Lepcha lineage is a consanguineal kin groups that traces common descent through known ancestors. Lepcha lineage is of two types – patrilineal and matrilineal. Theoretically matrilineal clan follows from all the offspring of one woman. All the sisters and brothers of the woman become the member of the same clan. In case of patrilineal clan, the man and his children both son and daughter are included. But the Lepcha clan is sharply different from the theoretical form of either matrilineal or patrilineal type. Lepcha girl child gets her mother's Moo while male child gets his father's Moo. Lepcha male Moos are different from those of the females. This is perhaps peculiar in the Lepcha society. Lepcha Moo is sex linked and unilineal in character. Within its patriarchal structure, Lepcha society got a peculiar mixture of both patrilineal and matrilineal character. Each lineage pattern is peculiar to the Lepchas where both the sexes could retain their identity in the society. Lepcha society gives equal honor, respect, importance and value to the female Moo along with that of the male Moo.

Moo is very significant and touchy for the Lepchas. They feel proud of carrying their ancestral Moo. Moo is used by the *Bongthing* and *Mun,* the priests and priestess during marriage or any other offerings to the Nature. Any Lepcha ritual starts with *Chi Faat* where the Bongthing or Mun offers Chi to the Almighty in the name of the worshipper by citing their Moo. After offering Chi to Fodongthing and Nazaongnyo, the primogenitor of the Lepchas, the Bongthing and the Mun offer Chi to the ancestors of each Moo. Moo plays an important role in regulating Lepcha marriage. A boy can not marry a girl belonging to his mother's Moo while girls can not marry the boy of his father's Moo. From the viewpoint of origin of family, Lepcha society consists of non consanguineous family structure where marriage between blood relations is forbidden. Veena Bhasin wrote that "Now a days primary function of Putso is to regulate marriage. In addition to not marrying a fellow Putso member, one can not marry a member of one's mother's Putso up to four generations; this rules out matrilineal cross-cousin marriage" (1989: p. 110).

Chi Nakane from the experience of Sikkim Lepchas observed restrictions on marriage within same clan without specifying any generation gap. "There is a strong tendency to avoid marriage, including any sexual connection, among members who have been related for several generations not only on the father's side but also the mother's side. And the members within these generations are all called 'brother' and 'sister' with a distinction between 'older' and 'younger', in the Lepcha kinship terminology. Kinship on the mother's side seems much less important in determining avoidance of marriage than that on the father's side; empirically there is, according to my data, no marriage whatsoever between members of the same patri-clan" (1966: p. 234). In Gitdabling area the author noted that the Lepchas "can not marry members of either father's or mother's clans, unless they are related within seven generations. (1966: p. 235).

Referring Gorer, Jenny Bently finds the role of Moo in Lepcha society mainly in case of marriage. She wrote that "today the main function of Lepcha clan is to regulate marriage and prevent incest" (2007: p. 90).

As per Lepcha custom, son receives their father's property while daughter gets mother's property. Traditionally land is owned by the male members of the society while the movable properties are possessed by the females. The movable assets like jewellary etc which a girl receives during marriage are to be handed over to the girl child. In case mother possesses some landed property, then that needs to be handed over to the girl child automatically. So Moo has its crucial role over the transfer of properties and it is unidirectional. Veena Bhasin remarks "previously Putso was a land holding group. Land in one Busti was divided among the members of only one Putso. In very small Busties the people usually belong to the same Putso" (1989: p. 240). Lepchas are so sensitive about their Moo that even in case of adopting child, they prefer to take a child from among their own Moo so that the land can remain within the same Putso name. The author could find that "if the couple has a daughter, a son-in-law is bought, all the expenses of the marriage are born by the girl's parents, and no bride price is paid" (1989: p. 241).

Lepchas so long commonly use 'Lepcha' as their surname but recently there is a tendency among the educated Lepchas to use their Moo as their surname eg. Passang Tshering Simik Moo, Lyangsong Tamsang etc. Females are usually using 'Lepcha' as their surname but there are a few exceptions among the Christians eg. Shera Pandi Mulom Moo etc. Lepcha Moo has become a mark of identification of their clan and community.

In recent times the concept of separate Moo is preserved and maintained mainly by the Buddhist Lepchas. Religious conversion makes no use of Moo in their day to day life and hence a sort of confusion and misunderstanding arises among the Christians. As Moo has no use in socio-cultural activities, Christians started forgetting their Moo to a large extent. Inter community marriage to a large extent responsible in using even the father's Moo by the girl child. The confusion, inconsistent, misunderstanding and misleading concept and use of Lepcha Moo is due to the followings:

i). Acculturation and modernization curtailed the activities of both Bongthing and Mun who are the main user of Lepcha Moo in the traditional culture and custom.

ii). Religious conversion and consequent use of alien religion – Christianity and Buddhism restricts the use of Moo. Buddhism particularly Mahayana group to a large extent liberal and allows the Lepchas to follow their traditional culture simultaneously and both Lama and Bongthing took part in most religious functions. But Christianity is Church oriented activity where Bongthing has no role to play. Moo lost all its religious value to the Christians.

iii). Inter-tribe marriage creates a sort of confusion in using Moo among the Lepchas. In case the mother is non Lepcha, the girl child has no alternate but to use the father's Moo which is not permitted. By marrying a non Lepcha boy, the Lepcha girl loose her mother's Moo and can not be carried out by her daughter for the future generations.

iv). The illiterate and ignorant Lepchas do not pass on their Moo among the future generations. There is no system of keeping the record of Moo in the Lepcha society.

v). Presence of good number of unmarried boys and girls crossing the marital age is another limiting factor responsible for transmitting Moo to the future generations.

The Study Area

Moo is considered to be more important for the females than to the males. In spite of the influx of large number of non –Lepcha girls in the Lepcha family through inter community marriage and religious conversion of the Lepchas from their original nature worshipper; females even today are preserving the Lepcha tradition of carrying female Moo. In their patriarchal form of society, Lepcha girls with their mother's Moo enter and stay in the new environment and the village. Naturally the number of female Moo in any village is more than that of the male Moo. Marriage of a boy adds the possibility of increasing the number of female Moo in the village. Male Moo can be increased with the entry of new member in the village by constructing new house which is almost nil in any village. For the last twenty five years there is no record of sale and purchase of Lepcha land in our study area. Land only changed hands by dividing among the family members. It is customary that Lepcha land is in the name of the male members of the family. Boys receive their father's landed properties while girls get their mother's movable properties like jewellaries etc. Thus the number of male Moo is more or less constant while female Moo has all the possibility of increasing variety. The following Table – 7.1 has been prepared to show the sex – wise distribution of Moo as a percentage of their population in our study area.

Table – 7.1
Sex-wise Distribution of Moo as a Percentage of their Population and Households

Year	*Type of Moo*			*Moo per Households*		
	Female	*Male*	*Total*	*Female*	*Male*	*Total*
Mani Gumba	27 (36.99)	9 (14.06)	36 (26.28)	0.96	0.32	1.28
Tashiding	12 (13.95)	11 (12.50)	23 (13.22)	0.35	0.33	0.68
Khamdung	13 (22.41)	9 (12.50)	22 (16.92)	0.50	0.35	0.85
Lower Beyong	31 (16.76)	18 (9.47)	49 (13.07)	0.48	0.28	0.76
Total	83 (20.65)	47 (11.35)	130 (15.93)	0.54	0.31	0.85

Source: Field Survey.

Table 7.1 shows that the female Moo as proportion to their population is more than the corresponding figure for the male Moo in all the villages separately and also as a whole. The proportion of female Moo compared to their population is the highest in Mane Gumba (36.77) followed by Khamdung (22.42 Per cent). It may be noted that both the villages are dominated by the Buddhists Lepchas who belief in Bongthimism. Simultaneous use of Lama and Bongthing necessities the use of Lepcha Moo in their day to day life. Buddhist dominated villages are the preservers of Lepcha Moo in general and female Moo in particular.

On the average Moo per household is 0.85. It is the highest in Mane Gumba (1.28 per cent), followed by Khandung (0.85 per cent); Lower Beyong (0.76 per cent) and Tashiding (0.68 per cent). Each household individually posses at least two Moo — one each for female and male. Marriage gains the number of female Moo in each family while number of male Moo remains the same. Lower variety of male Moo pulls their average figure per household less than that for female Moo. .

The above table also reveals that female Moo per household is more than male Moo in all the villages. It is highest in Mane Gumba (0.96 per cent), followed by Khamdung (0.58), Lower Beyong (0.48 per cent) and Tashiding (0.35 per cent).The study area reveals highly about the position of women in the Lepcha society.

Table 7.2 has been prepared to show details about the variety and strength of Lepcha Moo in our study area. It has been noted that female Moo is 1.77 times more than the male Moo. In Mane Gumba it is three times more than the male Moo. Female Moo is more spread over households than the male Moo. As Much as 57 households possess only one female while such number for the male Moo is only 19.This means that females are genealogically linked only within a particular family and least matrilineal relation with other members within the village. They enter the village through marriage. The male Moo is more confined while the female Moo is more spread among the large number of households. These confined male Moos are the original inhabitants of the village.

Table 7.2 reveals that there are very few common Moos present both among the males and females in the four study villages. But their variety is much more in case of female moo. There is hardly any similarity in female Moo between any two villages. In each village not only the number of female Moo is much more than male Moo but it is more diverse and peculiar than that of the male Moo.

It is a matter of great concern that a large number of female Moo falls under the items — not known, not given and non Lepcha. The largest number in this category is with

Tashiding village followed by Lower Beyong. Between the two, the first village is dominated by the Christians and the second one is inhabited by mixed religious group. It may further be noted that even in Christian village, all the male members have their own Moo but the exception is with the female Moo. It is a matter of great concern and proper steps should be taken in preserving the females Moo from its vanishing trend.

Table – 7.2
Details of Lepcha Moo in Study Area

Sl No	*Female Moo* Name of Moo	Popu-lation	House-holds	*Sl No*	*Male Moo* Name of Moo	Popu-lation	House-holds
1	*2*	*3*	*4*	*5*	*6*	*7*	*8*
A. Name of the village: Mani Gumba							
1	Bri Moo	3	2	1	Fyaongdi Moo	5	2
2	Chong Moo	3	1	2	Goulook Moo	23	10
3	Fyaongdi Moo	1	1	3	Haoloong Moo	21	8
4	Git Molaom Moo	2	1	4	Lyaang Moo	3	1
5	Jamyaong Moo	1	1	5	Naamchu Moo	4	3
6	Ling Taong Moo	3	3	6	Naami Moo	2	1
7	Lichong Moo	1	1	7	Shyaor Moo	1	1
8	Mi- Simik Moo	4	1	8	Simik Moo	1	1
9	Molaom Moo	5	4	9	Taarjaok Pasaong Moo	2	1
10	Maongmi Moo	2	1	10			
11	Maongbyo Moo	2	1	11			
12	Nani Moo	1	1	12			
13	Phaokli Moo	2	1	13			
14	Raonglo Moo	3	1	14			

(Contd...)

1	*2*	*3*	*4*	*5*	*6*	*7*	*8*
15	Sadaa Moo	3	1	15			
16	Saong Moo	1	1	16			
17	Shyer Moo	6	3	17			
18	Saompa Moo	4	3	18			
19	Sandyong Moo	2	1	19			
20	Shyer Faokli Moo	3	1	20			
21	Shing Saong Moo	1	1	21			
22	Simik Moo	1	1	22			
23	Song Moo Mong Moo	1	1	23			
24	Soomoot Moo	4	2	24			
25	Savyet Moo	1	1	25			
26	Yari Moo	2	1	26			
27	Yung Moo	1	1	27			
28	Not Known	2		28			
29	Not Given	5		29			
30	Non Lepcha	3		30			
31	TOTAL	73	38	31	TOTAL	62	28

B: Name of the village: Tashiding Busty.

1	Aadyen Moo	3	1	1	Fonyoong Rungsaong Moo	3	2
2	Ethan Moo	2	1	2	Joriboo Moo	9	4
3	Fee Moo	2	1	3	Karthaak Moo	5	2
4	Jori Boo Moo	2	1	4	Naamchu Moo	3	1
5	Molo Mayeng Moo	2	2	5	Sadaa Moo	34	12
6	Malaom Moo	2	1	6	Sungtim Moo	11	4

(Contd...)

1	*2*	*3*	*4*	*5*	*6*	*7*	*8*
7	Naamchu Moo	1	1	7	Saongtyen Moo	4	1
8	Sinthi Moo	2	1	8	Taaraang Moo	3	1
9	Somoot Moo	2	1	9	Tingboo Moo	7	1
10	Taamsaang Moo	2	2	10	Tookoo Chao Moo	2	11
11	Taamsaang Pajyeng Moo	3	1	11	Yaagen Moo	2	1
12	Tingboo Moo	2	1	12			
13	Not Known	45	—	13	Not Known	1	—
14	Not Given	7	—	14	Not Given	—	—
15	Non Lepcha	9	—	15	Non Lepcha	4	—
16	TOTAL	86	14	16	TOTAL	88	40

C: Name of the village: Khamdung.

1	Arampucho Moo	1	1	1	Fyung Moo	2	1
2	Ethan Moo	1	1	2	Fonyoong Rungsaong Moo	2	1
3	Emsaong Moo	4	1	3	Malaom Moo	4	2
4	Lik Moo	3	1	4	Naamchu Moo	16	4
5	Malaom Moo	12	7	5	Phepon Moo	5	2
6	Naom Gye Chu Moo	2	1	6	Somboo Moo	5	4
7	Naamchu Moo	2	1	7	Shyok Moo	24	8
8	Pothyaang Moo	2	1	8	Tingboo Moo	3	1
9	Sadaa Moo	3	1	9	Yung Moo	11	5
10	Sandyang Moo	2	1	10			
11	Simik Moo	5	2	11			
12	Shyok Moo	1	1	12			
13	Sungoot Moo	1	1	13			

(Contd...)

1	2	3	4	5	6	7	8
14	Not Known	—		14			
15	Not Given	8		15			
16	Non Lepcha	11		16			
17	TOTAL	58	20	17	TOTAL	72	28

D: Name of the village: Lower Beyong.

1	2	3	4	5	6	7	8
1	Bri Moo	4	3	1	Bri Moo	4	4
2	Brisaong Moo	2	1	2	Fodaong Moo	2	1
3	Chaong Moo	9	2	3	Genyaong Moo	2	1
4	Chaong Yaoksaom Moo	3	1	4	Gangtok Moo	10	3
5	Feng Moo	2	1	5	Goulook Moo	19	7
6	Faokli Moo	1	1	6	Kaabo Moo	10	3
7	Goulook Moo	1	1	7	Looyi Moo	46	14
8	Keng Moo	1	1	8	Malaom Moo	22	13
9	Keyaonggri Yukcho Moo	1	1	9	Numfock Moo	3	1
10	Koorook Moo	7	1	10	Sadaa Moo	9	3
11	Mungsaong Moo	3	1	11	Saongmaa Moo	6	2
12	Naamchu Moo	1	1	12	Sandyong Moo	1	1
13	Naomfaok Moo	1	1	13	Sheraa Moo	1	1
14	Naomfaok Kooraok Moo	6	4	14	Sambar Moo	1	1
15	Piting Moo	2	1	15	Taamsaang Moo	9	3
16	Raongding Sungdyaang Moo	4	2	16	Tihitaong Moo	36	10
17	Raongding Sungdyaang Moo	2	1	17	Tingboo Moo	3	2

(Contd...)

1	*2*	*3*	*4*	*5*	*6*	*7*	*8*
18	Saompa Moo	9	3	18	Tangee Taam Moo	6	4
19	Sambar Gen Moo	15	4				
20	Shara Moo	6	2				
21	Saong Moo Shee Moo	16	7				
22	SShey Moo Ye Moo	10	2				
23	Simik Moo	8	4				
24	Soongoot Moo	6	3				
25	Taamsaang Pajyeng Moo	3	2				
26	Tingboo Moo	1	1				
27	Tinggro Moo	7	2				
28	Tingro Moo	6	2				
29	Tihitong Moo	5	2				
30	Yari Moo	14	5				
31	Not Known	1	—				
32	Not Given	13	—				
33	Non Lepcha	15	—				
34	TOTAL	185	63		TOTAL	190	74

Source: Field Survey.

Epilogue

Moo places the females in a higher position in the Lepcha society. Females not only retain their identity in the society but separated themselves from the male counter part by possessing distinct Moo of their own. It honors, respects and recognizes the position of women in the Lepcha society. Existence of separate Moo is the other name of self respect and self reliance for the females in the society. They are neither dependent nor get Moo from the males. Females are no way inferior but maintain their equality and parity with male members in the Lepcha society. A female not only respects in inheriting her mother's Moo but she feels proud of transmitting it to her daughter. Mother lives in her daughter and hence girl child is welcomed in the society.

Moo has its practical use in case of traditional marriage where there is strong taboo in marrying with in the same Moo. A boy can not marry a girl who belongs to his mother's Moo. Similarly a girl can not marry a boy of her father's Moo. The Buddhist Lepchas are still following this restriction but the Christians have to some extent liberalized the restrictions of Moo in marriage. The high percentage of exogamous marriage and the presence of unmarried boys and girls are the two factors responsible for loosening the role of Moo in present Lepcha society. But the recent practice of using Moo as title is a step in reviving the position of Moo in Lepcha society. Any way, the presence of separate Moo among the women upholds their status in the Lepchas society. It not only gives a prestigious position of women in the society but keeps the women distinct and separate from the males. Women can be recognized by their separate Moo.

8

Economic Status of Women Among the Lepchas

Introduction

There is no denial of the fact that social status of women in general and that of the tribal in particular depends upon their economic empowerment. No development could be achieved on sustainable basis unless and until the women folk of the society are developed and equipped economically. The contribution and involvement of women in economic activity is related to their status and role in the family and in the society. An economically parasite women can not claim equal status with their counterpart in the family and in the society. Women's participation in the income earning activity creates awareness and changed the attitude of the family and the society towards health care, education program, standard of living and in all sphere of life. The total outlook of the women can be changed with their economic empowerment. Economic independence has a far reaching consequence in changing and providing necessary weapon for uplifting the society and the country.

The present chapter has been divided in three sections: Section I discusses the general overview of the women in tribal India; Section II deals with the economic status of women in Lepcha society from the viewpoint of existing literature and census data; Section III examines status of women among the Lepchas from the information collected from the study area.

Status of Tribal Women in India: A General Overview

India is the second largest country next to Africa in respect of tribal population. Tribes constitute 8.08 per cent of total population of our country. The Government of India after independence has taken a number of measures / policies to uplift the economic condition of tribes in India. One of the basic purposes of enlisting the tribes under the category of Scheduled Tribe of India was to extend special facilities and protection so as to keep them outside the purview of competition. Various approaches, models, concepts and thesis have been made and tested for tribal development. But even after sixty years of independence there are fresh demands for including different communities under the net of ST. Several ST communities demand for their inclusion in the category of Primitive Tribal Groups. Such demands are rooted in the fact that tribes are still backward and exploited class in comparison to the other ethnic groups of the country. The development plans so far undertaken are not just clicking or the appropriate plans as required for their development are not undertaken so far.

The sex ratio of ST population (972 female per thousand male) in India is better than for the total population (927 female per thousand male) as per 1991 census. To develop the tribes there is an urgent need of developing the tribal females. The irony of the fact that the work participation rate for the tribes (49.3 percent) is much better than that of the total population (37.5 per cent) of India in 1991 but their economic condition remain far neglected and as high as 51.9

per cent tribes are lying below poverty line compared to 37.3 per cent for the total population in India in1993 – 94. The participation rates in the working force of the tribal population by gender have been higher during the census period 1961—1991. The following Table- 8.1 shows gender-wise participation of population (in percentage) in India for the period 1961 – 91.

Table – 8.1
Gender-wise participation of tribal and total population in India , 1961 – 1991.

(In percentage term)

Census Year	*Total population*			*ST population*		
	Person	*Male*	*Female*	*Person*	*Male*	*Female*
1	*2*	*3*	*4*	*5*	*6*	*7*
1961	13.0	37.2	27.9	56.5	61.3	52.0
1971	33.1	52.6	12.1	38.5	55.9	20.8
1981	38.5	51.6	51.6	42.5	56.7	28.1
1991	37.6	51.5	51.5	42.0	53.7	30.0

Source: V.S.Upadhyay: Tribal Development in India P – 271.

In spite of high sex ratio and higher participation of women folk in economic activity, the economic condition of women are not only weak but it is pathetic. .

In order to safeguard and protect the interest of the tribes and the tribal areas, a number of Acts and Regulations had been passed right from the British rule in India.

Some such important acts during the British rule are:

1. Cleveland's Hill Assembly Plan of 1872.
2. Bengal Act, XIII, 1833.
3. Wilkinson Act

4. Act 1855.
5. Act 1870
6. Scheduled Area Act 1874 (Darjeeling, Jalpaiguri and Chitagong Hills)
7. Government of India Act 1919
8. Government of India Act 1935.

After independence, the government of India morally accepted to continue protective measures for the upliftment of the tribal population of the country. A number of programmes have been launched from time to time for the welfare of the underprivileged class in general and for tribals in particular. Some such programs are:

1. Community Development Programme, 1952.
2. Special Multipurpose Tribal Blocks, 1956.
3. Tribal Development Blocks, 1961.
4. Tribal Development Agencies, 1966.
5. Primitive Tribal Groups, 1971
6. Integrated Tribal Development Projects, 1978
7. Tribal Sub- plan, 1971.

A dozens of programs have been planned, launched, implemented, modified, revised, and executed under the broad as poverty alleviation drive by the central government. Among them the Swarna Jyanti Gram Sarojgar Yojna initiated in 1999 has proved to be much fruitful for the tribal women. Females can become self sufficient by forming Self Help Groups (SHG) and avail government subsidies up to fifty percent of the loan amount.

In spite of several affords the economic condition of the tribes in general and the women in particular could not improve much. The national seminar (1993) on status of tribal women organized by the Council for Social Development observed that:

"The tribal women have been more adversely affected than tribal men by the developmental projects and deforestation. It was argued that the negative effects of developmental programmes on tribal women included an increase in the workload of women, increase in unemployment of women as a result of the introduction of modern agricultural implements, increase in migration to other areas as labourers, marginalization of women due to restrictions regarding exploitation of forests, and exploitation of women in various ways, such as, marrying tribal women for receiving benefits meant for tribals, compensation for land given in terms of jobs for men, social and sexual exploitation, etc."

THE CASE OF THE LEPCHAS

Economic Status: Secondary Data

The secondary data examines the economic status of women in the Lepcha society over three different time periods: nomadic stage, shifting cultivation stage and settled cultivation stage.

Nomadic Stage

During this stage, the Lepchas used to subsist on hunting, fishing and gathering fruits and roots. Perhaps up to the 13th century and before the reign of *Khy Bumsa* who was the ruler and one of the signatories of *Blood Treaty* with the Tibetans, Lepchas led nomadic life. The economy was closely linked with the forest which provided with food, shelter and what not. They knew all the secrets of the forest and the hills. As children of Kanchanjunga they possessed full knowledge of the beasts, birds, trees, shrubs, flowers, fruits, funguses etc of the region. Lepchas were the born botanists and zoologists of the hills and possessed some chemical knowledge of freeing poison from the poisonous trees.

No systematic study has so far been conducted on the nomadic life of the Lepchas in general and on the status of women in particular. But some writers like G.B.Mainwearing, L.A.Waddell, A.Campbell and others have mentioned about the nomadic life of the Lepchas in the early days.

Regarding nomadic life G.B.Mainwaring wrote: "what and whatsoever might have been their original source, they appeared in the most simple, primitive, state, living in the midst of the vast wild, magnificent forests, old as the hills themselves.... From the forests they obtained fruits of numerous descriptions, edible and otherwise useful; thus all their wants were supplied. They knew no care, and but little sorrow, cheerful as the birds, and sturdy as the trees around them, they roamed through the forests inhaling health. They understood little about medicines and had not much use for them, sickness being almost unknown among them, but they possess some very efficacious roots &c., with which 1 believe Europeans are still unacquainted" (1876: p. IX).

In his travelogue, L.A.Waddell expressed the same opinion with A. Campbell regarding the nomadic life of the Lepchas. He wrote that before the invasion of the Tibetans "Lepchas were the original and sole inhabitants of Sikkim. At that time the Lepchas had a somewhat nomadic life and subsisted mainly on collection of roots, tubers, and fishing, hunting etc. (1899: p. 14).

Although the existing literature remained silent about the role of women in Lepchá nomadic life but it could safely be inferred that the women were no less important than the men in the primitive stage of Lepcha fife. In those days they led a communal life where the community, may be in different groups, lived and moved together in search of food, the basic necessity of life. Naturally the women might have also participated in different activities along with the male members of the society. The custom of carrying *Baanhoor*, a small sickle like knife, in the backside of their waist belt or girdle proves that women must have used the same in those days. It might have been used both for protecting and defending themselves from any attacks of enemies and wild lives. It might be used for the purpose of hunting and food gathering. Women also carry with them a pair of *Zet*, long, sharp and pointed silver safety pin for holding dam-bun, Lepcha female dress on both sides of their shoulders. The *Zet* , if required, can also be used as weapon to defend themselves from the attack of the enemies. It may be noted that Lepcha males carry *Baan-pook*, Lepcha knife which is bigger in size than *Baan-hoor*, the female knife. It may easily be inferred that hard and laborious works might had been done by the male members with use of *Baan-pook* while comparatively less laborious works were carried out by the female with the use of *Baan- hoor*. Beside carrying their sickle or knife both by the male and female members of the society, women were also expert in using bow and arrow, the communal weapon widely used during the hunting operation. Even today women took part in *Chongay*, archery competition which may be considered as the legacy of their primitive habit. In Lepcha *Chong* means arrow and *Sali* means bow; *Chongay* means archery competition. It may be noted that Paril Lepcha of Kalimpong is the recipient of gold medals at the sub Junior National Archery Competition, 2004-05. The traditional Lepcha society was matriarchal which itself is the indication of direct and active participation and involvement of women in economic activities.

Shifting Cultivation Stage

The entire period of Tibetan rule in Sikkim which started sometimes in the 13th century after the reign of *Khy Bumsa* and ended with the entrance of British in Darjeeling track in 1936 can roughly be identified as the period of shifting cultivation in the Lepcha economy. The process included firstly to select a plot of virgin land, clean the jungle and set fire to it. Their habit was to cultivate a particular plot of land for three to four years and then leave the land due to decrease in its fertility. They used rude wooden agricultural implements like hoe for cultivation of crops. The productivity of Lepcha cultivation on an average was comparatively low.

Description of shifting cultivation among Lepchas can be found in the writings of E.T.Dalton, A. Campbell, R. Temple, W.W.Hunter, J.D.Hooker, H.H.Risley, R.V. Nebesky, Chi Nakane, Haharaja and Maharani Dolma of Sikkim and others.

E.T. Dalton along with Campbell observed that Lepchas were "poor agriculturists. They form no permanent villages and cultivate barely sufficient for their subsistence. They seldom remain more than three years in one spot. They have no-plough, and the implements they employ do no more than scrap and soften for the reception of seed in the upper layer of vegetable mould." (1872: p. 9).

Richard Temple wrote: "they are poor for they have no idea of cultivation beyond cleaning a spot of virgin soil, and scrapping up its surface with the rudest of agricultural implements, repeating the process elsewhere as soon as that particular area is exhausted" (1875: p. 19).

In the words of W.W.Hunter shifting cultivation "consists in selecting a spot of virgin soil, cleaning it of forest and jungle, and scraping up the surface with the rudest agricultural implements. The productive power of the land becomes exhausted in a few years, when the cleaning is abandoned and a new site chosen, where the same operations are carried on de novo." (1876: p. 47).

H.H. Risley describes "Lepcha are poor agriculturists...they do not form permanent villages, and rarely remain longer than three years in one place, at the expiration of which they move into a new part of the forest, sometimes near, often distance, and there go through the labour of cleaning a new one, and preparing the ground for a crop. The later operations consists in cutting down the smaller trees, lopping off the branches of the large ones, which are burnt, and scratching the soil with the 'ban', after which, on the falling of a shower of rain, the seed is thrown into the ground" (1891:pp. 13-14).

Chi Nakane quoted Maharaja and Maharani of Sikkim and described Lepcha shifting cultivation as "a new patch of jungle would be cleared every year, and when dried set fire to. On the cleared space, paddy, kodo, and bhutta, as well as various white and black grains would be sown. Next year another patch of jungle would be cleared. The virgin soil of course yielded a very rich crop, and people used to gain their living very easily, and also enjoyed a good many sorts of fruits and herbs, which they can not get now. As they had not much call on them for free labour contribution or much of tax to pay, they were very happy". (1966: p. 216)

All the write ups confirm the practice of shifting cultivation among the Lepchas in the early days. But none of them could specify the role and participation of women in different stages of shifting cultivation. Two Lepcha folk tales are relevant in this context. The first one is about the division of women labor in Lepcha agriculture. It says the Lepcha traditional agriculture is popularly known as *Zomaal.* In Lepcha *Zo* means paddy and *Zomaal* means sowing of paddy in the dry land. Under this system, the males are engaged to dig the earth with pointed bamboo rod while the females are assigned the work of pushing the seed inside the holed or loosed earth. *Zomaal* is an example of division of labor and it identified the involvement and assigned work of the women in Lepcha shifting cultivation. It is believed that women are the lucky section of the society and plants can germinate better and yield more if they are sown by the women.

The second folktale is about the period of agricultural operation. It is told that around 1300 AD Lepcha king Ronji Pemo married queen Zolosy Pandi, daughter of Raja Dev Chandra of *Zolosy* means Jalpaiguri. Zolosy Pandi was born and brought up in the plains and knew nothing about the agricultural operation of the hills. When she came to the hills after marriage, she could not match the timing of the crops in the hills. She, thus, send a massage to her mother through river Teesta requesting her to inform her about the timing of the crops particularly about vegetable in the hills. It is told that mother queen send her message through a bird known as *Kurnook*. It is believed that during April-May when the bird comes from the plains, Lepchas consider the period important for the cultivation of vegetables. Lepchas of Mane Gumba even today wait for the *Kurnook* to come before they go for the cultivation of vegetables. The folk tale is an indication of women's involvement in the management, decision and policy making operation in Lepcha agriculture.

Settled Cultivation Stage

During the British period Lepchas were forced to adopt settled cultivation. O'Malley wrote "with the introduction of settle cultivation and the reservation of forest, they have had to give up their old nomadic cultivation, and have lost much of their jungle craft; but they have learnt in its place how to make terraces for rice fields and the methods of agriculture practiced by the Nepalese" (1907: p. 44).

Restriction of the use of forest compelled the Lepchas to depend solely on terraced based cultivation. Their economy became agriculture based subsistence one and they started producing those crops which were needed for their consumption. The major crops were: paddy, millet, maize, buckwheat, barley, and vegetable. They used small tools, domestic manure, domestic seeds, rain water and household labor. No investment as such was required for such cultivation. The concept of wage labor was totally absent and the entire operation was carried out with family labor.

With the influx of large number of immigrants, land became scarce to the Lepchas and they started to use land with care. Two categories of land – wet land and dry land— were used for the purpose of cultivation. Wetland (*Zo nyaot*) is used for the cultivation of paddy and dry land (*Moong nyaot*) for the cultivation of maize and millet. Beside the food crops, Lepchas started using cash crops like cardamom, ginger, vegetables etc. Food crops are tradition based and considered to be a household activity. Lepchas have shown some sort of commercial attitude for the production of cash crops where they started using some chemical fertilizer, HYV seed, and some mechanical tools. There are absolutely no assured irrigation facilities and the Lepchas are depending absolutely on rain water or on stream water for cultivation. Although some wage labor is used for cash crops but Lepcha agriculture is basically a household activity.

Quoting Morris, A.K.Das narrated the significant rôle of women in the Lepcha agricultural practice. "In Sikkim, both Lepcha men and women work in the fields, and there is no hard and fast divisions of labour between the sexes, although the heavier work is mostly done by males. They do not recognize any inherent distinction between the temperament of the sexes, there is with them practically no such things, as "men's work" and "women's work".

"A Lepcha woman does considerably more physical work than the man. This is not, however, to regulate then to the position of domestic slaves; and while the laws of the state do not permit a women to inherit land, she can and does, own other property, and is an equal partner with her husband in the management of the household affairs" (1978: pp. 52-53).

The nature of Lepcha agriculture can be discussed with the help of secondary data on industrial classification of Lepcha population for the state of West Bengal and for the district of Darjeeling.

Industrial Classification of Lepcha Population

Data on industrial classification of Lepchas are available with the years 1961, 1971 and 1981. Table 8.2 shows that the percentage of Lepcha workers for the state of West Bengal decreases from 51.59 to 48.69 and 42.23 over the decades 1961, 1971 and 1981 respectively; while it increases from 48.41 to 51.31 and further to 56.26 for that of non-workers. The situation is also more or less same for the Lepchas of Darjeeling district. Against decreasing percentage of workers 51.81, 49.78 and 42.38 respectively, the percentages of non-workers have increased from 48.19 to 50.22 and 56.11 per cent for the years 1961, 1971 and 1981 respectively. But the case is not the same among the Lepchas living in rural and urban areas. The fluctuations in the percentages of both workers and non-workers among the Lepchas of urban areas of the state and the district are due to the corresponding fluctuations in the female population. But for the rural Lepchas a decreasing trend among both the workers and non-workers can be noticed for both the males and females. Over the decades Lepchas, thus, are becoming unemployed and the trend is more among the females in both the rural and urban areas.

Table 8.3 shows industrial classification of Lepcha population for the state over the census periods 1961, 1971 and 1981. Highest proportion of population is engaged in cultivation (81.91 per cent in 1961; 34.01 per cent in 1971; and 73.23 per cent in 1981 respectively) followed by other services and agricultural labor. The proportion of population engaged in mining and quarrying, household industry, construction, trade and commerce, transport, communication is very negligible.

As cultivator, females are dominating over males for all the three decades. Their role is also important in case of livestock, forestry, fishing, hunting and plantation work. But in all other categories, the role of females cannot be ignored. The higher percentage of female population unequivocally shows the importance of female participation in working group.

Almost same trend has been marked among the Lepchas in the district level classification (table – 8.4) but the corresponding percentages for the cultivators are more than those of state level percentages. As the Lepchas of the state are residing mainly in Darjeeling, the district level statistics basically represent in the state level statistics. Combining cultivators and agricultural labor, it can be stated that nearly 85.16, 62.45 and 81.95 per cent of population are wholly depend on agriculture for the census period 1961, 1971 and 1981 respectively. The rest 14.84, 37.55 and 18.05 per cent of workers are engaged in activities other than agriculture. Lepcha economy, thus, can safely be identified as agricultural one. Adding engagement of Lepchas in Livestock, forestry, fishing, hunting, plantation and orchard sector, it is seen that as much as 88.93, 71.92 and 87.06 per cent of workers are engaged in activities connected with the exploitation of nature. Irrespective of ups and downs, Lepchas even during the modern periods are continued to maintain a close link and depend largely on nature for their livelihood and women continued to play an important and vital role in the Lepcha agricultural operation.

The secondary data unequivocally establish the fact that majority of the Lepchas are the agriculturists and the Lepcha economy is agricultural one where more than half of the work is carried by the women.

Table – 8.2

Workers and Non-workers among the Lepchas of West Bengal and Darjeeling – 1961-1981

		Population			*Worker*						*Non Worker*					
		1961	*1971*	*1981*	*1961*		*1971*		*1981*		*1961*		*1971*		*1981*	
		No.	*No.*	*No.*	*No.*	*%*	*No.*	*%*	*No.*	*%*	*No.*	*%*	*No.*	*%*	*No.*	*%*
WEST BENGAL																
RURAL	Male	6946	7526	10795	4292	61.79	4220	56.07	5830*	54.01	2654	38.21	3306	43.93	4857*	44.99
	Female	6883	5847	10133	3172	46.08	2328	39.82	3379*	33.35	3711	53.92	3519	60.18	6512*	64.26
	Total	13829	13373	20928	7464	53.97	6548	48.96	9209*	44.00	6365	46.03	6825	51.04	11369*	54.32
URBAN	Male	631	779	1216	288	45.64	356	45.70	483*	39.72	343	54.36	423	54.30	730*	60.03
	Female	849	416	1265	147	17.31	190	45.67	193*	15.25	702	82.69	226	54.33	1071*	84.66
	Total	1480	1195	2481	435	29.40	546	45.69	676*	27.25	1045	70.60	649	54.31	1801*	72.59
DARJEELING																
RURAL	Male	6761	7030	10560	4190	61.97	3982	56.64	5707*	54.04	2571	38.03	3048	43.36	4747*	44.95
	Female	6685	5409	9954	3104	46.43	2250	41.59	3341*	33.56	3581	53.57	3159	58.41	6375*	64.04
	Total	13446	12439	20514	7294	54.25	6232	50.10	9048*	44.11	6152	45.75	6207	49.90	11122*	54.22
URBAN	Male	624	708	1070	283	45.35	318	44.92	407	38.04	341	54.65	390	55.08	663	61.96
	Female	840	389	1165	147	17.5	188	48.33	185*	15.88	693	82.5	201	51.67	979*	84.03
	Total	1464	1097	2235	430	29.37	506	46.13	592*	26.49	1034	70.63	591	53.87	1642*	73.47

Sources: 1. Census of India 1961 – West Bengal Part V-4 (ii) Special Tables on Scheduled Tribes.
2 Census of India 1971 – West Bengal Special Table on Scheduled Tribe.
3. Census of India 1981 – West Bengal Series – 23 Part IX (IV) Special Tables on Scheduled Tribes.

Note: Figures with star mark indicate those items. which do not tally with their corresponding population figure if workers and non-workers are added together.

Table – 8.3
Industrial Classification of Lepcha Population of West Bengal – 1961-1981

Categories	1961						1971						1981					
	Male		Female		Total		Male		Female		Total		Male		Female		Total	
	No.	%	No.	%	No.	%	No.	%	No.	%	No.	%	No.	%	No.	%	No.	%
Total workers	4580	100.00	3319	100.00	7899	100.00	4576	100.00	2518	100.00	7094	100.00	6313	100.00	3571	100.00	9884	100.00
Cultivators	3590	78.38	2880	86.77	6470	81.91	1522	33.26	891	35.39	2413	34.01	4485	71.04	2753	77.09	7238	73.23
Agricultural Labourers	146	3.19	92	2.77	238	3.01	1382	36.20	574	22.79	1956	27.57	459	7.27	245	6.86	704	7.12
Livestock, forestry, fishing, hunting, plantation etc.	194	4.24	128	3.86	322	4.08	406	8.87	374	14.86	780	10.99	310	4.91	221	6.19	531	5.37
Mining, Quarring	-	-	-	-	-	-	-	-	-	-	-	-	-	-	-	-	-	-
Manufacturing, processing, servicing, Repair Household industry	29	0.63	6	0.18	35	0.44	10	0.22	8	0.32	18	0.26	23	0.37	12	0.34	35	0.35
Other than household industry	7	0.15	7	0.21	14	0.18	39	0.85	26	1.03	65	0.92	106	1.68	23	0.64	129	1.31
Construction	10	0.22	1	0.03	11	0.14	67	1.46	25	0.99	92	1.30	52	0.82	12	0.34	64	0.65
Trade and commerce	36	0.79	9	0.27	45	0.57	78	1.71	21	0.83	99	1.40	100	1.58	39	1.09	139	1.41
Transport, and communication	37	0.81	4	0.12	41	0.52	113	2.47	41	1.63	154	2.17	109	1.73	7	0.20	116	1.17
Other service	531	11.59	192	5.79	723	9.15	959	20.96	558	22.16	1517	21.38	669	10.60	259	7.25	928	9.39

Sources: Ibid.

Table – 8.4
Industrial Classification of Lepcha Population of Darjeeling – 1961-1981

Categories	1961						1971						1981					
	Male		Female		Total		Male		Female		Total		Male		Female		Total	
	No.	%	No.	%	No.	%	No.	%	No.	%	No.	%	No.	%	No.	%	No.	%
Total workers	4473	100.00	3251	100.00	7724	100.00	4300	100.00	2438	100.00	6738	100.00	6114	100.00	3526	100.00	9640	100.00
Cultivators	3572	79.86	2870	88.28	6442	83.40	1455	33.84	889	36.46	2344	34.79	4463	72.99	2747	77.91	7210	74.79
Agricultural Labourers	84	1.88	52	1.60	136	1.76	1306	30.37	558	22.89	1864	27.67	445	7.28	245	6.95	690	7.16
Livestock, forestry, fishing, hunting, plantation etc.	178	3.98	113	3.47	291	3.77	322	7.49	316	12.96	638	9.47	287	4.69	206	5.84	493	5.11
Mining, Quarring	-	-	-	-	-	-	-	-	-	-	-	-	-	-	-	-	-	-
Manufacturing, processing, servicing, Repair Household industry	29	0.65	6	0.18	35	0.45	10	0.23	8	0.33	18	0.27	23	0.38	12	0.34	35	0.36
Other than household industry	7	0.16	7	0.22	14	0.18	35	0.82	25	1.03	60	0.89	75	1.23	15	0.42	90	0.93
Construction	10	0.22	1	0.03	11	0.14	60	1.39	25	1.03	85	1.26	49	0.80	12	0.34	61	0.63
Trade and commerce	30	0.67	9	0.28	39	0.50	76	1.77	20	0.82	96	1.42	87	1.42	36	1.02	123	1.28
Transport, and communication	37	0.83	4	0.13	41	0.53	108	2.51	41	1.68	149	2.21	92	1.51	7	0.20	99	1.03
Other service	526	11.76	189	5.81	715	9.27	928	21.58	556	22.80	1484	22.02	593	9.70	246	6.98	839	8.71

Sources: Ibid.

Economic Status: Primary Data

The secondary data collected from census documents unequivocally established that the Lepcha economy is agriculture based. The following table- 8.5 shows the number and percentage of households consider either agriculture or non agriculture as their main sector of engagement in our study area.

Table - 8.5
Distribution of Households dependent on agriculture and Non-agriculture as Main sector of engagement

Name of village	*Agricultural*	*Non-agricultural*	*Total*
1	*2*	*3*	*4*
Mane Gumba	17(60.71)	11(35.29)	28(100.00)
Tashiding	10(29.41)	24(70.59)	34(100.00)
Khamdung	21(80.71)	5(19.23)	26(100.00)
Lower Beyong	55(84.62)	10(15.38)	65(100.00)
Total	103(67.32)	50(32.68)	153(100.00)

Source: Field Survey.

It is evident that 103 households comprising 67.32 per cent of the total are based on agriculture as their main sector of involvement. Almost all the households have their own landed property and carry out agricultural operation with the family labor and community labor. The two villages (Khamdung and Lower Beyong) located off the town are more dependent on agriculture. Tashiding is located near the town and its dependence on agriculture is the least (only 29.41 per cent households). Thus nearness to the town and dependence of household on agriculture is indirectly related. It has also been noted that land is comparatively scarce in those villages which are located near the town areas. The average possession of land holding per household is more in Lower Beyong followed by Khamdung, Mane Gumba and Tashiding. Thus, both land holding capacity and dependence on agriculture are indirectly related to nearness to the town areas. Scarcity of land compels the Lepchas to shift from their dependence from agriculture to non agricultural sectors both public and private. As high as 70.59 per cent of households of Tashiding village is non agricultural followed by Mane Gumba (939.29 per cent).

Table-8.5 does not give any idea about the involvement of women in economic activity. The following table- 8.6 shows sex-wise distribution of Lepcha population in the income earning activities in our study area.

It is clear that only 38.11 per cent of total population is directly engaged in income earning activities. The proportion of working population engaged in agriculture is 62.38 per cent but it is 23.77 per cent of total population of the study area.

The proportion of working female is only 17.04 per cent of total working population of the study areas. Out of this working female Lepchas 39.62 per cent are engaged in agriculture and the rest are spread over a large variety of activities. The percentage of working female to total female of the study area is only 13.19 per cent. Most of the working females are absorbed in state government services like teaching and nursing. Their engagement in central government and private jobs, self business and entrepreneurship are very negligible. It has been noted that some females are also engaged in Church oriented religious activities.

Village-wise highest percentage of females engaged in income earning activities are found in Lower Beyong (22.45 per cent), followed by Tashiding (21.79 per cent) and Mane

Table – 8.6
Sex-wise distribution of population in different income earning Activities

Category/	MANE GUMBA			TASHIDING			KHAMDUNG			LOWER BEYONG			TOTAL		
Sector of Job	M	F	Total	M	F	Total	M	F	Total	M	F	Total	M	F	Total
1	2	3	4	5	6	7	8	9	10	11	12	13	14	15	16
Central Govt	2 (66.67)	1 (33.33)	3 (100.00)	2 (66.67)	1 (33.33)	3 (100.00)	—	—	—	1 (50.00)	1 (50.00)	2 (100.00)	5 (62.50)	3 (37.5)	5 (100.00)
Stata Govt	5 (100.00)	—	5 (100.00)	9 (42.86)	12 (57.14)	21 (100.00)	3 (100.00)	—	3 (100.00)	2 (25.00)	6 (75.00)	8 (100.00)	19 (51.35)	18 (48.65)	5 (100.00)
Private Sector	3 (100.00)	—	3 (100.00)	10 (90.91)	1 (9.09)	11 (100.00)	5 (100.00)	—	5 (100.00)	11 (100.00)	—	11 (100.00)	29 (96.67)	1 (3.33)	5 (100.00)
Business	2 (100.00)	—	2 (100.00)	4 (66.67)	2 (33.33)	6 (100.00)	—	—	—	—	2 (100.00)	2 (100.00)	6 (60.00)	4 (40.00)	5 (100.00)
Agriculture	26 (96.29)	1 (3.71)	27 (100.00)	26 (100.00)	—	26 (100.00)	28 (96.55)	1 (3.45)	29 (100.00)	93 (83.04)	19 (16.96)	112 (100.00)	173 (69.18)	21 ()10.82	5 (100.00)
Religious Activities	4 (100.00)	—	4 (100.00)	3 (75.00)	1 (25.00)	4 (100.00)	2 (100.00)	—	2 (100.00)	4 (44.44)	5 (55.56)	9 (100.00)	13 (68.42)	6 (31.58)	5 (100.00)
Retired Person	2 (100.00)	—	2 (100.00)	7 (100.00)	—	7 (100.00)	1 (100.00)	—	1 (100.00)	3 (100.00)	—	3 (100.00)	13 (100.00)	—	5 (100.00)
TOTAL	**44 (95.65)**	**2 (4.35)**	**46 (100.00)**	**61 (78.21)**	**17 (21.79)**	**78 (100.00)**	**39 (97.50)**	**1 (2.50)**	**40 (100.00)**	**114 (77.55)**	**33 (22.45)**	**147 (100.00)**	**258 (82.96)**	**53 (17.04)**	**5 (100.00)**

Source: Field Survey

Gumba (4.35 per cent).In Lower Beyong 57.57 per cent females are engaged in agricultural activities while 70.59 percentage of working females are engaged in state government jobs. Both the village are Christian dominated with high rate of literacy rate which might have been helped the females to absorbed them in income earning activities.

It is interesting to note that except Lower Beyong, females in other villages have enlisted themselves in the category of household activities and considered agriculture as their secondary source of engagement. Lepcha agriculture is family oriented and all members as per their age and sex get involve in different types of agricultural operations

Like most tribal agriculture, Lepchas carry out agriculture on subsistence basis. Household is the main source of supply of labor for agriculture. Household comprises of members of married couple living together with their descendents and in some cases representatives of older generations. Two peculiarities have been noted in respect to the composition of population: a) presents of good number of unmarried persons both male and female and b) adoption of child both male and female by the households.

Almost all members irrespective of their age and sex involve in agricultural operation. It has been found that even the school going children help domestic agriculture during their off school time. Some light works like carrying meal/ Tiffin to the field for the labors rest on the children. During the peak agricultural season, many schools in the village areas arrange vacation and holidays according to the agricultural calendar year. It has been experienced that during the peak agricultural season the attendance of students become thinner.

The young, energetic female members of the households are directly engaged in different agricultural operations. Such members may be related with the head of the family as wife, daughter, sister etc. their earning can neither be measured in monetary units nor separated from the total earning from agriculture but their service is very crucial and vital for Lepcha agricultural operation. The aged females help agriculture by transmitting their experience to the younger generations. They also indirectly help agriculture by substituting and releasing the labor of the house wives and daughters for agriculture and shouldering the responsibilities of carrying out daily household activities.

Table- 8.7 shows agricultural operation and classification of work between male and female for different crops in our study area. A perusal of the table shows that different categories of works have been assigned to different types of labor. Comparatively hard and laborious works have been assigned to male members while females specialize in transplanting, broadcasting of seeds, weeding and plucking, pulverizing and storing grains. Females specialize in these works and such works are generally not been assigned to the male members of the Lepcha society. It has been observed that female's involvement is more in traditional crops like paddy, maize, and millet while for the newly introduced cash crops like ginger, cardamom, vegetables and floriculture the role of female is less significant. So modernization of agriculture and introduction of newer variety of crops have made the female labor less important in Lepcha agriculture.

During our field study it has been noticed that most females of all age group are involved in the agricultural operations. But they do not consider agriculture as their primary occupation and preferred to recognize themselves as household activities or as students as the case may be. The only exception is with Lower Beyong village where a good number of females recognized agriculture as their primary sector of engagement. The following Table-8.8 shows sex-wise involvement in agriculture as primary and secondary sector of engagement.

Table- 8.7
Sex-wise Agricultural Operation Among the Lepchas

Type of Operation	*Paddy*		*Maize*		*Millet*		*Ginger*		*Cardamom*		*Floriculture*		*Vegetables*	
	M	*F*	*M*	*F*	*M*	*F*	*M*	*F*	*M*	*F*	*M*	*F*	*M*	*F*
1	*2*	*3*	*4*	*5*	*6*	*7*	*8*	*9*	*10*	*11*	*12*	*13*	*14*	*15*
Cleaning	"				"		"		"	"	"			
Ploughing	"		"				"		"				"	
Levelling	"		"		"				"		"		"	
Pulverisizing	"		"	"	"	"	"				"			
Ridge-Making	"	"	"	"			"	"	"	"	"		"	"
Transplanting	"	"	"	"	"	"					"		"	"
Mud-play	"	"												
Weeding	"	"	"	"			"	"			"	"	"	"
Harvesting	"	"				"	"		"					
Threasging	"	"				"				"	"		"	"
Drying	"									"				
Plucking	"			"										
Weighting	"													
Carrying	"		"											
Stacking	"													
Storing	"	"	"	"		"	"				"			"
Total	15	7	8	6	4	5	7	2	5	4	8	1	6	5

Table 8.8
Sex-wise Involvement in Agriculture as Primary and Secondary occupation.

Name of Village	*Agriculture as primary Sector*			*Agriculture as secondary Sector*			*No involvement in Agriculture*		
	M	*F*	*Total*	*M*	*F*	*Total*	*M*	*F*	*Total*
1	*2*	*3*	*4*	*5*	*6*	*7*	*8*	*9*	*10*
Mane Gumba	26 (96.29)	1 (3.71)	27 (100.00)	15 (27.78)	39 (72.22)	54 (100.00)	41 (50.62)	40 (49.38)	81 (100.00)
Tashiding	26 (100.00)	—	26 (100.00)	15 (31.25)	33 (68.75)	48 (100.00)	41 (55.41)	33 (44.59)	74 (100.00)
Khamdung	28 (96.55)	1 (3.45)	29 (100.00)	16 (28.56)	40 (71.43)	56 (100.00)	44 (51.76)	41 (48.24)	85 (100.00)
Lower Beyong	93 (83.04)	19 (16.96)	112 (100.00)	38 (40.43)	56 (59.57)	94 (100.00)	131 (63.59)	75 (206)	206 (100.00)
Total	173 (89.18)	21 (10.82)	194 (100.00)	84 (33.33)	168 (66.67)	252 (100.00)	257 (57,62)	189 (42.38)	446 (100.00)

Source : Field Survey.

Primary occupation is the main or the basic involvement of an individual. Secondary occupations are those where the individuals are engaged during their off period and have other areas of their main engagement. For many people, agriculture is not the main occupation but they help in carrying out agricultural operation during their spare time. Sometimes they even take temporary leave from their main occupation and extend their help in agricultural operation. They do not receive any cash in return but share agricultural produce by consuming it.

Table- 8.8, constructed to show sex-wise involvement of the Lepchas in agriculture as primary and secondary sector of engagement, gives the following interesting results:

a). Involvement of females in agriculture as primary occupation is very negligible (10.22 percent). In some villages (Tashiding—0.00; Mane Gumba – 3.71: and in Lower Khamdung – 3.45 per cent), females do not consider agriculture as their primary sector of engagement.

b). Females in all the villages consider agriculture as secondary sector of their engagement. Female's involvement (66.67 per cent) in agriculture as secondary occupation far exceeds than that of the male's (33.33 per cent).

c). Overall involvement of females (42.38 per cent) in agriculture is slightly less than those of males (56.62 per cent). The lesser proportion of female's involvement in agriculture as primary sector (10.87 per cent) is compensated by their higher proportion of involvement as secondary occupation (66.67 per cent).

d). Villages with higher proportion of involvement of females in agriculture as primary occupation are accompanied by their lower engagement as secondary occupation. Conversely, the villages with lower proportion of their engagement as primary occupation have higher proportion of their involvement in agriculture as secondary source.

e). Female labour is inevitable in agricultural operation among the Lepchas.

Households remain the main source of labour for Lepcha agriculture. Two other sources are: wage labor and exchange labour.

Wage is paid both in cash and kind. Monetary wage is more common for the cultivation of cash crops like vegetables, ginger, cardamom, floriculture etc. Monetary wage is discriminated among the Lepchas on the basis of age and sex. The following is the average wage of the labour during the study period.

Adult Male — Rs 40/-

Adult female — Rs 35/-

Children (both sexes) — Rs 25/-.

Females are paid less than their counterpart, the male members for the same type of work. It has been taken for granted that female productivity and efficiency is less than those of the males. Females are less preferred in the modern cultivation (like floriculture, vegetables) where the Lepchas started using fertilizer, chemicals, pesticides etc. In case of traditional crops like paddy, maize, millet etc female's service is well recognized in specific categories of work mentioned in table 8.7.

Real wage i.e. wage in terms of kind is still prevails among the Lepchas in case of paddy cultivation. A labour has to wait till the harvest for his or her payment in terms of paddy. All irrespective of age and sex are paid equally and each labour is paid 1 *pathi* (=4 kg of paddy). In case of paddy cultivation equality is maintained to that extent that even a child labour is considered as important as those of the adult male or adult female labour. It may be noted that for some works like using them as weight during leveling the paddy field child labour is the only option. Lepchas do respect child labor and make no discrimination in paying them equally with other types of labour.

The other type of labour widely used in traditional Lepcha cultivation is exchange labour popularly known as *Tyaolmatheong* in Lepcha and *Parma* in Nepali.. Labour is exchanged basically in traditional crops like maize, millet, and paddy. Labor of all age and sex are accepted for exchange and only the head is counted and not the efficiency or productivity. In Lepcha agriculture human labour can also be exchanged with animal labour. Labour available for one crop can also be exchanged for other crop and other time period. In *Tyaolmatheong* all the four types of labour – male, female, child and animal labour – used in Lepcha traditional crop cultivation are considered to be the same and equally productive and important.

Thus, the treatment towards female labour in Lepcha agriculture is not uniform for all the crops and over all the periods. In case of traditional crops and method of cultivation where even today the exchange labour and real wage prevail, females are considered equally with the males. But in case of modern cash crops with modern technology female labour is considered inferior to male labour. It can be said that with the introduction of modern crop and method of cultivation females started loosing their position and importance in the Lepcha society. Modernization discriminates Lepcha females adversely.

Property Right and the Law of Inheritence

It has been seen that the females in the Lepcha society posses distinct Moo which is different from the male Moo. A girl inherits Moo from her mother while a son from his father. In the same way all properties, both movable and immovable, are also inherited in the same pattern from mother to daughter and from father to son. That means, mother's property is distributed among the daughters and that of the father's to the sons. But in practice the females are deprived because lands are generally in the name of the males and hence the girls are not inheriting the landed property but they are very well inheriting all types of movable properties of their mother.

As per Lepcha tradition after the dead of the head of the family i.e father the landed property which is normally in his name is distributed among the sons. In most cases the eldest son enjoys the ancestral house while the youngers are to construct new establishment in the plot of land specifically given for the purpose. Only the ornaments etc of the mother are to be given equally among the daughters. Land does not follow the matrilineal pattern but it follows patrilineal channel. J.R. Subba comments that "women have no right of inheritance. They have a great role however in the agricultural operation from sowing to harvesting" (2008; p. 253). S. Ghosal observed the issue minutely and comments that "according to Lepcha traditional custom, land can only be owned by men, in the event of a women or a group of women (usually co-wives) being left sole possessors of a property, they must acquire, either by marriage or by adoption, a male who can inherit the property. But today even a women, who does not have any male member to look after, can have land in her name" (1990: p. 110). D.C.Roy noted that "a Lepcha family without male offspring occasionally gifts land to the girl child and invites the son-in-law to reside with his bride who inherits the parent's property. Families either without male offspring or without any issue adopt child (*Ta-gri-kup-tsaop*) and with the permission of the *Keyong Sezong*, the village level organization accepts the child and allows inheriting all types of property. The non-Lepcha child is also adopted and assimilated into the society by giving moo or even ST certificate (2005: p. 91).

A.R. Foning also noted deprived condition of women in case of inheritance of landed property. "In our society, we follow the patriarchal system. The head of the family i.e., the father is the supreme in the family. The words spoken by him, or the decision given by him is unquestionable. All the property, both movable and immovable, belong to him. He may, during his life time dispose of some part, or keep the whole property as he may consider best. When he dies, normally the eldest of his sons, takes charge of the family properties, including cattle and other assets, rights, duties and everything....As far as property matters are concerned, except for their own movable personal belongings, females have no *locus standi*. However, it is seen that the unwritten norms of the society have ample provision for safeguarding the interests of the seemingly helpless female sex. As long as the girls are not married and taken away by their husbands, they have full right of protection and being looked after in their father's, brother's or uncle's place, whichever be their home, and whoever be their head of the family. Even after marriage we are supposed to keep an eye on the welfare of the girl's and their children and come to their assistance whenever necessary" (1987: pp. 194-197).

In another occasion Foning gave a detailed account of the law of inheritance among the females. "Speaking more on the subject of ownership of female property, there is a certain custom in our society called 'Atil'. Usually daughters, sisters, aunts, and near relations like cousins are given gifts in the form of livestock, chicken, ornaments, etc. Some are even allotted a piece of land to cultivate and enjoy the products, or even one or two fruit trees. The recipient may sell the products or dispose them off in any way she likes; nobody has any right to question her on that account. When they marry and go away, they have a right to take away their movable property with them. A widow who for some reason has not been applied with an 'a-ngop' and has only daughters in the family, is allowed to enjoy the property, both movable and immovable, during her life time. When she dies, the property reverts, to the nearest male agnate. Thus a women never possesses landed property as is understood in the legal terms of other people" (1987: pp. 196-107).

The Lepcha Customary Law is very restrictive in inheriting land only among the male members of the society. It also states about the complexities due to adoption of both Lepcha. "An adopted Lepcha son from the same clan shall be entitled to the ancestral land and property; however, an adopted Lepcha girl from the same clan or mother's clan, when she is married off or given in marriage, shall not be entitled to any ancestral land and property of her adopted parents. While she was living with her adopted parents, if she has made and accumulated her own personal wealth like gold, silver, money, domesticated animals like pig, cow, goat, chicken etc. she may take them with her after marriage with the consent and permission from her adopted parents" (2003: p. 4).

Complexities in case of adoption of non-Lepcha child are much more from the angle of inheriting the landed property. The Lepcha Customary Law states that "Disputes shall arise over the possession of the ancestral land and property between the non-Lepcha adopted child and the rightful, lawful, full blooded Lepcha next of kins.

The Lepcha ancestral land shall not be passed on to a non-Lepcha at all. If it happens, the very existence of the Lepchas is jeopardized, threatened, and endangered" (2003: p. 4).

Somewhat different procedure in distributing land is observed by H.H. Risley. "In matters of inheritance and succession the Lepchas follow a tribal custom of their own, which is administered by the panchayats of the tribe, and rarely comes before the regular courts. At a man's death his property is supposed to be divided equally among his sons, but the rule of equal division is liable in practice to be modified by other considerations. Thus the widow and daughters of the deceased usually live with the eldest son, and where this is the case he gets an extra share of the property. In Sikkim, again, it is held that the rule of equal division only applies where the sons render equal service to the Raja of the country, so that if one son does service and the others do not, that one gets an extra share of the property. A similar principle is recognized by the Lepchas of Darjeeling. In dividing an inheritance account is taken by the panchayat of the extent to which the different heirs have contributed to the improvement of the property, and their shares are adjusted accordingly. Brothers have no claim by right of descent, but shares may be awarded to them by the panchayat in proportion to the work they have done during the lifetime of the deceased. Wills are unknown: but a father may make a verbal declaration in favour of a particular son, and the panchayat will give effect to this declaration of his wishes. If sons survive, the unmarried daughters are maintained by them, and neither they nor married daughters take any share in the property. If, however, there are no sons, a married daughter may succeed, provided that she and her husband have lived in her father's house. The whole system, however, is extremely fluid and indefinite, and the rules stated above are in practice constantly modified by the panchayat with the object of doing substantial justice to the various claimants" (1891: pp. 9,10). But in our study we could observe that all lands are inherited and shared equally by the sons irrespective of their contribution in making the family property. Even the minors are getting equal proportion to that of his eldest brother. The role of village panchayat is limited only as witness to equal distribution of property so that no one deprives the other.

Epilogue

The type of activities performed by the Lepcha women over different stages of their economy has never remained the same but it has been observed that the women played an important role in Lepcha economic activity. Women are the integral part of Lepcha economy and they contributed positively at different stages of economic development. During the hunting and food gathering stage when there was no permanent settlement, women not only move from one place to another along with the male counterpart but actively involved and participated in collecting fruit, root and hunting animals. Carrying *Baanhoor*, sickle like knife at the back and possessing chemical knowledge of freeing poison from poisonous roots to make them edible proved women's participation in day to day economic activity. During the Tibetan rule when the Lepchas practiced shifting cultivation, women beside their participation in different types of economic activities also involve in management and decision making operations. The folktales of *Zomaal* and *Zolosy Pandi* give enough reasons to establish that women had changed the type of economic activity in the new system of livelihood but they are responsible partner of the male members in the economic operation. The British rule forced the Lepchas to adopt terraced based settled cultivation.

The industrial classification of Lepcha population for the year 1961 – 1981 shows that Lepcha economy is basically agriculture based. Women dominate over men in the categories of cultivation, agricultural labor, livestock, fishing but their involvement in other activities like transport, commerce and communication can not be ignored. Information on agricultural operation and classification of work as per sex reveals that women are involve in comparatively less laborious works like plantation of sapling, weeding, threshing, harvesting, storing plucking of fruits, flowers, drying of crops etc. It has also been observed that the role of women is more important in traditional crops like paddy, maize and millet. In case of modern cash crops like cardamom, ginger, floriculture and vegetables etc women's role is insignificant but they continued to extend some service for the cultivation of these crops. In a word, although the involvement of women in different stages of economic activities has changed but still they are the indispensable part of the Lepcha agricultural economy.

In spite of their important role in agriculture, women were neglected in distributing land among the descendents. Roshina Gowloog observed "a girl could possess land the way she possessed animals but on being married she could only take away her animals and make no claims on the land. Till her marriage, the harvest from her land would be kept separately and utilized for buying her jewels and other things but this arrangement would discontinue as soon as she was married" (1995: p. 74). The pattern shows patrilineal bias in the Lepcha society in case of inheritance of landed property but their role, involvement and contribution of women in agricultural operation is unquestionably accepted in the Lepcha society.

9

Political Status of Women in the Lepcha Society

Introduction

The three terms 'Status', 'Participation' and 'Empowerment' are quite often referred and used synonymously but they are conceptually different and carry separate meaning altogether. The term 'Status' is generally used by the social scientists to show the 'social status' of any group or community compared to others. Economic status has become an out dated term and is recently been replaced by the term 'economic empowerment'. Similarly political scientists prefer to use the term 'political empowerment' instead of the days old 'political status'.

Status is a relative term which is used to mean how much power and authority the women can enjoy in a society. It also denotes the amount of right and role the women play vis a vis their counterpart men in the society. Empowerment is an intra community / gender term where one aims to examine the amount of extra power the community / gender added to those of the existing ones. It is the process of "endowing women, who otherwise are powerless, with the necessary dosage of capacity to act, influence, and decide. To others it is a further step in reinforcing and strengthening the constitutional provisions of equality and rights, democratic processes and secular polity in India so as to increase women's equality and rights ..... Political empowerment is a process of equipping women with more fuel and power to emerge in positions of decision making." (Susheela Kaushik 2001: p. 183).

Initially the present chapter was designed to identify the political empowerment of women among the Lepchas from the angles of using the reservation policies of the Constitution in different political bodies like Panchayats, Municipalities, Legislature and Parliament. Details about a cross section study in respect of women filling candidature, withdrawn, contested, elected etc in all the different tiers of election in the village, municipality and council level was expected to give a clear picture of the political empowerment of women among the Lepchas. But the existing human and financial resources are not sufficient to collect information as required. Hence we slightly divert our attention in finding an alternate set of information where the women participate and engage in the tribal level organizations and institutions.

Lepchas are a minority community in all the countries where their population is very negligible fraction to the total population of the concern state / country. The mind set up of the Lepchas is also apolitical. They do participate in exercising adult franchise; there may be long queue in the polling booth and the women may be very eager to caste their votes but they are not politically conscious and rationally equipped to exercise political game. Political analysts opine that Lepchas prefer to wait, observe and caste their votes only at the last moments. The fruits of 73rd and 74th amendments of Indian Constitution have not been reached to the Lepchas. The Amendments reserve the seats for women and ST candidates in the Panchayets and Municipalities but it is reported that the quota and reservations are being used and filled by the other women and Scheduled Tribe candidates and not by the Lepchas. Roshina Gowloog could find insignificant role of women in political arena in Sikkim. "With the headman interfering in a lot of family matters the importance of women at least in the political field was probably not significant. There never was a female headman, nor would a woman normally be consulted in any village matter. It was always the male heads of the family who were called upon to do various things by the headman" (1995 : P - 74). So, instead of political empowerment of women among the Lepchas in the form of capturing political power in the statutory bodies, we prefer to discuss here the empowerment of women in the decision making processes in the community level organizations and institutions. The following institutions have been chosen for the present study:

Lepcha Association and the Women

The Lepcha Association, head quarter Kalimpong was established in 1925 and has registered under Certificate of Registration of Societies Act XXI, 1860 vide No S/18713/909 dated 27.3.1950. Later on the alteration was accepted u/s 9 (2) of WBSR Act 1961 vide Memo No S/1048 dated 13.7.1995 of the Registrar of Firma and Societies and Non- trading Corporations, West Bengal. It has been affiliated to the Akhil Bharatiya Adivasi Vikash Parisad Vide Registration No 49/ 1967—68 with effect from 23.3.1997. The Lepcha Association has been renamed as Indigenous Lepcha Tribal Association (ILTA) with effect from 8th March 2004.

Organizationally the Association comprises of three tiers: Keyong Shezoom, Thom Shezoom and Poom Shezoom. Keyong Shezoom is the village level organization; Thom Shezoom is the sub-divisional level and Poom Shezoom is the highest level organization of the Lepchas. Each Shezoom is linked with the next higher tier both organizationally and functionally. The Executive members of each Shezoom are elected democratically through direct voting by the General Body members. Lepchas by paying monthly subscription of Rs 10/- can become a member of the General Body of the concerned Keyong Shezoom. Members of the Executive Body of all Keyong Shezooms constitute the General Body of Thom Shezoom. Similarly the General Body of the Poom Shezoom is constituted with all the Executive Body members of all the Thom Shezooms. All the Keyong Shezoom and Thom Shezooms are to get official recognisition from the ILTA.

The Executive Body of the Keyong Shezoom comprises of a President, Secretary and three to four other members depending on the strength of the Keyong Shezoom. At present there are 106 Keyong Shezooms under Kalimpong Thom Shezoom. Followings are some of the women members holding the posts of President and Secretary in different Keyong Shezooms for the period May, 2006 to May, 2008:

1. Renue Simit Lepcha, President, Dr Graham's Home Keyong Shezoom.
2. Renue Songmit Lepcha, President, Pudung Keyong Shezoom.
3. Renue Juleemit Lepcha, Secretary, Long Dyop Keyong Shezoom.
4. Renue Rizamo Lepcha, Secretary, Mayal Keyong Kashyon Keyong Shezoom.
5. Renue Somit Lepcha, Secretary, Ecchhey Dungla Keyong Shezoom.
6. Renue Mayalmit Lepcha, Secretary, Mani Gumba Keyong Shezoom.
7. Renue Sukdim Lepcha, Secretary, Suntuk Keyong Shezoom.
8. Renue Phup Lhamu Lepcha, Secretary, Upper Minchu Keyong Shezoom.

9. Renue Indu Lepcha, President, Khamdung Keyong Shezoom.

10. Renue Lhamu Lepcha, Cultural secretary, Khamdung Keyong Shezoom.

The Executive Body of the Thom Shezoom comprises of President, Secretary and other Executive members. Some Thom Shezooms depending on their necessity create posts of Vice President, Assistant secretary, Treasurer, Cultural Secretary, Literary Secretary etc. All the Presidents of the Keyong Shezooms automatically become member of the Executive Body of Thom Shezoom and they hold the post of Vice President. The number of Vice Presidents in any Thom Shezoom depends upon the number of Keyong Shezooms under it.

At present there are ten Thom Shezooms under ILTA. They are:

1. Kalimpong Thom Shezoom.
2. Kurseong Thom Shezoom
3. Mumring Thom Shezoom
4. Sokhyam – Pokhibong Thom Shezoom.
5. Mirik Thom Shezoom, wef. 4th June, 2005.
6. Darjeeling Thom Shezoom.
7. Oodlabari Thom Shezoom.
8. Sittong I &II Thom Shezoom wef 11th December, 2001.
9. Kolkata Thom Shezoomwef 31st May 2003.
10. Delhi Thom Shezoom wef April, 2004.

Organizationally the Keyong Shezooms are directly linked with and controlled by the Thom Shezoom but there is no uniformity about the number of Keyong Shezoom under one Thom Shezoom. Kalimpong Thom Shezoom has highest number (106) of Keyong Shezoom while Kolkata and Delhi Thom Shezooms have no Keyong Shezoom under them. The number of Keyong Shezoom under any Thom Shezoom is region specific and depends upon the concentration of the Lepchas in that region.

Anyway, following is the list of women personality holding different designations in different Thom Shezooms under ILTA in different times:

1. Renue Namchermit Lepcha — Joint Treasurer, Sittong I &II wef. 11th December 2001.
2. Renue Mingfong Lepcha – President, Kolkata Thom Shezoom wef. 2nd November, 2003.
3. Renue Lingom Lepcha – Asstt. Treasurer, Kolkata Thom Shezoom wef. 2nd November, 2003.
4. Renue Ewpundeei Lepcha – Cultural Secretary, Kolkata Thom Shezoom wef. 2nd November, 2003.
5. Renue Jyermit Lepcha – Vice President, Mirik Thom Shezoom wef. 4th June, 2005.
6. Renue Mekina Lepcha – Joint Secretary, Mirik Thom Shezoom wef. 4th June, 2005.
7. Renue Dawa Lamu Lepcha – Joint Secretary, Darjeeling Thom Shezoom wef. 22 July, 2006.
8. Renue Neeta Lepcha – Cultural Secretary, Darjeeling Thom Shezoom wef. 22 July, 2006.
9. Renue Pema Lamu Lepcha – Executive Member, Darjeeling Thom Shezoom wef. 22 July, 2006.
10. Renue Rosa Lepcha — Executive Member, Darjeeling Thom Shezoom wef. 22 July, 2006.

11. Renue Mingkit Lepcha – Executive member, Delhi Thom Shezoom, wef. 2nd October, 2007.
12. Renue Colonel (Retd) P S Lepcha – Executive member, Delhi Thom Shezoom, wef. 2nd October, 2007.
13. Renue Remi Lepcha – Executive member, Delhi Thom Shezoom, wef. 2nd October, 2007.
14. Renue Ling Om Lepcha – Treasurer, Kolkata Thom Shezoom wef. November, 2006.
15. Renue Anuja Lepcha – Cultural Secretary, Kolkata Thom Shezoom wef. November, 2006.
16. Renue Josephine Lepcha – Advisor, Kolkata Thom Shezoom wef. November, 2006.
17. Renue Pauline Lepcha – Advisor, Kolkata Thom Shezoom wef. November, 2006.

The Poom Shezoom is the highest non-political body in the Lepcha Association. It is named as Indigenous Lepcha Tribal Association (ILTA). The Executive Body of the Thom Shezoom comprises of President, Secretary, Treasurer, Cultural Secretary, Game Secretary, Literary Secretary and other Executive members. All the Presidents of Thom Shezoom are the ex-officio Vice Presidents of the Poom Shezoom. All other Executive members are elected by the General Body comprising of the executive members of the Thom Shezoom.

At present there are no women portfolio holders in ILTA. Except Renue Azem Rebeka Lepcha who was President during 1940's and 1950's nobody could remember and give an account of any other women holding any portfolio in Poom Shezoom. It is a matter of great concern from the view point of women empowerment among the Lepchas. ILTA is the highest policy making body among the Lepchas and the women in no way take apart in policy making. It indicates very low degree of political empowerment of women among the Lepchas. But women are found to be very active and holding important posts in both Keyong Shezoom and Thom Shezoom.

Education and the Lepcha Women

There is no denying the fact that education is the engine of all round development of an individual, a community and a society. For the weaker section of any society education opens up better socio-economic opportunities and leads to faster economic development. It reduces poverty and helps in improving standard of living of the individual and the society. The nexus between education and development is so close and multifarious that it is difficult to quantify the effect of education on any specific aspect of development. Apart from physical capital investment, non-physical factors such as health, research, knowledge, organization and administration etc. play an important role in human quality and development. Education helps in socialization of a child and the development an individual in respect of human personality, social mobility, occupational change and the placement in professional life. Status of women both in the family and society depends to a large extent to their educational attainment. Education among the women is positively related with their comparative position in the social, political and economic sphere of life.

Literacy Rate

Table 9.1 shows literacy rate among the Lepchas, both man and woman, for the census period 1961-1981.

A perusal of table 9.1 shows that the literacy rate among the Lepchas has increased from 24.67 per cent in 1961 to 25.89 per cent in 1971 and further to 41.47 per cent in 1981. The proportionate rate for the females has slightly decreased initially from 25.00 per cent to 24.30 per cent and then increased to 39.00 per cent during the same period. It can be noted that over the decades the literacy rate among the Lepchas has increased but it is much better among the females than among the males. This is a sign of improvement of the women status in the Lepcha society.

Table 9.1
Literacy Rate Among the Lepchas of West Bengal

Census Year	*Lepcha population*			*Literacy Rate*		
	Male	*Female*	*Total*	*Male*	*Female*	*Total*
1961	7577 (49.49)	7732 (50.51)	15309 (100.00)	2833 (75.05)	942 (24.95)	3775 (100.00)
1971	8305 (57.01)	6263 (42.99)	14568 (100.00)	2855 (75.67)	918 (24.33)	3773 (100.00)
1981	12011 (51.31)	11398 (48.69)	23409 (100.00)	5900 (60.77)	3808 (29.23)	9708 (100.00)

Source: Census of India : 1961; 1971; 1981

A survey of Lepcha students studying in the government aided primary and secondary schools of Darjeeling district has been by Indigenous Lepcha Tribal Association for the session 2005-06. The following table 9.2 shows a comparative analysis between the male and female students among the Lepchas:

A perusal of table 9.2 reveals that the girl students of Darjeeling district in no way he behind the boys in case of either primary or secondary education. In fact, in case of secondary education the girls are at par with the boys while in primary education they are slightly behind the boys. Both in Darjeeling and Kurseong subdivisions the girls are performing better and they are ahead of the boys in respect of both primary and secondary education. Although in Kalimpong the number of girl students is remarkably high but they are slightly behind in proportion to the boys.

Literacy rate in our study area (Table – 4.3) is remarkably high with 82. 35 per cent. Although the male literacy rate

Table - 9.2
State of Education Among the Lepcha Students in Darjeeling: 2005-06

Sub-division	*Primary Education*			*Secondary Education*			*Total Students*		
	Boys	*Girls*	*Total*	*Boys*	*Girls*	*Total*	*Boys*	*Girls*	*Total*
DarjeelingSubdivision	173 (47.92)	188 (52.08)	361 (100.00)	210 (46.46)	242 (53.54)	452 (100.00)	383 (47.11)	430 (52.89)	813 (100.00)
Kalimpong Subdivision	1631 (52.92)	1451 (47.08)	3082 (100.00)	1104 (50.99)	1061 (49.01)	2165 (100.00)	2735 (52.13)	2512 (47.87)	5247 (100.00)
KurseongSubdivision	196 (46.23)	228 (53.77)	424 (100.00)	179 (48.38)	191 (51.62)	370 (100.00)	375 (47.23)	419 (52.77)	794 (100.00)
TotalStudents	2000 (51.72)	1867 (48.28)	3867 (100.00)	1493 (49.98)	1494 (50.02)	2987 (100.00)	3493 (50.96)	3361 (49.04)	6854 (100.00)

Source: King Gaeboo Achyok Magazine, 2005 P- 19.

(87.44%) is much higher than the female literacy rate (77.11%) but it is much higher than the all India average of 65.38 per cent (as per 2001census). Without much of complacency one can say that the females among the Lepchas are maintaining an above average standard in respect of educational attainment.

Lepcha Night School and the Women

Under the guidance and monitoring of ILTA, the Keyong Shezooms are running Night Schools to spread the Lepcha language, literature and culture to the young generations. Lepchas have their own scripts and literature. Except in Sikkim Lepcha language has not been recognized and introduced in the school curriculum in any state or country. In Sikkim Lepcha language is taught up to degree level. Under the leadership of ILTA at present as much as 40 Night Schools are functioning without any Government help whatsoever. Most of such schools are located in the remote villages which are dominated by the Lepchas.

After getting permission from ILTA it is the liability of the Keyong Shezoom to organize and run the schools. ILTA supplies some study materials and give some guide lines for uniformity in the schools. Workshops and Seminars are also organized from time to time to train the teachers of the schools. But the basic liability remains with the Keyong Shezoom. The fees from the students are very nominal and the remunerations for the teachers are almost nil.

The staff pattern of the schools depends upon the student strength but in most cases it consists of one Head teacher and two or three Assistant teachers. It has been found that a good number of women volunteered in extending free service for the cause of spread of Lepcha language and literature. The following list shows the involvement of women in different Lepcha Night Schools:

1. Renue Sanumit Lepcha – Asstt. Teacher, Pochok Lepcha Night School
2. Renue Jeongmit Lepcha – Asstt. Teacher. Pochok Lepcha Night School
3. Renue Ong Clyonum Lepcha – Asstt. Teacher, Lower Beyong Lepcha Night School
4. Renue Sanchalmit Lepcha -- Asstt. Teacher, Nok Lho Lepcha Night School
5. Renue Mangalmit Lepcha – Head Teacher, Shihor Aom Lepcha Night School, Lyangsa.
6. Renue Phurmit Lepcha – Asstt. Teacher, Shihor Aom Lepcha Night School, Lyangsa.
7. Renue Poemit Lepcha – Asstt. Teacher, Samsing (Pokang) Lepcha Night School
8. Renue Samthomit Lepcha – Asstt. Teacher, Dubling Lepcha Night School
9. Renue Sukmit Lepcha -- Head Teacher, Santook Lepcha Night School
10. Renue Lourmit Lepcha – Asstt. Teacher, Prektam Lepcha Night School
11. Renue Julie Lepcha -- Asstt. Teacher, Loangdeop. Lepcha Night School
12. Renue Nomit Lepcha – Head. Teacher, Upper Pembling Lepcha Night School
13. Renue Chongmit Lepcha – Asstt. Teacher, Upper Pembling Lepcha Night School
14. Renue Tikamit Lepcha – Asstt. Teacher. Kangkibong Lepcha Night School
15. Renue Nirkit Lepcha – Asstt. Teacher, Reon Lepcha Night School

16. Renue Doma Lepcha -- Asstt. Teacher, Pashyor Lepcha Night School

17. Renue Pemula Lepcha -- Head. Teacher, Zo Lepcha Night School (Samthar)

18. Renue Songmit Lepcha – Head Teacher, Pudung Lepcha Night School

19. Renue Songkit Lepcha – Head Teacher, Chyo Panol Lepcha Night School, Sitong

20. Renue Klara Lepcha – Asstt. Teacher, Pafan Kyong Lepcha Night School, Mirik.

21. Renue Meekina Lepcha – Head Teacher, Pasang Silu Keyong Lepcha Night School, Mirik.

22. Renue Neetamit Lepcha – Asstt. Teacher, Jasbir Keyong Lepcha Night School, Mirik.

23. Renue Chumit Lepcha -- Head Teacher, Palzar Keyong Lepcha Night School, Mirit.

24. Renue Rongmit Lepcha – Asstt. Teacher,Palzar Keyong Lepcha Night School, Mirik.

The role of women as Head teacher and Assistant teacher in the Lepcha Night School is very crucial. The leadership quality of women not only restricts within the house but also in the schools where their role is very appreciating. The leadership quality is not measured in monetary terms but it attaches a great value of preservation and maintenance of true Lepcha culture, custom and literature.

Women in Lepcha Language Board Examination

Lepcha language is yet to be recognized in the school curriculum in Darjeeling district. The government of Sikkim has recognized and introduced Lepcha language in the schools since 1975 and successively up to the graduation level since 2002. In order to facilitate the Lepcha children in their mother tongue, ILTA takes initiative in opening and running Night Schools in different villages. One of the problems associated with the Night School remained in the availability and recruitment of qualified teacher. ILTA under the guidance and supervision of its Literary Secretary has established a board known as Lepcha Language Educational Development Board to conduct examination on Lepcha language and literature and issue certificate to the successful candidates.

Women are found to be very enthusiastic in attending and a good number of them have successfully completed the board examination conducted by ILTA. They have been found to come from far off remote villages, took the trouble of staying over night in the Lepcha hostel but were very enthusiastic and serious in appearing the examination. This shows the contribution of women in maintaining, preserving and upholding Lepcha language and literature. The following table 9.3 shows details about the board examination and the case of the women for the years 2005-06:

Table – 9.3
Result of Language Board Examination, 2005 & 2006

YEAR	*APPEARED*			*PASSED*		
	Male	*Female*	*Total*	*Male*	*Female*	*Total*
2005	66 (58.93)	46 (41.07)	112 (100.00)	60 (59.41)	41 (40.59)	101 (100.00)
2006	—	—	—	22 (61.11)	14 (38.89)	36 (100.00)

Source: 1. Indigenous Lepcha Tribal Association, Kalimpong.
2. Aachuley. Vol 11. No 2. July, 2007.

It is evident that the percentage of women passed the Language Board Examination has slightly decreased from 40.59 to 38.89 over the year 2005 – 2006. But the determination, dedication, trouble and effort the women give for the Examination are really appreciable and deserve special mention. For a strong literary world the role of women in any society is very crucial and indispensable and the Lepcha women are found to be preparing themselves to shoulder the responsibility.

Historical Personalities and the Women

No written documents are available on the significant role played by the Lepchas in general and by the women in particular. Actually history about the Lepchas has not been written extensively and systematically. But using oral source and going through hearsay we could identify three strong women personalities among the Lepchas who contributed positively for the growth of the community in the region. They are: Azem Rebeka Namchu, Helen Lepcha, and Ruth Karthak Lepchani. Let us introduce these personalities and see in brief their course of action in Darjeeling and Sikkim areas.

Azem Rebeka Namchu: Social Worker

Azem Rebeka Namchu (1884 – 1958) was popularly known as David Babuni in Kalimpong. Originally she was from Sitong under Kurseong sub-division but after marrying David Chandra Mohan Babu she was permanently settled at 'Kanchanjunga Kothi' in Kalimpong and named after her husband, 'David Babu'.

David Babuni was a tall lady with huge physical figure. She had no formal education but acquired the skill of speaking and understanding five languages: Lepcha, Nepali, Bengali, Hindi and English. All the officials and dignitaries visited Kalimpong during the British and post independence period had close contact with Babuni. She used to invite all of them for lunch / dinner and used the opportunity in obtaining the maximum from them. She met Pandit Jawaharlal Nehru, the then Prime Minister of India, Krishna Menon, then Defense Minister, Dr B. C. Roy, then Chief

Minister of West Bengal, P.C. Sen, the then Chief Minister and the others and utilize them the best for the benefit of the community. All the local level officials were personally linked with her. When Kalimpong Municipality was formed in 1945, David Babuni became the first women nominated member. She even today is the only lady to remain elected commissioner of the Municipality for three consecutive terms. Her contribution as a social worker in the capacity of a commissioner has well recognized by the people of Kalimpong. She was dedicated and impartial in her activities.

Babuni was the President of the Lepcha Association during the initial period of its formation. It is during her tenure the Association was registered under the Societies Act in March 1950. She led a delegation to meet the Namgyel (king) of Sikkim and collected ten thousand rupees for the growth of the Association. She was a leader per excellence and fought hard in including the Lepchas under the category of Scheduled Caste of Indians constitution. She introduced three sources of income for the association and the people: Grain Gola (a sort of Cooperative sale centre), Diary Farming and Transport business for making profit for the Association. She could collect funding for buying a vehicle to ply between Kalimpong and Darjeeling for earning profit.

David Babuni had a dedicated soul and was a Lepcha by heart. She was a Christian by religion, but never neglected Lepcha traditional culture. She did not allow the exogamous marriage of her beloved niece even to a good boy. She always wore Daam– Dyam, Lepcha female dress and prefer to talk in Lepcha with her fellow tribe. The Lepchas of Kalimpong in particular and that of the district in general will remember her long for her strong personality and dedicated soul.

Helen Lepcha: The Lone Freedom Fighter

Helen Lepcha (1902/03 —1980) is popularly known as Sabitri Devi not only in the hills but throughout the country as her rename was done none other than Mahatma Gandhi. Mrs. Indira Gandhi called her Saili Didi (in Nepali saili is the third daughter of a person).

Sabitri Devi was the first and the only Lepcha lady from Darjeeling hills who took active part in Indian freedom fighting. Inspired by Gandhiji's non-violence movement, Sabitri Devi left for Calcutta in 1918 and stayed with her elder sister and joined one centre to learn the art of making thread with 'charka' (spinning wheel). She became so efficient and expert within very short period of time that the Bengal Board of Charka made her leader to take part in one Khadi and Charka Exhibition organized at Muzaffarpur, Bihar. Her expertise in the exhibition made her popular not only in Bihar but she became familiar to the leaders of the all India congress party. Later on in 1920 her dedicated service for the flood affected areas of Bihar made her an all India leader. As a result Mahatma Gandhi invited her to visit Sabarmati Ashram where Helen Lepcha was renamed as Sabitri Devi by Bapuji. Most probably Gandhiji smelt some foreign touch in the name of Helen and made her Swadeshi by pure Indian name. Following Gandhiji's instruction, her areas of activity extended over different coal field areas of Bengal, Bihar and Uttar Pradesh but she was confined to Patna, Danapur, Bankipur and Jharia. The common people in these areas accepted her leadership and joined Indian freedom fighting. She attended All India Congress Conference held at Ahmedabad and met top leaders of congress including Sarojini Naidu. Later she led a procession from coal field area of Jharia to the gathering at Mahammad Ali Park, Calcutta and there met Mahatma Gandhi, Chittaranjan Das, Moulana Abul Kalam Azad, Smt Urmila Devi, Smt Swarup Rani and others. Due to all these activities she was disliked by the British ruler and was kept under observation and restraint by the police. But this could not control her from taking part in different non violent activities, processions and boycott of foreign goods. During one boycott of foreign good and setting them fire at Siliguri, Sabitri Devi and with twelve others were arrested and accused for three months laborious imprisonment in Darjeeling jail. The Amrita Bazer Patrika in its issue on 30th January 1922 wrote "Sabitri Devi with the Congress Secretary and E. Ahmed and Gorkha volunteers have been arrested". After release from jail she was home interned and was not allowed to leave Kurseong. Even then she was not stepped back from her involvement in direct freedom struggle. She remained one of the undisputed leader of congress party and freedom fighter of the hill district of Darjeeling.

To meet ailing C.R.Das, Mahatma Gandhi came to Darjeeling sometime during 1925-26. It is told that when Sabitri Devi met Gandhiji she was dressed herself with gold ornaments. Gandhiji was annoyed with Sabitri Devi and told her to live simple life and urged to donate all her ornaments for the Swaraj Fund. Sabitri Devi instantly donated all her ornaments for the Swaraj Fund. Since then she never used any sort of golden or silver ornaments in her life time. She was a dedicated freedom fighter and true follower of Mahatma Gandhi. She led a simple life and never used and sort of luxury articles in her life even after independence. She was a congresswoman by the true sense of the term. The Darjeeling district is proud of having such a dedicated lady freedom fighter and patriot of the nation.

Netaji Subash Chandra Bose spent sometimes at Gidde hills, Kurseong where Sarat Chandra Bose, elder brother of Netaji had a residence. Sisir Kumar Bose, nephew who accompanied Netaji during his escape, mentioned in his book *Mahaniskraman* about Netaji's stay at Kurseong. He mentioned that after his gall bladder operation, Netaji came to Kurseong for rest in June 1936 and left for Calcutta before winter started. For the second and last time, Netaji along with Sarat Chandra Bose, elder brother, Sisir Kumar Bose, nephew and others visited Kurseong during puja vacation (October- November of 1937) and left for Calcutta to attend General Conference of Congress where Mahatma Gandhi, Jawaharlal Nehru and others attended. He was house arrested by the British police and Sabitri Devi was assigned the work of supplying bread etc for Netaji. It is said that Sabitri Devi played an important role in supplying secret letters, information and even dresses for Netaji during his house arrest.

Besides her involvement in freedom struggle, Sabitri Devi was a social worker and worked for the common people. She was elected as Commissioner of Kurseong Municipality in 1936 and worked for the betterment of the municipal area. She was reelected as the commissioner for the second term also. She was the leader not only for the Lepchas but she was above all communal feelings and worked for all communities of the hill people. She was unanimously and simultaneously worked as the president of the Lepcha Association, Sherpa association, Anjuman Islamia of Kurseong and District Congress party. Till her death she worked as the Mandal of Kurseong region. Involvement and holding highest position in different organizations show strong personality, acceptable leadership and secular character of her life. She was well accepted and respected by all sections of the people of Kurseong. It was so much so that different religious groups in Kurseong demanded her dead body for performing the last rites according to their respective religious norms and customs. She was so close to each religion that all considered her to be the believer of their religion. This shows that Sabitri Devi never neglect or ignore any religion. She was secular by heart and may be considered as a role model for the others. She was a leader by herself.

During silver jubilee celebration of Indian independence, the Government of India honored and awarded Sabitri Devi with Tamra Patra and conferred pension meant for the freedom fighters. Mrs Indira Gandhi, the then Prime Minister honored and handed over the same to her beloved Sailididi on 15th August 1972. The Tribal Welfare Department, Government of West Bengal honored and recognized her with the 'Reward to Tribal Headman of the district'. The Governor of West Bengal handed over the reward on 1st June 1958 at Shurbery ground, Raj Bhawan, Darjeeling.

Azem Rebeka Lepcha may be considered as a liberal leader who wanted change but wanted to do it orderly and peacefully. She preferred change in terms of equal opportunities and basic rights to all. She established good rapport with the officials and dignitaries of both the British and independent Indian. She believed in using the situation and gets the maximum benefit for the Lepchas out of that.

Helen Lepcha was a radicalist leader who wanted to revolutionize against the British rule and believed that the downfall of the Lepchas was mainly due to the British rule in the region. It may be noted that the Lepchas are dying race and their downfall started with the Tibetan invasion and the final blow was given by the British and thereafter Lepchas could not stand any more. So Helen Lepcha joined hands with the Congress party to make an end of British Raj in the country.

Ruth Karthak Lepchani: Leader of Democratic Movement in Sikkim

Ruth Karthak Lepchani, the lone Lepcha heroine of Sikkim democratic movement, was born on 12th May 1934 (or 1936) at Arithang, Gangtok, Sikkim. Her father Chandralal Karthak was a Lepcha but her mother was a Bhutia from Gyansapa clan from West Sikkim.

During her school days, Ruth Karthak Lepchani was a brilliant student of Paljor Namgyal Girl's High School,

Gangtok and passed School Seminar in 1951. She then joined P.G. Hospital (now Seth Suklal Karnani Hospital) in Calcutta for five years advanced course in nursing.

During those days Sikkim was under monarchical rule. Ruth came back to Sikkim in 1955 as a young, energetic nurse with the intension to serve the people of the state particularly the Lepchas. She was deeply shocked by the pathetic socio-economic condition of the Lepchas of Sikkim under the monarchical rule. She noticed how the Lepchas lost their land and became helots in their own land. Although she was carrying the blood of her Bhutia mother but she was moved by the Chogyel's tyrannical rule towards the simple, innocent and aboriginal Lepchas of Sikkim. She inherited more of Lepcha heart from her father than those of Bhutia heart from her mother or Nepali heart from her grand mother. In fact, Ruth Karthak Lepchani was very soft and kind hearted person and after judging the socio-economic condition of the different ethnic groups of Sikkim she became very much sympathetic towards the Lepchas. She observed and touched by the pathetic condition of the Lepchas living in the village areas. All the intruders are found to be much better and well off at the cost of the aboriginal simple Lepchas.

Before Namgyal rule Lepchas were the rulers of their own land which was spread from Kanchanjunga in the north up to Titalia (now in Bangladesh) in the south and from Tagang La, Thong La and Rudak river (now in Bhutan) in the east up to Tamar river, Arun river and Koshi river (now in Nepal) in the west. The boundary of the original Lepcha land was next to fixed. Although Lepchas have their own language and script but no detail records of the rulers are available. It is told that all authentic Lepcha records and documents were burnt to ashes by the then Namgyal rulers near Gayzing which caused a big crack in the stone.

Ruth Karthak Lepchani had no faith in monarchical rule of Sikkim because she believed that rulers were imported from Tibet only to rule and suppress the indigenous Lepchas. She strongly recommended that the condition of the Lepchas can be improved only by releasing them out of the clutches of the Tibetan rulers. She played an important role in the field on democratic movement in Sikkim and was one of the key personalities in merging Sikkim with the Indian Union. She was a horror to the Chogyals of Sikkim.

Ruth Karthak Lepchani was a leader of the common people. She was jailed and interned for six times within 12 years for the cause of the common people of the state. Although details about her arrest and successive happenings are not available, but it may be inferred with certainty that she had to suffer a lot both during the Chogyal's monarchical rule and Kazi's democratic rule. She was first arrested by the Royal Police on March 23, 1967 in Singtam on ground of sedition. The judgment for her arrest came after nearly 20 months of detention in Gangtok jail. Without mentioning any cause, the Sikkim police also arrested Ahsan Abdul Halim, the husband of Ruth Karthak and send him to jail along with his wife.

On November 15, 1968, Ruth was sentenced to undergo two years rigorous imprisonment by the Chief Magistrate of Sikkim. But before the completion of the sentence she was expelled from Sikkim with injunctions not to enter Sikkim again. During this time she stayed sometime in Kalimpong and thereafter left for Calcutta to join her husband.

After 1973 things in Sikkim began to change and atmosphere was created for setting up democratic structure in Sikkim. Ruth entered Sikkim with the expectation of getting back her house, property and to regain her lost political position. But Ruth was expelled by an Order issued by B.B.Lal, the Chief Executive, Government of Sikkim under the provision of Home and Police Department notification No 4081/ H.P. Jan. 1956.

In 1966, Ruth formed *The Sikkim Independent Front*, a new political Party to fight against the Chogyal rule in Sikkim. She became the first General Secretary of the party. She formed the party basically to fight and save the Lepchas against the tyrannical Chogyal rule. She believed that the condition of the Lepchas can be improved by establishing democracy in the state. She continued her struggle even after merger of Sikkim with India and took part in election process for forming government in the state. She was the leader of the poor and deprived section of the society.

Sikkim became the 22nd state of India since April 26, 1975. Ruth entered Sikkim during the parliamentary election of 1977 with the expectation of contesting the election as Janata Party candidate. But again she was arrested. After a lot of harassesment from the Sikkim administration, Ruth filed her nomination paper as independent candidate but failed to win the election may be because of her long absence from the state and hence lack of close connection with common people.

Ruth Karthak Lepchani is the lone Lepcha women from Sikkim who could dedicate her life for the common people particularly for the Lepchas of Sikkim. Her sufferings for the people of Sikkim are legendary and make history in Sikkim. She spearheaded the sense of consciousness among the Lepchas and placed them with honour and rehabilitation in their own homeland. She took upon herself indescribable sufferings in jail in Gangtok and internment from Sikkim. She is the most self sacrificing champion of the Lepcha cause. She should be identified as one of the foremost freedom fighters that India has produced so far. She nullified all such statements that made by different authors on Lepchas as shy, docile, simple, introvert, lazy, accommodative etc etc. She was as strong, both physically and mentally, as any other leaders and was above the average standard of any women leader of the country. She possessed an exemplary character which makes all the Lepchas proud. Her dedication, commitment and loyalty towards the common people particularly towards the Lepchas are unquestionable and for which she will be remembered in the history of the country for a long period. Her grand father adorned Ruth as the reincarnated 'Daughter of the Goddess Kanchanjunga'. She will be remembered for her work and contribution on Lepcha – Nepali harmony in Sikkim. Her position and role as social reformer and rescuer of the Lepchas of Sikkim surpassed her involvement in the political affairs of the state. She was more a leader of the Lepchas than a leader of the state. In fact, her political affiliation was intentional and targeted to acquire power for the betterment of the Lepchas. She considered herself as a leader of the Lepchas and joined politics as a stepping stone to bring back the lost status and position of the Lepchas in the state.

Ruth Karthak Lepchani was a revolutionary social worker not only for the state of Sikkim but in a sense for the country as a whole. During Janata rule she established good rapport and relations with the central ministers and leaders. She along with her husband formed an 'All India Forum for the Unemployed Youths'. They believed that there can be no equality so long as the system of inheritance exits. They believed in the revolutionary idea that after one's death, his/her property should become public property. During her exile in Calcutta, Ruth was fortunate in meeting people who have dedicated themselves in rebuilding India – morally, economically and she received their blessings for her work in Sikkim. She was a leader par excellence and will be remembered in the history of India for rebuilding Sikkim from authoritarianism to its present democratic shape.

Ethnic Revolt and the Women

Lepchas are basically simple, shy, silent and peace loving people. By nature they accept whatever is happened to them and consider everything as gift or curse of Almighty. So doing anything against what has happened is something like going against nature or God. They are very pious. One version of their name, Lepcha, means 'to wait' they are waiting for justice to be given to them by God.

In recent past the Lepchas under the leadership of Indigenous Lepcha Tribal Association have started protesting and organizing movements on a number of issues. Among the charter of demands, three are considered to be important and the Association is pressurizing hard for their fulfillment. They are: (i) recognition and introduction of Lepcha language in the schools, (ii) inclusion of the Lepchas under the category of Primitive Tribal Group and (iii) scrapping of hydro electric power project from Dzongu.

The Association has organized a number of processions, protest rally and relay hunger strike in different places like Kalimpong, Kurseong, Darjeeling, Gangtok etc. The leaders of the Association have arranged their meetings with state and central leaders and submitted memorandum in respect to their demands. In all protest rallies and processions, the presence of women is noteworthy. On their demand of scrapping the Hydro project, the Lepchas are undergoing relay hunger strike in three places – Gangtok (since 27th June, 2007 till date), Kalimpong (from 23rd August, 2007 to 30th November, 2007), Darjeeling (1st September, to 30th November, 2007). It is reported that women along with the male members have joined hands in the hunger relay protest in Gangtok. In Kalimpong and Kurseong, women have not joined as hunger striker but their role as volunteer is well recognized. In Kalimpong, most volunteers were the women who assist in all organizational respects to make the program a success. Women voluntarily joined from different far off villages and served all through hundred days on shifting basis. It is reported that some girls were interested in joining the group of hunger strikers and go far fasting but the Association leaders somehow prevented them from joining as hunger striker and engaged them to help in organizational activities.

Epilogue

Empowerment and Participation are the two buzz words which are very commonly used by the modern political scientists. Both the terms are quantified and measured in terms of number of women contested, elected, represented etc in different public political organizations. Empowerment is positively related with the number of women representatives in different political organizations.

Lepchas in general are not directly involved in politics. Their interest in politics is confined among some of the educated males. They do cast votes but not at all conscious in political matters. Buι the women have been found to take keen interest in ethnic organizations. Now, involvement and participation of women in ethnic organization can better be treated as 'status' rather than empowerment. No ethnic elements can be quantified in numerical numbers but can be expressed in qualitative or relative terms. Two types of qualitative study can be conducted: (i) position of women vis -a- vis men and (ii) change in the position of women over two time periods

In order to examine the status of women among the Lepcha we could identified some ethnic organization and areas of action among the Lepchas. They are: Keyong Shezoom, Thom Shezoom, Poom Shezoom, Literacy rate, Lepcha Night School, Lepcha language Board Examination, historical leadership and ethnic revolt etc.

It has been found that women are playing increasing role in the Keyong Shezoom, Thom Shezoom, Language Board Examination and in Lepcha Night School. Women's participation in Lepcha Ethnic Revolt deserve special attention. The lone Lepcha freedom fighter in Indian independence was from the women and no male members are found to represent it. Sikkim democratic movement would not have been matured without the direct and aggressive involvement of common Lepchas under their female leader. In all ethnic movements, girls are found to be at the forefront of the procession, rally and hunger strike. As women are not taking part in direct politics and political organizations, the concept of empowerment of women is unsuitable for the present study but it can undoubtedly be said that women possess a notable status in the Lepcha society. Involvement of women in any ethnic organization, except in Poom Shezoom, has an increasing trend and the young generations are found to be more active in the regard. Women hold a commendable position in Lepcha ethnic organizations and their ethnic political status and awareness in the society is well recognized.

10

Conclusion

Introduction

Participation of women is sine qua non of any development. Without adequate concern of women the developmental efforts, so far taken by the government, will be derailed. Integrating women in the main developmental process is of vital importance for the overall development of the country. It has been realized and accepted, both theoretically and legally, that the equal standing of women with their male counterpart is the pre condition of any development.

Women play a very important and significant role in the tribal society. The actual status of women depends upon the type of the society. In a matriarchal society, the status of women is comparatively higher than that of in the patriarchal society. Again, women under all matriarchal society do not enjoy same social status. Even they enjoy higher social status, they may not enjoy similar type of economic and political status. So, the position of women in any society particularly in case of tribal society can be viewed from three angles: social, economic and political. All the three aspects are so closely and mutually correlated that only an integrated approach can reveal the actual position of women in the society.

Lepchas are the little known aboriginal community of the southern face of the Eastern Himalayas. After political division of their country, at present Lepchas are the residents of India, Nepal and Bhutan. In India they are recognized as Scheduled Tribe in three states: Sikkim, West Bengal and Tripura. But the main concentration of the Lepchas remains in the North district of Sikkim and Darjeeling district of West Bengal.

There is no single agency to collect demographic details of the Lepchas but from different sources it is found that they are mostly confined in Sikkim (40,568), followed by Darjeeling (32,377), Nepal (3,660) and Bhutan (34700). In no country or state, Lepchas are the sizable proportion of the concerned population. Lepchas are as low as 0.01 percent of total population in Tripura; 0.02 per cent in Nepal; 1.88 per cent in Bhutan; 1.94 per cent in Darjeeling and 7.51 per cent in Sikkim. Without questioning about the validity of the demographic details we may just note the insignificant proportion of Lepcha population in all the countries / states. The strength of Lepcha population vis a vis total population of the concerned country / state has an important bearing upon their economic development, social status and political empowerment.

The sex composition of Lepchas in Sikkim for 2001 is 945 female per thousand male. Sikkim is recorded lowest female sex ratio in India. But the sex composition of the Lepchas in the state (945) is higher than the overall sex ratio for the state (832) and the all India average (933). In West Bengal, the sex composition of Lepcha population shows very irregular trend over the decades 1961 – 2001. From 1020 female per thousand male in 1961 the sex ratio falls to 754 in 1971 and then again increased to 949 in 1981 and further falls to 880 in 1991 and ultimately stands at 981 in 2001. Any way, both in Sikkim (945) and in West Bengal (981), the sex ratio of female per thousand male is higher than that of all India average (933) for the year 2001. It shows that the rate of inequality between male and female is much less among the Lepchas than that of so called Indian civilized society. The sex composition reflects the underline social, economic and political pattern of the society. It is an important indicator to measure the extent of equity between male and female in the society.

Although both primary and secondary data have been collected and used as and when necessary but the study is basically based on primary data collected from four Lepcha dominated villages of Kalimpong, the stronghold of the Lepchas in the district of Darjeeling and to the state of West Bengal. Basic information of the study area shows that 54.53 per cent Lepchas are Buddhists, 41.54 are Christians and 3.39 per cent are nature worshippers. Lepchas were originally nature worshipper and this high degree of religious conversion has an important long term bearing upon the socio-cultural life of the Lepchas. The high sex ratio of female per thousand male (971) in the study area hints upon high degree of equality between the two sexes and the prestigious position of women in the Lepcha society. Mane Gumba, the Buddhist dominated village recorded 1141female per thousand male. It simply implies that even today the girls are welcomed in the family and in the Lepcha society. Literacy rate, 82.35 per cent (87.44 % for the male and 77.11% for the female), in the study area may be considered to be satisfactory but their percentages for the higher and technical educational levels are not at all satisfactory. The high rate of drop out is a matter of great concern for both the sexes.

The present study aims at examining the dynamism of status of women in Lepcha society. The status of women has been examined from three angles: social, political and economic. The main findings of the study are discussed in the following paragraphs:

Social Status of Women Among the Lepchas

Women hold a prestigious and respected position in the Lepcha society. Beside their high sex ratio and literacy rate, we could identify three aspects which are not only peculiar among the Lepchas but they contribute heavily in upholding the prestigious position of women in the Lepcha society. They are: Moo, Mun and Bride Price. All the three are related to traditional Lepcha religion of nature worshipper and are related to their traditional culture, custom, rituals, values and beliefs, but even today they can be identified as important indicators which uphold the prestigious position of women in the Lepcha society.

In Lepcha vocabulary some common forms of address without making any sex linked division are used in the kinship relationship. In this connection G.Gorer wrote that "for people younger than speaker, too, they do not make any distinction of sex; the same word is used for a younger brother or a younger sister, for a son or a daughter, for a nephew or a niece. Only in the case of children's spouses are different words used for son-in-law and daughter-in-law" (1938: p. 143). This indicates comparative social equality between men and women in the Lepcha society.

Moo and the status of women

Lepchas call their clan as *Pu–tso* or *Agith* but it is popularly known as Moo. Lepcha society is casteless society. There are no upper or lower castes among the Lepchas and all are equal. Except Karvo Moo there is no caste wise division in the Lepcha society and all can perform any kind of profession in their day to day life. There is no bar in marriage among the different Moos. The clan or Moo is an important component in the Lepcha social organization. Lepcha Moo is an extensive form of lineage constituted of blood relations. There are some unilineal types of small groups who are the relatives and linked in terms of blood.

Moo is dyadic relations between person and person. In Lepcha society male Moo differs from female Moo and the genealogical relations among the Lepchas can better be shown with the help of Moo. Each Moo relates with particular ancestor and hence persons belonging to same Moo have some sort of relation among themselves, may be of very distance type. The same blood is running in the veins of the same Moo. Unlike the Hindu *Gotra*, the Lepcha Moo can not be changed even after marriage. Moo is obtained by birth and under no circumstances it can be changed. The girls carry the mother's lineage while the boys carry their father's lineage. Although Lepcha society is patriarchal but in case of Moo there is a peculiar blending of both patrilineal and matrilineal.

In Lepcha society female Moo is different from male Moo. It is as if the mother lives in her daughter and the father in his son. Naturally a mother is very keen to give birth a girl child. Birth of a girl child reduces the mental pressure of the mother and thereby become relaxed by transmitting Moo to her daughter which she inherits from her mother. The modern concepts of abortion and destroying girl foetus carry no sense in Lepcha society rather the family and the society celebrates at the birth of a girl child.

In traditional society, Moo plays a crucial role in a number of socio-cultural and religious occasions.

Moo is the first concern in the selection of life partner. A girl can not marry a boy whose mother belongs to the same Moo to that of her. Similarly a boy can not marry a girl whose fathers moo is same to his own moo. It is believed that marriage within the same Moo in the cause of both physical and mental disorder among the offspring.

After death the soul of the departed female go to the original Chu, peak for eternal rest. Mun plays an important role in collecting soul and guiding it to reach the appropriate Chu. Moo is the identity which acts as passport for meeting the ancestors after death.

In all religious rites, the Bongthing or the Mun acts as a mediator and offers prayer and presents gifts on behalf of the devotee. To establish link between Rum, good soul or Mung, bad soul and the devotee, Moo works a sort of identification of the Lepchas. Moo is the identity of the Lepchas and is the only wave to link them with their ancestors. In some cases Moo is linked with the place or locality and all living within the particular areas posses same Moo. A Lepcha feels proud of mentioning his / her Moo. Thus Moo is very peculiar feature in Lepcha society and all irrespective of sex are proud of belonging to a specific Moo.

Our study area, comprising 816 persons, has 130 Moos. Here female Moo is 1.77 times more than the male Moo. In a village, there is less possibility of changing the number of male Moo but the female Moo can always be increased by marrying girls from outside the village and obviously from among outside the Moo of groom's mother. Marriage of each boy, thus, enhances the possibility of adding female moo in the existing moo structure of the village.

Sex-wise arrangement of Moo indicates some sort of confusion and anomaly in the sense that in some cases girls are found to use male Moo which as per true Lepcha tradition is strictly prohibited and not acceptable. There is a sharp line of distinction between the male and female Moo and Lepcha Moo is sex linked. A girl can inherit Moo from her mother so there is no chance, whatsoever, of using male Moo by a female. But due to inter- community / exogenous marriage where Lepcha boys marry non-Lepcha girls, the offspring particularly the girl child find problem of inheriting Moo as there is no system of female Moo among the non Lepchas. The girl child in such cases is found to use her father's Moo and thus derailed the entire very scientific system of Lepcha Moo structure. In recent times, a system known as 'Aali Oom' has been evolved in which the non – Lepcha bride can be Lepchanised by adopting and gifting Moo of a motherly Lepcha lady of the locality. The whole process need to be performed by a Bongthing and hence Christians are found to be reluctant while the Buddhists are following the procedure and are the preserver of Lepcha traditional Moo. Beside this, Moo is ritually and socially related to the Buddhists while Christianity is Church oriented and lost all the importance of Moo.

There is a recent tend among some of the Lepchas to use Moo as surname. This is a good endeavor in saving and the reviving the vanishing value of Moo. But in the process one should be very careful in using it most appropriately and scientifically and should not create confusion.

Mun and the status of Women

Lepcha religion is known as *Bongthimism* or *Munism* according to the important role played by Bongthing, the Lepcha priest and the Mun, their priestess or the priest. From birth till the soul reach to heaven, the role of Bongthing and Mun is so important and inevitable that their religion is known by their name.

As per Lepcha mythology, *Nyolik Nyosong Mun*, the first Mun was created by *Itbu moo*, the mother creator to punish the *Mungs,* the devils. Mun may both be male and female but female Mun is believed to be more powerful and common in the Lepcha society. Mun can neither be created nor trained. Mun is divinely ordained power and gift of Almighty.

Lepchas believe in soul and spirits. There are two types of spirits: Rum, the good spirit and the Mung, the bad spirit.

Mun acts as a mediator between the spirit world and the common Lepchas. The good spirits are believed to protect and act for the betterment of the Lepchas. They cause no harm but the Lepchas worship them in routine manner for their blessings. The bad spirits are offered as and when necessary. They are the cause of all harms and misfortunes of any degree and need to be pleased by offerings. Mun offers hen for blood and other articles like Chi, fish, egg, fruits, rice, etc. to Mung.

The role of Bongthing and Mun is indispensable for all sorts of religious offerings and celebrations from cradle to grave. But Mun plays some specific power which the Bongthing does not possess. Mun is divinely ordained person who can talk with the spirits. Lepchas believe that after death their soul returns to their respective Chu, peak, to meet their ancestors for eternal rest. It is the duty of the Mun to catch the soul of a departed person and guide them to meet their ancestral Chu. This specific work can be done only by a Mun, known as Pildon Mun, and for which she is well recognized in the locality and is indispensable in the Lepcha society.

A Mun beside her proficiencies in religious rituals also possesses divinely gifted knowledge of herbal medicine. She is the bare footed doctor in the village who beside her act of mediator with the evil spirits causing harm also prescribes herbal medicine for the disease. Villagers near and far assemble her place and take her advice before going for medical treatment.

Mun is considered to be the gift of Almighty and the prestige of the village is closely related with the availability and power of the Mun. Many villages are known and identified by the name of the Mun. She is the representative of the females in the society who upholds the status of women in the Lepcha society.

The role and position of Mun has changed over the different phases of religious conversion. Church oriented religious activities make the Mun non-functioning among the Christian Lepchas. Buddhism is to some extent liberal and allows Mun to perform most religious functions along with Lama in the Monastery. In the Monastery oriented activities, Lama dominates over the religious activities but in domestic rituals the Lepchas mostly call Mun or Bongthing. In death ritual, Mun is the only choice.

Mun plays an important role, especially among the Buddhists, in preserving the traditional Lepcha culture, custom and rituals. She is the only mediator for guiding the soul of the departed person to reach their respected Chu where their ancestors are waiting. She is also the orator, well versed in Lepcha literature, language, and acknowledged with Lepcha folk tales, folk songs, mythology, tradition, custom, religion, language and what not about the Lepchas. The hymn and chanting of the Mun is considered to be purely God gifted and are used in Lepcha folk songs. There is no written form of prayers and everything is performed orally but all are as per the Lepcha tradition and custom. Mun as a representative of the females acts as the preserver of Lepcha language, literature culture and custom. In most major religions of the world, females are not allowed to act as priestess but Lepchas are exceptional and honors the females by assigning the top most responsibility and prestige. Females feel proud of the Mun.

Bride Price and the status of Women

Lepchas still maintain their days old system of bride price (*Taya – Kup – Afaar* or *Myaok Panol*). It symbolizes both the utility of women to men and the compensation to the parents for giving the girl in marriage. Each Lepcha family welcomes the girl child and the society celebrates at the birth of a girl child in the village. The logic behind bride price is that the parents take lot of pains in bringing up the girl child and they should be rewarded at the time of leaving the house after marriage. It is also a loss of working hand in both the farm and household activities and should be compensated for the loss by one time payment.

In earlier days Lepcha marriage (*Bri*) was considered to be a service marriage where the groom rendered physical service in his in-law's family. It is customary that in order to qualify himself as a groom, a Lepcha boy needed to serve in the bride's house even for seven long years. There are seven stages in the Lepcha marriage and they need seven long years to complete it. The groom generally extended physical labor in the agricultural field and thereby compensated in advance the loss of the bride's labor in her parent's field. But this system has been faded away with the passage of time due to the non availability of sufficient agricultural land. The service marriage in course of time has been transferred to marriage by purchase where the groom had to pay in terms of both cash and kind to his in laws for compensating the absence of the girl in the family whom they brought up with so much of care.

The bride price (*Taya - Kup - Afaar*) still prevails in the Lepcha society but its amount and magnitude has reduced to such an extent that it can now better be considered as a symbol of girl's position in the society. Beside some cash, the groom needs to present *Chi, Aamoo Dum - Dyem* (mother's dress), silver coin, front leg of bull, hind right leg of bull, liquor, dress and jewelry of the bride. The bride price is considered as security of the girl child in her in laws house. Under any circumstances if the bride returns to her parent's house, the bride price need to be returned to the groom. The bride price is to be preserved and may be used by the groom as interest free loan to meet the emergent financial crisis.

As per their folk tale marriage in Lepchas society started by seeking hands of *Naripnom,* the girl by *Tarbongmoo,* the boy after the payment of good number of gifts and presents like Chi, pig, ox; copper vessel, new cloth etc. The system of bride price thus has its mythological origin and is continuing even today.

Lepcha marriage is Moo exogamous and race endogamous. It means they prefer to marry within the Lepcha community but there is strong taboo in marrying within the same Moo, clan. It is customary that a boy should not marry a girl belonging to his mother's Moo and also the girl should not marry a boy belonging to her father's Moo. Lepcha Moo is gender specific and females are the carriers of their mother's Moo while males carry their father's Moo.

Altogether 227 cases of Lepcha marriage has been recorded is our study area. The percentage of race exogamous marriage is 41.41 while for race endogamous it is 58.59. The high rate of race exogamous marriage in a small tribal community like the Lepchas is a matter of great concern. Out of total exogamous marriage as high as 65.96 percent Lepcha boys are found to marry non – Lepcha girls while 34.04 per cent Lepcha girls marry non – Lepcha boys. Out of total girls marriage 64.44 per cent has been recorded as race endogamous and 35.56 per cent as race-exogamous. In both the cases it has been found that Lepcha girls are contributing more than the boys in preserving the traditional culture and custom.

Among the eight types of marriage as found in the Lepcha society, marriage by test, junior levirate, marriage by exchange, widow marriage, and marriage by service are the types of the past and are rarely practiced in the present day. The types of marriage which are commonly practiced are – arranged marriage, marriage by elopement and love marriage. Arranged marriage is widely practiced by the Buddhists and is most common in the village areas. The Christians who mostly live in the town areas undergo with the other two types of marriage. Love marriage and marriage by elopement are mostly exogamous in nature and create a lot of identity crisis in the Lepcha society. The slow growth rate of population in the Lepcha society may be due to the increasing number of exogamous marriage where a Lepcha girl looses her capacity of transmitting her mother's Moo among the future generations. This is a matter of great concern for the Lepchas and deserve special attention.

Lepcha society follows monogamous marriage (95.92 per cent) while polygyny (4.57 per cent) and polyandry (0.51 per cent) are only the exceptional cases and individualistic in nature.

In Lepcha marriage, two match makers, *Peeboo* (representing the groom's side) and *Pamiboo* (representing the bride's side) play very crucial and important role. There are seven different stages through which Lepcha marriage should pass for its completion and at each stage *Peeboo* and *Pamiboo* conduct all procedures and formalities in pure traditional style. *Pamiboo* always gets upper hand over Peeboo and dominates in the marriage ceremony. He is the most respectable person in the Lepcha marriage and placed next to Bongthing, the Lepcha priest. *Pamiboo* takes the detail accounts of the bride price from *Peeboo* as per the traditional marriage and imposes fine or punishment in the evént of any default. He upholds the position of bride price in Lepcha society.

Over the passage of time. bride price lost its earlier weight and status in respect of its volume and variety. In the traditional marriage by service, a boy needed to serve as much as seven consecutive years to be qualified himself as the groom for the marriage. In course of time, the hard physical labor has been replaced by bride price. The system of modernization and exogamous marriage compel the Lepchas to follow a sort of bride price which is very nominal and just a token amount. But its presents upholds the comparative position of women in the Lepcha society.

In Lepcha society females are integral part of the family set up. They are associated in almost all types of social and family affairs and activities. But they are recognized either by the name of their children or husband or even by the name of the village where they were born. Very occasionally they were called by their names (G.Gorer: p. 144). This, in a sense, do not place the females highly but from the point of retaining and carrying their mother's Moo in the new family and the society, Lepchas place the females highly in their society.

Economic Status of Women Among the Lepchas

Economically the Lepchas pass through different stages: nomadic, shifting cultivation and settled cultivation. The type of activities performed by the women over different stages of their economic growth has never been remained the same but they are the integral part of the economy and contributed positively in the process of economic growth. During the hunting and food gathering stage when there was no permanent village, the women not only move together from one place to another with their male counterpart but actively involved and participated in collection of food, root and hunting animals. Carrying *Baanhoor*, sickle like knife at the back and knowledge of freeing poison from poisonous roots to make them edible proved women's participation in day to day economic activity. During the Tibetan rule when the Lepchas practiced shifting cultivation, women beside their participation in different types of economic activities also involved in management and decision making operation. The folk tales of *Zomaal* and *Zolosy Pandi* give enough reasons to believe that women had changed the type of economic activity in the new system of livelihood but they were the responsible partner of the male members in the economic operation. The British rule forced the Lepchas to adopt terraced based settle cultivation. The industrial classification of the Lepcha population for the year 1961 – 1981 proved that Lepcha economy is basically agriculture based. Women dominate over men in the categories of cultivation, agricultural labor, livestock and fishing but their involvement in other categories like commerce, transport and communication can not be ignored. Information on agricultural operation and classification of work as per sex reveals that women are involved in comparatively less laborious work like plantation, weeding, harvesting, threshing, storing, plucking and drying the crop. It has been observed that the role of women is more in case of traditional crops like paddy, millet and maize. In modern cash crops, like floriculture, vegetable, ginger and cardamom women's role become insignificant but they continued to participate in agricultural operations.

Primary data collected from four villages unequivocally establishes the fact that Lepcha economy is agriculture based. As high as 67.32 per cent households are directly dependent on agriculture and they have landed properties of their own. Females comprise of only 17.04 per cent of total working population of the study area. 39.62 per cent working females are engaged in agriculture. Except Lower Beyong females in rest three villages consider their involvement in agriculture as secondary activity. Lepcha agriculture is subsistence based and females consider their involvement as a normal routine household activity. All the female members of the family like house wife, daughter, sister, mother etc are engaged in different types of agricultural operations as per their capacity and efficiency. Even the school going students during their off school season contribute in completing the agricultural operation.

In our study area 42.38 per cent females are involved in agriculture but only 10.82 per cent consider it as their primary occupation and 66.67 per cent as secondary occupation. All the females are engaged in their own cultivable land where agriculture is carried out on subsistence basis and they are not paid separately for their engagement. But in case of *Tyaolmaatheong*, exchange of labor, both male and female are treated equally. Each labor unit, irrespective of sex, is paid 1 *pathy* (= 4 Kg) of rice after the harvest. No discrimination, whatsoever, is made in respect of age, sex, efficiency and productivity of the worker. Even child labor is paid equally and the Lepcha wage structure is an example of perfect socialism. But wage is discriminated on the basis of age and sex in case of modern cash crops where females are paid less than the males even for the same type of work.

Thus, in the Lepcha dualistic economy women are treated differently in different situations. In the traditional hunting and food gathering stage and even in case of traditional food crop, women's participation in different agricultural operations remains indispensable and they occupy a prestigious position. This high degree of participation is one of the essences of any tribal economy. But in capitalistic farming where things are measured in monetary terms, women started loosing their earlier position. Their high degree of participation and involvement in agriculture are accompanied by comparative low degree of empowerment.

Political Status of Women Among the Lepchas

Empowerment and Participation are the two buzz words which are very commonly used by the modern political scientists. Both the terms are quantified and measured in terms of number of women contested, elected, represented etc in different public political organizations. Empowerment is positively related with the number of women representatives in different political organizations.

Lepchas in general are not directly involved in politics. Their interest in politics is confined among some of the educated males. They do cast votes but not at all conscious in political matters. But the women have been found to take keen interest in ethnic organizations. Now, involvement and participation of women in ethnic organization can better be treated as 'status' rather than empowerment. No ethnic elements can be quantified in numerical numbers but can be expressed in qualitative or relative terms. Two types of qualitative study can be conducted: (i) position of women vis – a – vis men and (ii) change in the position of women over two time periods

In order to examine the status of women among the Lepcha we could identified some ethnic organization and areas of action among the Lepchas. They are: Keyong Shezoom, Thom Shezoom, Poom Shezoom, Lepcha Night School, Lepcha language Board Examination, historical leadership and ethnic revolt etc.

It has been found that women are playing increasing role in the Keyong Shezoom, Thom Shezoom, Language Board Examination and in Night School. Women's participation in Lepcha ethnic revolt deserves special attention. The lone Lepcha freedom fighter in Indian independence and the lone Lepcha leader in Sikkim democratic movement were from the women and no male members are found to represent it. In all ethnic movements, girls are found to be at the forefront of the procession, rally and hunger strike. As women are not taking part in direct politics and political organizations, the concept of empowerment of women is unsuitable for the present study but it can undoubtedly be said that women possess a notable status in the Lepcha society. Involvement of women in any ethnic organization, except in Poom Shezoom, has an increasing trend and the young girls are found to be more active in this regard.

Overall Status of Women Among the Lepchas

In the traditional Lepcha society, Moo, Mun and Bride Price were the three main pillars which kept the position of women high among the Lepchas. Lepcha society passes through a number of stages where religious conversion, foreign rule, demonstration effect etc pressurized the socially weak Lepchas from different angles. In the process all the three pillars become weak and could not retain their original glory. The tremulous effect of religious conversion destroy all the three strong pillars of women identity among the Christian Lepchas. Buddhists on the other hand are the followers of Lepcha tradition and hence could retain some of the glorious aspects of women in their society. The present decade may be identified as the decade of revival where the Indigenous Lepcha Tribal Association under the joint leadership of the office bearers attempted a number of measures to uphold the status of women in particular and the traditional Lepcha culture, custom and tradition in general.

Lepcha economy is agriculture based and it has been found to be an example of dualistic in nature. Women in the Lepcha economy have been treated differently in different stages of its growth. In the traditional hunting and food gathering stage and even in case of traditional food crop, women's participation in different agricultural operations remains indispensable and they occupy a prestigious position. This high degree of participation is one of the essences of any tribal economy. But in capitalistic farming where things are measured in monetary terms, women started loosing their earlier position. Their high degree of participation and involvement in agriculture are accompanied by comparative low degree of empowerment.

Lepchas are not involved in direct politics. Even the reservations in Panchyet etc are not properly utilized by the women. But women are found to play increasing role in their ethnic organizations. Their role in Keyong Shezoom, Thom Shezoom, Language Board Examination and in Night School are very appreciable. Women's participation in procession, rally, hunger strike etc deserve special attention. The lone

Lepcha freedom fighter in Indian independence was from the women and no male members are found to represent it. In all ethnic movements, girls are found to be at the forefront. As women are not taking part in direct politics and political organizations, the concept of empowerment of women is unsuitable for the present study but it can undoubtedly be said that women possess a notable status in the Lepcha society. Involvement of women in any ethnic organization, except in Poom Shezoom, has an increasing trend and the young generations are found to be more active in the regard.

In a word, modernization and religious conversion have reduced the traditional social status of women in the Lepcha society. Even then existence of Bride Price, Moo and Mun placed the women in a high and prestigious social position in the Lepcha society. In the Lepcha dualistic economy, women are treated differently under different situations. High degree of participation and involvement place the women a prestigious position in the traditional agriculture. Modernization reduces the previous position of women in agriculture. In spite of their high degree of involvement in modern cash crops, women enjoy low degree of empowerment. The political empowerment of women among the Lepchas is very insignificant but they posses commendable status in their ethnic organizations. In the hierarchy of statuses, a Lepcha woman is placed next to God and enjoys high degree of social status followed by comparative low degree of economic and least amount of political status. Thus, from social, economic and political angles, women are not only indispensable part of the Lepcha society but they occupy a prestigious and higher position in their society with high degree of involvement in all spheres of life. Women in the Lepcha society are never neglected, ignored, unnoticed, unwanted, disregarded, ill treated, ill behaved in any occasion but they are always welcomed and respected. As early as 1925 C.De.Beauvoir Stock noticed the important place of the females in the Lepcha society. "The birth of a girl for the first child is considered very lucky, as a girl helps the parents much more than a boy, who plays the whole day" (1925 : P - 464). Beside this material gain, the Lepcha society even today welcomes the birth of a girl child and the villagers celebrate and enjoy more at the birth of a girl child than a male child in the village. Mayal Clymit Lepcha of Bong Busty, in brief, narrated the status of women in Lepcha society as: "In our society, at birth a female baby is always welcomed both in the family and society; in the matrimonial relation the bride is highly placed and bride-price is to be given; as wife she is honoured and involves in all social and economic matters and also a part of decision making body; as mother she remains alive in her girl child by transmitting her moo to the girl which is unchangeable at any cost. I am sure in no other community girls are getting such a wide variety of high position in the society compared to their male counterpart. So, I am proud to be a Lepcha".

Bibliography

A. Literature on the Lepchas

BAGCHI, G.C. (1982), 'From Semi Nomadism to Settled Agriculture: An Appraisal of Lepcha Economy' in K.S. Singh, ed., *Economics of Tribe and Their Transformation.* Concept Publications, Delhi.

BANERJEE, A.K. & OTHERS (1980), West Bengal District Gazetteer: Darjeeling. Govt. of West Bengal. Calcutta.

BASNET, L.B. (1974), Sikkim : *A Short Political History.* S.Chand and Co. (Pvt.) Ltd., New Delhi.

BELL, C.A. (1905), *Final Report on the Survey and Settlement of the Kalimpong Government Estate in the District of Darjeeling – 1901-1903.* Bengal Secretariate Press, Calcutta.

BENTLEY, J. (2007), *The Lepcha Cause.* Unpublished Thesis. Central Anthropology and Philosophical Faculty of University of Zurich.

–Do–(2007), Change and Cultural Revival in a Mountain Community of Sikkim. *Bulletin of Tibetology,* Vol. 43. No 1 and 2.

CAMPBELL, A. (1840), 'Note on the Lepchas of Sikkim with a Vocabulary of Their Language' in *Journal of Asiatic Society of Bengal IX.* Part 1, Calcutta.

CHATTOPADHYAY, T. (1990), *Lepchas and their Heritage.* B.R.Publishing Corporation, Delhi.

CENSUS OF INDIA. (1961), *West Bengal.* Vol.XVI, Part V-A (ii), Special Tables on Scheduled Tribes.

——, (1961), *Village Survey Monograph on Upper Pedong.* Vol. XVI, Part VI (10), West Bengal and Sikkim.

——. (1971), *West Bengal, Special Table on Scheduled Tribes.*

——, (1971), *Tripura, Social and Cultural Table.* Part II C(I) – VA, Special Tables on SC and ST.

——, (1981), *West Bengal.* Series-23, Part IX (IV), Special Tables for Scheduled Tribes.

——, (1991), *District Census Handbook : Darjeeling.* Series-26, Part XII-B, West Bengal.

——, (1991), *Village and Town wise Primary Census Abstruct, Darjeeling District.* District Census Handbook, Part XII, B, Series-26, West Bengal.

DAHAL, D.D. (1984), *Sikkim Ko Rajnaitik Itihas* (in Nepali). Subba Prakashan, Gangtok, Sikkim.

DALTON, E.T. (1872), *Descriptive Ethnology of Bengal.* Govt. Printing Press, Calcutta.

DAS, A.J. (1947), *Bengal District Gazetteers, Darjeeling.* Bengal Govt. Press, Alipur, Bengal.

DAS, A.K. and BANERJEE, S.K. (1962), *The Lepchas of Darjeeling District.* Tribal Welfare Department, Govt. of West Bengal.

DAS, A.K. (1978), *The Lepchas of West Bengal.* Editions Indian, Calcutta.

DONALDSON, F. (1900), *Lepcha Land or Six Weeks in the Sikkim Himalayas.* Sampson, Low Marston, London.

DOZEY, E.C. (1916), *A Concise and Complete History of the Darjeeling District since 1835*. Darjeeling. Reprint Jetsun Publishing House . Calcutta 1989.

FIRTH, R. (1939), *Primitive Polynesian Economy*. George Routledge, London.

———,(1967), *Themes in Economic Anthropology*. Tavistock Publications, London.

FONING, A.R. (1987), *Lepcha : My Vanishing Tribe*. Sterling Publishers Pvt. Limited, Delhi.

GHOSAL, S. (1990), *Lepchas of Darjeeling and Sikkim : A Study in Cultural Ecology and Social Change*. Unpublished Ph.D. Thesis, North Bengal University, Darjeeling, West Bengal.

GORER, G. (1938), *The Lepchas of Sikkim*. Reprint 1984, Central Publishing House, Delhi.

GOWLOOG, R.P. (1995), *Lingthem Revisited : Social Change in a Lepcha Village of North Sikkim*. Har Anand Publications, Delhi.

HOOKER, J.D. (1855), 'Notes of a Naturalist in Bengal, The Sikkim and Nepal Himalayas, The Khasi Mountains & C' in *Himalayan Journal*. Vol.2, Murry, London.

HUNTER, W.W. (1876), *A Statistical Account of Bengal*. Vol.X, Trubner & Co., London, Reprint, 1984, Concept Publishing Company, Delhi.

HUTTON, J.H. (1931), *Census of India*. Vol.II, Reprint, 1986, Gyan Publishing House, Delhi.

INDIGENOUS LEPCHA TRIBAL ASSOCIATION (2003), *The Lepcha customary Law*. ILTA. Kalimpong.

LEPCHA, P. (1999), *A Study of the Scottish Mission Work in Kalimpong Sub-division with Special Reference to the*

Lepcha Tribe. Unpublished Thesis Submitted for the degree of Bachelor of Divinity, Faculty of the Union Biblical Seminary, Pune, Maharashtra.

LEPCHA, S.W. (1979), *The process of Detribalisation of an Indian Tribe and Problems of Modernisation : A Sociological Study of the Lepchas of Darjeeling District*. Unpublished Ph.D., Thesis, Department of Sociology, Bhagalpur University, Bihar.

MAHARAJA, H.H. and MAHARANI DOLMA OF SIKKIM. (1908), *History of Sikkim*. Unpublished Manuscript.

MAINWARING, G.B. (1876), *A Grammer of the Lepcha (Rong) Language*. Reprint 1971, Manjusri Publishing House, Delhi.

MAITRA, A. (1974), Lepcha: the Original Tribe of Sikkim.(in Bengali). A. Mukherjee and Co Pvt Ltd. Calcutta.

NAKANE, C. (1966), 'A Plural Society in Sikkim : A Study of the Interrlations of Lepchas, Bhotias and Nepalis' in C.V.Furer Haimendorf, ed., *Caste and Kin in Nepal, India and Ceylon*. Asia Publishing House, Bombay.

NEBESKY, R.V.W. (1956), *Where the Gods are Mountains : Three Years among the People of the Himalayas*. Translated from German by Micheal Bullock Weildenfeld and Nicolson, London.

NIROULA, B.P. (1988), 'Caste/Ethnic Composition of Population of Nepal' in *CNAS Journal*. Vol.25, No.1, January, Kathmandu, Nepal.

O' MALLEY, L.S.S. (1907), *Bengal District Gazetteers : Darjeeling*. The Bengal Secretariate Book Depot, Reprint, 1989, Logos Press, Delhi.

PERRY, C.L. (1997), *Nepali Around the World*. Ekta Books . Kathmandu. Nepal.

PHILPOT, H.C.V. (1925), *Final Report on the Survey and Settlement of Kalimpong Government Estate – 1919-1922.* Bengal Secretariate Book Depot, Calcutta.

PORTER, A.F. (1931), ed., *Census of India : Bengal and Sikkim*. Part II, 1933, Central Publishing Branch.

RISLEY, H.H. (1891), *Tribes and Castes of Bengal Ethnographic Glossary*. Vol.II, Bengal Secretariate Press, Calcutta, Reprint, 1981, Firma Mukhopadhyay, Calcutta.

——, (1928), *The Gazetteer of Sikkim*. Bengal Government Secretariate, Calcutta. Reprint Low Price Publications. Delhi 2001.

ROY, D.C. (2005), Dynamics of Social Formation Among The Lepchas. Akansha Publishing House. Delhi.

SANKRITYANAYAN, R. (1950), *Darjeeling Parichay* (in Hindi). Adhunik Pustak Bhawan, Calcutta.

SIINGER, H. and RISCHEL, J. (1967), *The Lepchas ; Cutural and Religion of a Himalayan People.* Part I, II, The National Museum of Denmark Copenhagen.

SPRIGG, R. K. (2005), *Shedding some light on the history, Language and Literature of the Lepchas.* Indigenous Lepcha Tribal Association. Kalimpong.

STEINMANN, B. (1996), Mountain Deities: The Invisible Body of Society: A Comparative Study of the Representations by the Tamsang and the Thami of Nepal, the Lepcha and Bhutia of Sikkim. In Reflection of the Mountain : Essays on the History and Social meaning of the Mountain Cult in Tibet and the Himalayas.

STOCKS, C.DE.B. (1925), 'Folk-lore and Customs of the Lepchas of Sikkim' in *Journal and Proceedings Asiatic Society of Bengal*. New Series, Vol.XXI, No.4., Issued on 6th May 1927.

SUBBA,J.R. (2008). History, Culture and Customs of Sikkim. Gyan Publishing House. Delhi.

TAMSANG, K.P. (1983), *The Unknown and Untold Reality about the Lepchas*. Luen Sun offset Printing Co. Ltd., Hong Kong.

TAMSANG, L.S. (1997-2009), Editor, *Aachuley*. A Quaterly Lepcha Bilingual News Magazine. The Lepcha Literary Organisation, Kalimpong, Darjeeling.

TAMSANG, L.S. (2008), Lepcha Folk Lore and Folk Sons. Sahitya Academy. Kolkata.

THAKUR, R.N. (1988), *Himalayan Lepchas*. Archives Publishers, Distributors, Delhi.

WADDELL, L.A. (1899), *Among the Himalayas*. Constable, London. Reprint, 1978, Ratna Pustak Bhandar, Kathmandu, Nepal.

B. Literature on Tribes

AGARWAL, A & NARAIN, S. (1985), 'Women and National Resources'. Article in . *Social Action* 35. (n-4) Oct – Dec 18 301 – 325.

AGGARWAL, K. S. (ed) (1993), Dynamics *of Identity and Inter Group Relations in North East India*. Indian Institute of Advanced Study. Shimla.

ALLEN, M. & MUKHERJEE, S.N. (2006), *Women in India and Nepal*. Starling Publication.

BAGCHI, T. (1994), *Profile of Some Indian Tribes*. Punthi Pustak, Calcutta.

BAIG, T.A. (1976), India's *Women Power*. S. Chand and Co. New Delhi.

BAKSE, D.N. (1987), *Tribal Society of West Bengal*. (in Bengali) Vol I. Subarna Rekha. Calcutta.

BARUYA, A. (2005), *Belief in Witch – Witch Killing in Doors*. Northern Book Centre, New Delhi.

BASU, A. (1976), *Indian Women*. Vikash Publishing House. Delhi.

BETEILLE, A. (1977), 'The Definition of Tribe' in Ramesh Thapar, ed., *Tribe Caste and Religion in India*. Macmillan Company of India Ltd., Meerut.

——, (19740, *Six essays in Comparative Sociology*. Oxford University Press. New Delhi.

——, (1986), 'The Concept of Tribe with Special Reference to India'. Article in Arch. Europe. Social XXVII

BHATTY, Z. (1981), *The Economic Role and Status of Women in the Beedi Industry in India*. ILO Publications. New Delhi.

BHOWMICK, P.K. (1993), *Dynamics of Tribal Development*. Inter India Publications. Delhi.

BOSE, A.; SINHA, U.P. & TYAGI, R.P.(ed), *Demography of Tribal Development*. B.R.Publishing Corporation. New Delhi.

BOSE, N. K. (1980), *Tribal Life in India*. National Book Trust. New Delhi.

CHAMBE, N.P. (ed), *Tribal Techniques, Social Organisation and Development*. Indian Academy of Social Sciences. Allahabad. India.

CHATTAPADHYAY, K. D. (1978), *Tribalism in India*. Vikash Publishing House. New Delhi.

CHATTOPADHYAY, K.D. (1978), *Tribalism in India*. Vikash Publishing House Pvt. Ltd., Delhi.

CHAUDHURI, S. K. (2004), *Constraints of Tribal Development*. Mittal Publications, New Delhi.

CHOUBE, R. & SAINI, K. (ed) (2002), *Status of Women in Rural Societies*. Gyan Books Pvt. Ltd. New Delhi.

CHOUDHURI, B. (ed) (1992), *Tribal Transformation in India*. Vol-III. Inter India Publications. New Delhi.

CHOUDHURI, B (ed) (1990), *Tribal Development in India*: Problems and Prospects. New Delhi.

DANDA, A.K. (1973), *Tribal Economics And Their Transformation*. Indian Council on Social Science Research. New Delhi.

DANDE, A.K. (1991), *Tribal Economy in India*. Inter India. New Delhi.

——, (1988), 'Tribes in India' .Article in *Man in India*. Vol 68. No. 4.

DAS, A.K.; ROY B.K. & RAHA, M.K. (1966), *Hand Book of Scheduled Castes and Scheduled Tribes of West Bengal*. Tribal Welfare Department Govt. of West Bengal. Calcutta.

DAS, A.K.; RAHA, M.K. & DEY, S. (1990), *Tribal Situation In West Bengal*. Firma KLM Pvt Ltd Calcutta.

DAS, A.N. (1992), *India Invented: A Nation in the Making*. Monohar Publishers and Distributors. Delhi.

DESAI, A.R. (1971), 'Tribes in Transition' in Ramesh Thapar, ed., *Tribe, Caste and Religion in India*. Macmillan Company of India Ltd., Meerut.

DESAI, N. (1967), *Women in Modern India*. Vora and Co. Bombay.

DESAI, N. & MAITHERY, K. (1987), *Women and Society in India*. Ajanta Publications. Delhi.

DEVADAS, R.P. (1999), *Women and Development*. Centre for Women's Studies. Aninashilinam Deemed University.

DHAR, S.N. (2005), Micro Finance for Women. Northern Book Centre, New Delhi.

DODKEY, M.P. (1999), 'SHG's and Micro Credit Sustaining Rural Women'. Article in *Social Welfare* Vol 45.No12.

DUBE, S.C. (1977), *Tribal Heritage of India*. Vikash Publishing House. New Delhi.

ELWIN, V. (1943), *The Aboriginals*. Oxford University Press, Bombay.

FOBRES, G. (1998), *Women in Modern India*. Cambridge University Press. Cambridge, UK.

GHOSH, R. (2005), Facets of Feminism. Northern Book Centre, New Delhi.

GHURYE, G.S. (1963), *The Scheduled Tribes*. Popular Prakashan, Bombay.

——, (1943), *The Aboriginals So Called And Their Future*. Gokhal Institute of Politics and Economics. Poona.

HAIMENDORF, C. V. F (1982), *The Tribes of India.: The Struggle for Survival*. O.V.P. Bombay.

HASNAIN, N. (1983), *Tribal India Today*. Harman Publications. New Delhi.

JAIN, D. (ed) (1975), *Indian Women*. Publication Division; Ministry of Information and Broadcasting, Govt on India. New Delhi.

JHA, U.S. & PUJARI, P. (ed) (1996), *Indian Women Today, Tradition, Modernity and Challenge*. Kanishka Publishers & Distributors. New Delhi.

KATTAKAYAN, J.J. (1983), *Social Structure and Change Among the Tribes : A Study among the Uralies of Idukki District of Kerala*. D.P.Publications, Delhi.

KAUSHIK, S. (ed) (1993), *Women's Participation in Politics*. Vikash Publishing House. New Delhi.

KUNHAMAN, N. (1989), *Development of Tribal Economy*. Classical. New Delhi.

LAL, M and S.P.KUMAR (ed) (2002), *Women Studies in India*. Indian Institute of Advanced Study. Shimla.

LIETEN, G.K. et al (1989), *Women, Migrants and Tribals: Survival Strategy in Asia*. Monohar. New Delhi.

MAHAPATRA, A. (2005), *Demographic Perspectives on Indian Tribes*. Oxford University Press. New Delhi.

MAHAPATRA, L.K. (1994), *Tribal Development in India: Myth And Reality*. Vikash Publishing House Pvt Ltd New Delhi.

MAJUMDAR, D.N. (1937), *A Tribe In Transition: A Study in Cultural Pattern*. Langmans Green & Company London.

——, (1950), *Affair of A Tribe: A Study in Tribal Dynamics*. Universal Publications New Delhi.

MANDAL, A. (2005), *Women Workers in Brick Factory*. Northern Book Centre, New Delhi.

MANDAL, S.R. (2005), *Rural Muslim Women*. Northern Book Centre, New Delhi.

MEHTA, P.L. (1999), *Constitutional Protections to Scheduled Tribes in India in Retrospect and Prospects*. H.K. Delhi.

MENON, G. (1987), 'Tribal Women: Victims of the Development Process'. Article in *Social Action*. 37. No. - 4. Oct – Dec p 373 – 390.

MENON, G. (1993), 'Tribal Women The Ignored Sector in the Developmental Debate'. Article in Mrinal Miri (ed) *Continuity And Change*. Indian Institute of Advanced Study. Shimla.

MIRI, M. (1997), *Continuity And Change In Tribal Society*. Indian Institute of Advanced Study. Shimla.

MISRA, K.K. & LOWER, J.H. (ed) (2007), *Recent Studies on Indian Women: Empirical Work of Social Scientists*. Eastern Book Corporations. Delhi.

MISRA, K. & LOWER, J.H. (ed) (2007), *Recent Studies in Indian Women.: Empirical Work of Social Scientists*. Eastern Book Corporation, New Delhi.

MOORTHY, R. K. (2001), *Capacity Building for Women*. Saga Publications New Delhi.

NAIR, N.K. SUKUMARAN (1987), *Tribal Economy in Transition.: A Study of Meghalaya*. Inter—India Publications. Delhi.

NARASIMHAM, S. (1999); *Empowering Women: An Alternative Strategy for Rural India*. Saga Publications New Delhi.

NARASIMHAN, S. (1999), *Empowering Women: An alternate Strategy for Rural India*. Saga. New Delhi.

NATHAN, D. (ed) (1997), *From Tribe to Caste*. Indian Institute of Advanced Study. Shimla.

NAYEK, T.B. (1988), 'Tribe? What is a Tribe?' in S.B.Chakraborty, ed., *Social Science and Social Concern*. Mittal Publications, Delhi.

PACHAURI, S.K. (1984), *Dynamics of Rural Development in Tribal Areas*. Concept. New Delhi.

PARAMHANSA, V.R.K. (ed) (1975), *Perspectives on Tribal Development And Administration*. NICD. Hyderabad.

PATEL, M.L. (1984), *Planning Strategy for Tribal Development*. Inter India New Delhi.

PATHY, J.(1984), *Tribal Peasantry : Dynamics of Development*. Inter India Publications, Delhi

PATHY, J. (1984), *Tribal Peasantry: Dynamics of Development*. Inter India Publication Delhi.

PATHY, J. (1992), 'The Idea of Tribe and the Indian Scene' . Article in Choudhuri, B (ed) *Tribal Transformation in India*. Vol- III. Inter India Publications. New Delhi.

PATI, R.N. & JENA, B. (ed) (1989), *Tribal Development in India*. Ashigh. New Delhi.

PATI, R. N. & JAGATDEV, L. (ed) (1991), *Tribal Demography in India*. Ashish Publishing House. New Delhi.

PFETTER, G. & BEHERA, D.K. (ed) (1997), 'Contemporary Society'. Article in *Tribal Studies*. Vol-2 Concept Publishing Company. Delhi.

PRASAD, K. (ed) (2006), *Women in Rural Development.: Contemporary Social Policy and Practice*. Eastern Book Corporation. Delhi.

PRASAD, K. (ed) (2006), *Women in Rural Development: Contemporary Social Policy and Practice*. Eastern Book Corporation, New Delhi.

RAMAIAH, P. (1988), Issues *in Tribal Development*. Chugh Publications. Allahabad.

RAO, D.V.V.R. (1992), *Tribal Development: New Approaches*. Discovery. New Delhi.

RAZA, M. & AHMED, A. (1990), *An Atlas of Tribal India*. Concept Publishing Company. New Delhi.

RISLEY, H.H. (1871), *The Tribes and Caste of Bengal*.. Vol. II Calcutta.

ROY BURMAN, B.K.; CHUDHURI, B. & MISHRA, K. K. (ed) (2004), *Encyclopedia of Indian Tribes and Castes*. Vol- 3. Cosmo Publications. New Delhi.

ROY MUKHERJEE, S. (ed) (2006), *Indian Women,: Status, Participation and Empowerment*. Northern Book centre.

ROY, S. (2005), Tribes Education And Gender Question. Northern Book Centre, New Delhi.

ROY, U.K. ; DAS, A.K. & CHOWDHURI, M.K. (1982), *Planning for the Scheduled Tribes and Scheduled Castes: A West Bengal Perspectives.* Cultural Research Institute. Govt of West Bengal. Calcutta.

SACHCHIDANANDA (1964), *Culture Change in Tribal Bihar: Munda And Oraon.* Firma K.L.Mukhopadhyay. Calcutta.

SAHAY, S.P. (1988), *Tribal Women Labours: Aspects of Economic and Physical Exploitation.* Gyan Publishing House. New Delhi.

SAHLINS, M.D. (1968), *Tribesmen.* Prentice Hall. New Jersey.

SAKSENA, H.S. (2006), *Scheduled Tribes and Development.* Eastern Book Corporation. Delhi.

SAKSENA, H. S. (ed) (2006), *Scheduled Tribes and Development.* Eastern Book Corporation, New Delhi.

SAMANTA, R.K. (ed) (2005), *Empowering Rural Women: Issues, Opportunities and Approaches.* The women Press. Delhi.

SANDAY, P.R. (1973), *Towards a Theory of Status of Women.* American Anthropologists. 75: 1682 – 7000.

SENGUPTA, P. (1960), *Women Workers in India.* Asia Publishing House. Bombay.

SHARMA, B.D. (1978), *Tribal Development.* The Concept and the Frame. Prachi Prakashan . New Delhi.

——, (1984), *Planning for Tribal Development.* Prachi Prakashan. New Delhi.

SHARMA, K. (2002), 'Women's Studies in the Hall of Academy' Article in Malashri Lal and S.P. Kumar (ed) *Women Studies in India.* Indian Institute of Advanced Study. Shimla.

SIKDAR, C. (1990), *Economic Development of Tribal India.* Ashish. New Delhi.

SINGH, A.K & JABBI, M.K. (ed) (1997), *Tribals In India.* Har Anand Publications Pvt. Ltd. New Delhi.

SINGH, K.S. (1996), *Peoples of India, The Scheduled Tribes.* National Series, Vol.III, Anthropological Survey of India, Oxford University Press, Delhi.

——, (1982), *Tribal Movement in India.* Vols 1&2. Monohar Publication. New Delhi.

——, (1982), Economics of Tribes. Concept Publication Company. New Delhi

——, (1983), *Tribal Movement in India.* Monohar New Delhi

——, (1985), Tribal *Society in India: An Anthropo—Historical Perspective.* Manohar Prakashan. New Delhi.

SINGH, S. (2001), *Empowerment of Women: Miles to Go.* International Centre of Gandhian Studies & Research. Gandhi Smriti and Darshan Samiti. New Delhi.

SINGH,K. S. (1982), 'Transformation of Tribal Society :Integration vs Assimilation'. Article in *Economic And Political Weekly.* 17 (33) 1319 – 25: 17(34) 1376—84.

SINHA, S. (1965), 'Tribe – Caste and Tribe – Peasant Continua in Central India'. Article in *Man in India.* 45 (1).1.

SONI, J. K. (2006), *Women Empowerment: Exploring the Facts.* Eastern Book Corporation. Delhi.

SONI, J. (2006), *Women Empowerment; Exploring the Facts.* Eastern Book Corporation, New Delhi.

SRINIVAS, M.N. (1978), *The Changing Position of Indian Women.* Oxford University Press Bombay.

SRINIVAS, M.N. (1977), 'The Changing Position of Indian Women.'. Article in *Man.* 12: 221 – 38.

THAKUR, D. & THAKUR, D.N. (ed) (1994), *Tribal Life in India*. Vol - 6. Deep and Deep Publications. New Delhi.

TIWARI, G. (2006), *Role of Women in Family*. Eastern Book Corporation Delhi.

TIWARI, G. (2006), *Role of Women in Family*. Eastern Book Corporation, New Delhi.

TIWARI, P.P. & Tripathi, R.S. (ed) (1992), Dimensions *of Scheduled Tribes Development in India*. Uppal. New Delhi.

UNIVERSITY OF DELHI, (2000), *Hand Book*. Women's Studies and Development Centre, Delhi.

UPADHYAY, H.C. (1991), *Reservation For Scheduled Castes and Scheduled Tribes*. Anmol. New Delhi.

UPADHYAY, V.S. & PANDEY, G. (2003), *Tribal Development in India*. Crown Publications. Ranchi.

VAID, N.K. (2004), *Who Cares for Tribal Development?* Mittal Publications. New Delhi.

VIDYARTHI, L.P. (1964), *Cultural Contours of Tribal Bihar*. Punthi Pustak. Calcutta.

VIDYARTHI, L. P. (1981), *Tribal Development And its Administration*. Concept. New Delhi.

——, (1968), *Study Of Tribal Labours—Both Agricultural And Industrial In And Around Ranchi*. Manager of Publication. Delhi.

XAXA, V. (2003), 'Tribes in India.'. Article in Das, V. (ed) *The Oxford Indian Companion: Social and Social Anthropology*. Oxford University Press. New Delhi.

C. Literature on Women

AGARWAL, A & NARAIN, S. (1985), 'Women and National Resources'. Article in . *Social Action* 35. (n-4) Oct – Dec 18 301 – 325.

ALLEN, M. & MUKHERJEE, S.N. (2006), *Women in India and Nepal*. Starling Publication.

BAIG, T.A. (1976), India's *Women Power*. S. Chand and Co. New Delhi.

BARUYA, A. (2005), *Belief in Witch – Witch Killing in Doors*. Northern Book Centre, New Delhi.

BASU, A. (1976), *Indian Women*. Vikash Publishing House. Delhi.

BHATTY, Z. (1981), *The Economic Role and Status of Women in the Beedi Industry in India*. ILO Publications. New Delhi.

BHOWMICK, P.K. (1993), *Dynamics of Tribal Development*. Inter India Publications. Delhi.

CHOUBE, R. & SAINI, K.,(ed) (2002), *Status of Women in Rural Societies*. Gyan Books Pvt. Ltd. New Delhi.

CHOUDHURI, B. (ed) (1992), *Tribal Transformation in India*. Vol-III. Inter India Publications. New Delhi.

DAS, A.N. (1992), *India Invented: A Nation in the Making*. Monohar Publishers and Distributors. Delhi.

DESAI, N. (1967), *Women in Modern India*. Vora and Co. Bombay.

DESAI, N. & MAITHERY, K. (1987), *Women and Society in India*. Ajanta Publications. Delhi.

DEVADAS, R.P. (1999), *Women and Development*. Centre for Women's Studies. Aninashilinam Deemed University.

DHAR, S.N. (2005), Micro Finance for Women. Northern Book Centre, New Delhi.

DODKEY, M.P. (1999), 'SHG's and Micro Credit Sustaining Rural Women'. Article in *Social Welfare* Vol 45.No12.

FOBRES, G. (1998), *Women in Modern India*. Cambridge University Press. Cambridge, UK.

GHOSH, R. (2005), Facets of Feminism. Northern Book Centre, New Delhi.

JAIN, D. (ed) (1975), *Indian Women*. Publication Division; Ministry of Information and Broadcasting, Govt on India. New Delhi.

JHA, U.S. & PUJARI, P. (ed) (1996), *Indian Women Today, Tradition, Modernity and Challenge*. Kanishka Publishers & Distributors. New Delhi.

KAUSHIK, S. (ed) (1993), *Women's Participation in Politics*, Vikash Publishing House. New Delhi.

LAL, M and S.P.KUMAR (ed) (2002), *Women Studies in India*. Indian Institute of Advanced Study. Shimla.

MANDAL, A. (2005), *Women Workers in Brick Factory*. Northern Book Centre, New Delhi.

MANDAL, S.R. (2005), *Rural Muslim Women*. Northern Book Centre, New Delhi.

MISRA, K.K. & LOWER, J.H. (ed) (2007), *Recent Studies on Indian Women: Empirical Work of Social Scientists*. Eastern Book Corporations. Delhi.

MISRA, K. & LOWER, J.H. (ed) (2007), *Recent Studies in Indian Women.: Empirical Work of Social Scientists*. Eastern Book Corporation, New Delhi.

MOORTHY, R. K. (2001), *Capacity Building for Women*. Saga Publications New Delhi.

NARASIMHAM, S. (1999), *Empowering Women: An Alternative Strategy for Rural India*. Saga Publications New Delhi.

NARASIMHAN, S. (1999), *Empowering Women: An alternate Strategy for Rural India*. Saga. New Delhi.

PATHY, J. (1992), 'The Idea of Tribe and the Indian Scene' . Article in Choudhuri, B (ed) *Tribal Transformation in India*. Vol- III. Inter India Publications. New Delhi.

PATI, R. N. & JAGATDEV, L. (ed) (1991), *Tribal Demography in India*. Ashish Publishing House. New Delhi.

PFETTER, G. & BEHERA, D.K. (ed) (1997), 'Contemporary Society'. Article in *Tribal Studies*. Vol-2 Concept Publishing Company. Delhi.

PRASAD, K. (ed) (2006), *Women in Rural Development.: Contemporary Social Policy and Practice*. Eastern Book Corporation. Delhi.

PRASAD, K. (ed) (2006), *Women in Rural Development: Contemporary Social Policy and Practice*. Eastern Book Corporation, New Delhi.

RAZA, M. & AHMED, A. (1990), *An Atlas of Tribal India*. Concept Publishing Company. New Delhi.

ROY MUKHERJEE, S. (ed) (2006), *Indian Women: Status, Participation and Empowerment*. Northern Book centre.

ROY, S. (2005), Tribes Education And Gender Question. Northern Book Centre, New Delhi.

SAMANTA, R.K. (ed) (2005), *Empowering Rural Women: Issues, Opportunities and Approaches*. The women Press. Delhi.

SANDAY, P.R. (1973), *Towards a Theory of Status of Women*. American Anthropologists. 75: 1682 – 7000.

SENGUPTA, P. (1960), *Women Workers in India*. Asia Publishing House. Bombay.

SHARMA, K. (2002), 'Women's Studies in the Hall of Academy' Article in Malashri Lal and S.P. Kumar (ed) *Women Studies in India*. Indian Institute of Advanced Study. Shimla.

SINGH, S. (2001), *Empowerment of Women: Miles to Go*. International Centre of Gandhian Studies & Research. Gandhi Smriti and Darshan Samiti. New Delhi.

SONI, J. K. (2006), *Women Empowerment: Exploring the Facts*. Eastern Book Corporation. Delhi.

SONI, J. (2006), *Women Empowerment; Exploring the Facts*. Eastern Book Corporation, New Delhi.

SRINIVAS, M.N. (1978), *The Changing Position of Indian Women*. Oxford University Press Bombay.

SRINIVAS, M.N. (1977), 'The Changing Position of Indian Women.'. Article in *Man*. 12: 221 – 38.

TIWARI, G. (2006), *Role of Women in Family*. Eastern Book Corporation Delhi.

TIWARI, G. (2006), *Role of Women in Family*. Eastern Book Corporation, New Delhi.

UNIVERSITY OF DELHI, (2000), *Hand Book*. Women's Studies and Development Centre, Delhi.

D. Literature on Tribal Women

ADHIKARI, A. K. (1978), 'Status and Role of Women Among the Birhor: A Nomadic Hunting and Gathering Communities of Eastern India.' Article in *Tribal Women in India. Indian* Anthropological Society. Calcutta. No 4.

CHAUHAN, A. (1996), 'The Status of Tribal Women In India'. Article in *Trends in Social Science Research*. 3(2).

CHOUDHURY, D. (2000), *Tribal Girls: Aspirations, Achievements, and frustration*. Pointer Publications. Jaipur.

CHOUDHURY, N.C. (1978), 'Women hood in Tribal India.'. Article in *Tribal Women in India*. Indian Anthropological Society. Calcutta.

DUTTA, P.C. & OTHERS (1978), *Tribal Women in India*. Indian Anthropological Society. Calcutta.

FERNANDES, W. & MENON, G. (1987), *Tribal Women And Forest Economy. Deforestation, Exploitation and Status Change.* Social Institute. New Delhi.

GARG, B.M. (1960), *Status of Women in Tribal Communities in India.* Article in Indian Journal Social Work. 21 (2).

LODHA, N. (2000), *Status of Tribal Women*. Mangal Deep . New Delhi.

MANN, K. (1987), *Tribal Women in Changing Society.* Mittal Publications. New Delhi.

MAWAN, N. et al (1993), *Understanding Employment, Income in relation of Tribal Women.*: A case Study of Gonds in Madhya Pradesh. Article in Social Change. 23 (4).

MISHRA, K. (1991), *Women in Tribal Community: A Study of Arunachal Pradesh.* Vikash Publishing House. New Delhi.

PANDEY, B.B. (ed) (1997), *Status of Women in Tribal Society.* Directorate of Research Govt of Arunachal Pradesh. Itanagar.

RAO, V. M. (2002), 'Socio Economic Status of Tribal Women in Arunachal Pradesh'. Article in *Kurukshetra.* Ministry of Rural Development. Govt of India. New Delhi.

RAO, V. M. (2003), *Tribal Women in Arunachal Pradesh: Socio Economic Status.* Mittal Publications. New Delhi.

RIZVI, B.R. (1978), *Role of Women in Tribal Economy: A Study of the hill Korwa of Sarguja.* Article in Tribal

Women in India: Indian Anthropological Society. Calcutta.

ROY BURMAN. B. K. (1988), 'Challenges of Development and Tribal Women in India'. Article in Singh J.P.& Others (ed) *Tribal Women and Development*. MLU Tribal Research and Training Institute. Tribal Area Development Department. Udaipur. Rajasthan.

——, (1978), 'Emerging Humanity and Tribal Women in India'. Article in *Tribal Women in India*. Indian Anthropological Society. Calcutta

——, (1987), 'Development And Tribal Women in India'. Article in *Mainstream*. 19 & 20 November 25.

SHARMA, S.P. & MITTAL, A.C. (1998), *The Tribal Women in India*. 3 Vols. Eastern Book Company. Delhi.

SINGH, J. P. & VYAS, N.N. (ed) (1988), *Tribal Women and Development*. Jaipur. Rawat.

TRIPATHI, S.N. (2005), *Tribal Women in India*. Dominant Publishing House. New Delhi.

WHYTE, M. (1978), *The Status of Women in Pre Industrial Societies*. Princeton University. France.

Appendix - I

Table – 1
Details of population of four Surveyed Villages: Mani Gumba, Tashiding Busty, Khumdung and Lower Beyong

A. Name of the Village: MANI GUMBA.

Sl No	*Name*	*Age*	*Sex*	*Religion*	*Edu-cation*	*Primary Occupation*	*Moo*
1	*2*	*3*	*4*	*5*	*6*	*7*	*8*
1	O.T Naamchu	57	M	Nature Worshipper	VII	Retd Teacher	Naamchu Moo
2	Nimkit Lepcha	52	F	Do	VII	Household	S o n g m o o Mongmoot Moo
3	Sonamkit Lepcha	25	F	Do	XII	Student	Do
4	Yakit Lepcha	24	F	Do	XII	Do	Do
5	Tsheringkit Lepcha	22	F	Do	BA	Do	Do
6	Thupden Tsh Lepcha	49	M	Do	BA	State Govt	Naamchu Moo
7	Passangkit Lepcha	41	F	Do	HS	Do	Ling Taong Moo
8	Aghai Lepcha	63	M	Buddhist	MP	Retd	Haoloong Moo
9	Phurba Lepcha	30	M	Christian	HS	Agriculture	Do
10	Taramit Lepcha	50	F	Do	X	Household	Naani Moo
11	Ombimit Lepcha	62	F	Buddhist	—	Household	Aeri Moo
12	Keepa Lepcha	25	M	Do	HS	Agriculture	Haoloong Moo
13	Jeena Lepcha	20	F	Do	BA	Student	Aeri Moo
14	Rinchen Lepcha	19	M	Do	HS	Agriculture	Haoloong Moo
15	Reemit Lepcha	49	F	Nature Worshipper	MP	Household	Shyaor Moo
16	S.T. Lepcha	50	M	Do	MP	Agriculture	Taarjaok Passong Moo
17	Chusang Lepcha	17	F	Do	BA	Student	Shyaor Moo
18	Somi Lepcha	19	F	Do	XII	Do	Do
19	Lyanduk Lepcha	15	M	Do	XI	Do	Taarjaok Passong Moo
20	Dawa Tsh Lepcha	77	M	Do	IV	Agriculture	Haoloong Moo
21	Norkit Lepcha	69	F	Do	—	Household	Saompa Moo
22	Ong Tsh Lepcha	42	M	Do	BA	CentralGovt	Haoloong Moo
23	Rikmit Lepcha	35	F	Do	BA	Household	Ling Taong Moo
24	Chyoom Lepcha	7	M	Do	II	Student	Haoloong Moo
25	Lugten Lepcha	5	M	Do	LKG	Do	Do
26	Dorjee Tsh Lepcha	37	M	Do	BCom	State Govt	Do

(Contd...)

1	2	3	4	5	6	7	8
27	Dukmit Lepcha	22	F	Do	HS	Household	Ling Taong Moo
28	Rapten Lepcha	24	M	Do	HS	Agriculture	Haoloong Moo
29	Namcharmit Lepcha	20	F	Do	IX	Household	Savyet Moo
30	Nim Lhanu Lepcha	77	F	Buddhist	III	Do	Chong Moo
31	Nimkit Lepcha	67	F	Do	II	Do	Do
32	Jamit Lepcha	57	F	Do	II	Do	Do
33	Lusong Lepcha	37	F	Do	VIII	Agriculture	Fyaongdye Moo
34	Sanchamit Lepcha	32	F	Do	III	Household	NA
35	Labusong Lepcha	3	M	Do	—	—	Fyaongdye Moo
36	Chokit Lepcha	32	F	Do	VII	Household	Mi Simik Moo
37	Mayal Lepcha	27	F	Do	BCom	Do	Do
38	Sangkit Lepcha	52	F	Do	III	Do	Do
39	Suk Tsh Lepcha	22	M	Do	V	Lama	Fyaongdye Moo
40	Mayalmit Lepcha	18	F	Do	IX	Household	Jamyaong Moo
41	Bunumit Lepcha	18	F	Do	VI	Do	Mi Simik Moo
42	Nim Dorjee Lepcha	52	M	Do	HS	Agriculture	Fyaongdye Moo
43	Dorati Lepcha	45	F	Do	VII	Household	Raonglo Moo
44	Sumit Lepcha	17	F	Do	XI	Student	Do
45	Chumit Lepcha	15	F	Do	X	Do	Do
46	Rumjong Lepcha	10	M	Do	V	Do	Fyaongdye Moo
47	Chungdup Tsh Lepcha	12	M	Do	—	Household	Do
48	Pari Lepcha	59	M	Nature Worshipper	V	Business	Naani Moo
49	Aimit Lepcha	57	F	Do	VI	Household	Saompa Moo
50	Lagen Lepcha	22	F	Do	BA	Student	Do
51	Passang Lepcha	17	M	Do	X	Do	Naani Moo
52	Sonamkit Lepcha	15	F	Do	IX	Do	Saompa Moo
63	Tshemit Lepcha	73	F	Do	—	Household	Bri Moo
54	Ongmit Lepcha	44	F	Do	VI	Do	Do
55	Som Tsh Lepcha	41	M	Do	IX	Agriculture	Haoloong Moo
56	Gen Tsh Lepcha	38	M	Do	XII	Do	Do
57	Kusang Lepcha	24	M	Do	HS	Do	Do
58	Munna Lepcha	49	F	Buddhist	—	Household	Ling Taong Moo
59	Tshering Lepcha	22	M	Do	III	Pvt Service	Haoloong Moo
60	Chenchu Lepcha	59	M	Do	IV	Agriculture	Goulook Moo
61	Manika Lepcha	47	F	Do	—	Household	Bri Moo
62	Northen Lepcha	28	M	Do	VI	Agriculture	Goulook Moo
63	Annu Lepcha	20	F	Do	V	Household	Sadaa Moo
64	Limu Lepcha	4	F	Do	—	Do	Do
65	Nali Pandi Lepcha	2	F	Do	—	Do	Do

(Contd...)

1	2	3	4	5	6	7	8
66	Som Lepcha	25	M	Do	XII	Agriculture	Goulook Moo
67	Mingma Tsh Lepcha	73	M	Christian	MP	Retd	Haoloong Moo
68	Sukmit Lepcha	57	F	Do	VIII	Household	Maongmi Moo
69	Ongden Lepcha	39	M	Do	VIII	Agriculture	Haoloong Moo
70	Ranju Lepcha	27	F	Do	VI	Household	—
71	Aksha Milim Lepcha	2	F	Do	—	---	—
72	Safia Pandi Lepcha	22	F	Do	X	Household	Maongmi Moo
73	Tshering Lepcha	58	M	Buddhist	X	Agriculture	Haoloong Moo
74	Biramit Lepcha	48	F	Do	III	Household	Malaom Moo
75	Aimit Lepcha	64	F	Do	III	Do	Yung Moo
76	Ugyen Lepcha	28	M	Do	V	Lama	Haoloong Moo
77	Zimi Lepcha	19	F	Do	VI	Household	Malaom Moo
78	Rinzing Lepcha	17	M	Do	XII	Student	Haoloong Moo
79	Dugel Lepcha	29	M	Do	X	Agriculture	Goulook Moo
80	Punam Lepcha	22	F	Do	VII	Household	Maongbyo Moo
81	Kessang Lepcha	4	F	Do	—	—	Do
82	Naamchu Lepcha	21	M	Do	VIII	Army	Goulook Moo
83	Sankit Lepcha	25	F	Do	BA	Household	Saong Moo
84	J.B.Thapa	47	M	Do	III	Agriculture	NL
85	Pravimit Lepcha	37	F	Do	—	Household	Shyer Faokli Moo
86	Pravitra Lepcha	19	F	Do	V	Do	Do
87	Pranita Lepcha	15	F	Do	II	Do	Do
88	Prasant Lepcha	5	M	Do	—	—	—
89	Dip Sing Lepcha	57	M	Do	IV	Agriculture	Goulook Moo
90	Sankit Lepcha	47	F	Do	II	Household	Malaom Moo
91	Nima Lhamu Lepcha	48	M	Do	—	Do	Simik Moo
92	Saongden Lepcha	27	M	Do	HS	Agriculture	Goulook Moo
93	Dowden Lepcha	25	M	Do	VII	Lama	Do
94	Budhamit Lepcha	75	F	Do	—	Household	Shing Saong Moo
95	Chugyel Lepcha	25	M	Do	VI	Agriculture	Goulook Moo
96	Namgyel Lepcha	19	M	Do	XII	Do	Do
97	Nima Lepcha	30	M	Do	VII	WB Police	Do
98	Joymit Lepcha	35	F	Do	MP	Household	Malaom Moo
99	Nipon Lepcha	3	M	Do	—	—	Goulook Moo
100	Pendi Lepcha	42	M	Do	VII	Lama	Lyaang Moo
101	Dumit Lepcha	37	F	Do	III	Household	Sundyaang Moo
102	Karchen Lepcha	22	M	Do	VII	Agriculture	Lyaang Moo
103	Rumi Lepcha	18	F	Do	X	Student	Sundyaang Moo
104	Nawang Lepcha	15	M	Do	II	Agriculture	Lyaang Moo

(Contd...)

1	2	3	4	5	6	7	8
105	Duk Tsh Lepcha	46	M	Do	XI	Do	Goulook Moo
106	Saongmit Lepcha	37	F	Do	IV	Household	Phaokli Moo
107	Chinlop Lepcha	22	M	Do	BA	Student	Goulook Moo
108	Kinchun Lepcha	20	F	Do	XII	Do	Phaokli Moo
109	Budhamit Lepcha	74	F	Do	—	Household	—
110	Pandu Lepcha	38	M	Do	V	Driver	Goulook Moo
11	Jamuna Lepcha	32	F	Do	III	Household	—
112	Mullam Lepcha	8	M	Do	III	Student	Goulook Moo
113	Pemu Lepcha	3	F	Do	I	Do	—
114	Passang Lepcha	55	M	Do	IV	Agriculture	Goulook Moo
115	Usha Lepcha	50	F	Do	—	Pvt Job	—
116	Appu Lepcha	25	M	Do	V	Business	Goulook Moo
117	Martina Lepcha	20	F	Do	IX	Student	—
118	Dorjee Tsh Lepcha	65	M	Do	—	Agriculture	Shyaor Moo
119	Mina Lepcha	55	F	Do	—	Household	Songmoo Mongmoo Moo
120	Choden Lepcha	42	M	Do	BA	Agriculture	Haoloong Moo
121	Indramit Lepcha	35	F	Do	—	Household	—
122	Somrip Lepcha	6	F	Do	UKG	Student	—
123	Nimshong Lepcha	3	M	Do	LKG	Do	Goulook Moo
124	Marmit Lepcha	40	F	Do	MP	Household	Shyaor Moo
125	Y.T. Lepcha	42	M	Do	BA	Service	Naamchu Moo
126	Ziki Lepcha	18	M	Do	XII	Student	Do
127	Sandup Lepcha	42	M	Do	HS	Agriculture	Goulook Moo
128	Remit Lepcha	37	F	Do	V	Household	Shyaor Moo
129	Runmit Lepcha	16	F	Do	III	Do	Do
130	Tshewang Lepcha	12	M	Do	VII	Student	Goulook Moo
131	Purnal Lepcha	9	M	Do	V	Do	Do
132	Ong Tsh Lepcha	55	M	Do	BA	Teacher	Do
133	Premkit Lepcha	46	F	Do	X	Household	Malaom Moo
134	Kenzong Lepcha	19	M	Do	BE	Student	Goulook Moo
135	Chomit Lepcha	85	F	Do	—	Household	Git Malaom Moo
136	Norkit Lepcha	68	F	Do	—	Do	Do
137	Numkum Lepcha	12	F	Do	III	Student	—

Source: Field Survey.

Table – 2
Name of the Village : TASHIDING BUSTY

Sl No	*Name*	*Age*	*Sex*	*Religion*	*Edu-cation*	*Primary Occupation*	*Moo*
1	2	3	4	5	6	7	8
1	Lha Tsh Lepcha	63	M	Christian	II	Agriculture	Sadaa Moo
2	Rosa Lepcha	47	F	Do	IV	Household	Fee Moo
3	Daniel Lepcha	31	M	Do	X	Agriculture	Sadaa Moo
4	Elezabath Lepcha	29	F	Do	BA	Nurse	Fee Moo
5	Nuel Lepcha	22	M	Do	HS	Student	Sodaa Moo
6	John Tsh Lepcha	42	M	Do	HS	Teacher	Tookoo Chao Moo
7	Lusy Lepcha	36	F	Do	III	Household	--
8	Susan Lepcha	16	F	Do	X	Student	—
9	Yorusa Lepcha	7	F	Do	II	Do	—
10	Run Tsh Lepcha	62	M	Do	HS	Retd	Tookoo Chao Moo
11	Duklas Lepcha	42	F	Do	II	Household	---
12	Renu Lepcha	37	F	Do	MP	Nurse	—
13	Aju Lepcha	33	F	Do	HS	Household	—
14	Mashi Lepcha	30	F	Do	X	Do	—
15	Bar Sing Lepcha	72	M	Do	MP	Retd	Tingboo Moo
16	Mangal Mit Lepcha	67	F	Do	II	Household	—
17	Yugen Lepcha	52	M	Do	MP	Agriculture	Tingboo Moo
18	Ruben Lepcha	37	M	Do	BCom	Do	Do
19	Ruth Lepcha	25	F	Do	VIII	Household	—
20	Sudan Lepcha	35	M	Do	BSc	Pastor	Tingboo Moo
21	Geeta Lepcha	26	F	Do	X	Household	—
22	Anu Lepcha	32	M	Do	BSc	State Govt	Tingboo Moo
23	Habil Lepcha	46	M	Do	V	Pvt Job	—
24	Munna Lepcha	43	F	Do	II	Household	—
25	Elisa Lepcha	21	F	Do	VIII	Student	—
26	Yakub Lepcha	17	M	Do	VI	Do	—
27	Goel Sing Lepcha	67	M	Do	III	Retd	Sadaa Moo
28	Mangal Mit Lepcha	57	F	Do	—	Household	—
29	Paul Lepcha	35	M	Do	BD	Pastor	Sadaa Moo
30	Pandimit Lepcha	30	F	Do	BA	Household	—
31	Nabi Lepcha	27	M	Do	VIII	Driver	Sadaa Moo
32	Yanathan Lepcha	22	M	Do	VII	Pvt Job	Do
33	Amosh Lepcha	20	M	Do	IX	Agriculture	Do
34	Den Tsh Lepcha	52	M	Do	MP	Do	Do
35	Gamu Lepcha	46	F	Do	X	Household	Somoot Moo
36	Christopher Lepcha	24	M	Do	VIII	Agriculture	Do

(Contd...)

1	2	3	4	5	6	7	8
37	Anjana Lepcha	20	F	Do	VI	Household	—
38	Andrish Lepcha	20	M	Do	IX	Agriculture	Sadaa Moo
39	Ashish Lepcha	17	M	Do	XI	Student	Do
40	Aksha Lepcha	15	F	Do	VI	Do	Somoot Moo
41	Sarjan Lepcha	47	M	Do	VIII	Agriculture	Sadaa Moo
42	Arun Lepcha	24	M	Do	VI	Do	Do
43	Rinki Lepcha	22	F	Do	X	Household	—
44	Alrina Lepcha	19	F	Do	VI	Do	—
45	Odila Lepcha	81	F	Do	—	Do	Taamsaang Pajeng Moo
46	Sofia Lepcha	48	F	Do	MP	Teacher	Do
47	Mitho Lepcha	63	M	Do	VIII	Agriculture	Sadaa Moo
48	Gyanthop Lepcha	38	M	Do	BCom	Business	Do
49	Nirmala Lepcha	28	F	Do	X	Household	Malaom Moo
50	Fabina Lepcha	42	F	Do	X	Church Sister	Taamsaang Pajeng Moo
51	Joel Rippon Lepcha	4	M	Do	UKG	Student	Sadaa Moo
52	Erica Rippondi Lepcha	2	F	Do	—	—	Malaom Moo
53	Looyisa Lepcha	59	F	Do	—	Household	—
54	Sevastine Lepcha	24	M	Do	BA	Agriculture	Sadaa Moo
55	Bunu Lepcha	22	F	Do	VIII	Household	—
56	Justine Lepcha	22	M	Do	X	Agriculture	Sadaa Moo
57	Chypon Lepcha	64	M	Do	—	Do	Taaraang Moo
58	Churmit Lepcha	62	F	Do	—	Household	Molo Mayang Mo
59	Chipon Lepcha	27	M	Do	VIII	Agriculture	Taaraang Moo
60	Nurpun Lepcha	22	M	Do	VII	Do	Do
61	Subash Lepcha	47	M	Do	IX	Do	Sadaa Moo
62	Nimamit Lepcha	37	F	Do	—	Household	—
63	Rubin Lepcha	21	M	Do	VI	Driver	Sadaa Moo
64	Looyisa Lepcha	18	F	Do	X	Student	—
65	Albinash Lepcha	14	M	Do	VI	Do	Sadaa Moo
66	Gayboo Lepcha	45	M	Do	—	Agriculture	Do
67	Gyan Tsh Lepcha	52	M	Do	VIII	Govt Job	Do
68	Elezebeth Lepcha	47	F	Do	III	Household	—
69	Francis Lepcha	28	M	Do	BA	Teacher	Sadaa Moo
70	Hilda Lepcha	27	F	Do	MP	Do	—
71	Elvisa Lepcha	8	F	Do	III	Student	—
72	John Lepcha	23	M	Do	VII	Agriculture	Sadaa Moo
73	Fteidy Lepcha	18	M	Do	X	Do	Do
74	Rabi Lepcha	67	M	Do	VII	Retd	Sungtim Moo

(Contd...)

1	*2*	*3*	*4*	*5*	*6*	*7*	*8*
75	Pravitra Lepcha	55	F	Do	V	Household	—
76	Ningma Lepcha	45	F	Do	II	Do	—
77	Ranjana Lepcha	28	F	Do	BA	Nurse	—
78	Biden Lepcha	25	M	Do	BSc	Pvt Job	Sungtim Moo
79	Northen Lepcha	23	M	Do	X	Agriculture	Do
80	Runchi Lepcha	40	F	Do	III	Household	Ethan Moo
81	Laku Tsh Lepcha	42	M	Do	IV	Agriculture	Saongtyen Moo
82	Nima Lepcha	23	F	Do	—	—	Ethan Moo
83	Pascal Lepcha	21	M	Do	—	—	Saongtyen Moo
84	Gay Tsh Lepcha	67	M	Do	BSc	Agriculture	Karthaak Moo
85	Urmila Lepcha	62	F	Do	VIII	Household	—
86	Seon Tsh Lepcha	37	M	Do	BSc	Agriculture	Karthaak Moo
87	Gayboo Lepcha	32	F	Do	BA	Teacher	Do
88	Anjana Lepcha	30	F	Do	BA	Do	—
89	Raju Lepcha	52	M	Do	BCom	Agriculture	—
90	Rumgay Lepcha	2	M	Do	—	—	Karthaak Moo
91	Laban Tsh Lepcha	77	M	Do	LE	Retd	Do
92	Lhamu Lepcha	67	F	Do	—	Household	—
93	Dekiamit Lepcha	33	F	Do	X	Do	—
94	Keshar Lepcha	43	M	Do	—	Carpenter	Tingboo Moo
95	Songmit Lepcha	37	F	Do	—	Household	Sungtim Moo
96	Ezra Lepcha	26	M	Do	HS	Indian Army	Tingboo Moo
97	Hazel Lepcha	17	F	Do	X	Student	Sungtim Moo
98	Yahan Tsh Lepcha	50	M	Do	MP	Agriculture	—
99	Kabita Lepcha	47	F	Do	—	Household	—
100	Dongmit Lepcha	36	F	Do	BA	Teacher	—
101	Anmit Lepcha	34	F	Do	BA	Do	Sungtim Moo
102	Danial Lepcha	25	M	Do	MA	Bhutan gvtjob	—
103	Kamal Lepcha	20	F	Do	MA	Do	—
104	Marry Lepcha	24	F	Do	BA	Household	—
105	Rakel Lepcha	22	F	Do	VIII	Do	—
106	Sahath Sing Lepcha	84	M	Do	III	Agriculture	Sungtim Moo
107	Mangalmit Lepcha	72	F	Do	II	Household	Aadyen Moo
108	Dawat Lepcha	46	M	Do	XII	State Govt Job	Sungtim Moo
109	Omika Lepcha	37	F	Do	VIII	Pvt Job	—
110	Ashish Lepcha	11	M	Do	V	Student	Sungtim Moo
11	Marry Lepcha	43	F	Do	V	Household	Aadyen Moo
112	Denmo Lepcha	40	F	Do	V	Do	Do

(Contd...)

1	2	3	4	5	6	7	8
113	Len Tsh Lepcha	37	M	Do	X	Post office	Sungtim Moo
114	Chhomu Lepcha	30	F	Do	BA	Teacher	—
115	Mangalmit Lepcha	63	F	Do	VI	Household	—
116	Barmit Lepcha	42	F	Do	II	Do	—
117	Chilas Lepcha	10	M	Do	VIII	Student	—
118	Elias Lepcha	50	M	Do	III	Driver	Naamchu Moo
119	Nimkit Lepcha	43	F	Do	—	Household	Do
120	Mahima Pandi Lepcha	18	F	Do	X	Student	—
121	Salani Lepcha	12	F	Do	II	Do	—
122	Enos Lepcha	26	F	Do	VIII	Household	—
123	Sujit Lepcha	30	M	Do	VIII	Business	—
124	Afia Lepcha	11	M	Do	VI	Student	—
125	Sammuel Lepcha	8	F	Do	III	Do	—
126	Duk Tsh Lepcha	70	M	Do	X	Retd	Sungtim Moo
127	Passangkit Lepcha	65	F	Do	III	Household	—
128	Robert Lepcha	38	M	Do	VII	Driver	Sungtim Moo
129	Durga Lepcha	35	F	Do	VI	Household	—
130	Engel Lepcha	12	F	Do	VII	Student	—
131	Edwin Lepcha	9	M	Do	II	Do	Sungtim Moo
132	Henry Lepcha	33	F	Do	V	Household	—
133	Albert Lepcha	30	M	Do	VIII	Business	Sungtim Moo
134	Do Tsh Lepcha	37	M	Do	M Sc	Household	Sadaa Moo
135	Sankit Lepcha	28	F	Do	HS	Do	—
136	Zafed Lepcha	7	M	Do	II	Student	Sadaa Moo
137	Eman Lepcha	25	M	Do	VI	Agriculture	Do
138	Chomit Lepcha	20	F	Do	V	Household	Molo Mayeng Moo
139	Yelsong Lepcha	4	M	Do	I	Student	Sadaa Moo
140	Yeldoop Lepcha	2	M	Do	—	—	Do
141	Yahana Lepcha	31	M	Do	VIII	Driver	Do
142	Sarika Lepcha	26	F	Do	III	Household	—
143	Margarate Lepcha	62	F	Do	—	—	—
144	Pempo Lepcha	45	M	Do	X	WB Police	Fonyoong Rungsaong Moo
145	Omit Lepcha	39	F	Do	XII	Nurse	Taamsaang Moo
146	Dimpo Lepcha	6	F	Do	II	Student	Do
147	Dawa Fonning	56	M	Do	MP	WB Police	Fonyoong Rungsaong Moo
148	Karma Lepcha	48	F	Do	X	Household	—
149	Dayment Lepcha	19	M	Do	HS	Student	Fonyoong Rungsaong Moo

(Contd...)

1	*2*	*3*	*4*	*5*	*6*	*7*	*8*
150	Nagtu Lepcha	52	M	Do	VII	Agriculture	Sadaa Moo
151	Indra Maya Lepcha	46	F	Do		Business	
152	Sing Lepcha	62	M	Do	BA	Retd	Sadaa Moo
153	Lha Tsh Lepcha	56	M	Buddhist	X	Business	Yaagen Moo
154	Asha Lepcha	50	F	Do	X	Do	
155	Norja Lepcha	23	M	Do	X	Household	Yaagen Moo
156	Norjim Lepcha	20	F	Do	BA	Student	
157	Chedup Lepcha	65	M	Do	X	Household	-
158	Premit Lepcha	50	F	Do	MP	Post Office	--
159	Bir Bhr Lepcha	54	M	Do	MP	Tel Exchange	Joriboo Moo
160	Pampa Lepcha	50	F	Do	VII	Household	--
161	Riwash Lepcha	24	M	Do	BA	Student	Joriboo Moo
162	Ritesh Lepcha	26	M	Do	VII	Do	Do
163	Tshering Lepcha	48	M	Do	MP	Household	Do
164	Dolma Lepcha	45	F	Do	VI	Do	.
165	Saongay Lepcha	10	M	Do	VIII	Driver	Joriboo Moo
166	Dolmu Lepcha	12	F	Do	VII	Student	--
167	Ugen Lepcha	42	M	Do	VIII	Agriculture	Joriboo Moo
168	Doma Lepcha	39	F	Do	III	Household	—
169	Nitish Lepcha	13	M	Do	VI	Student	Joriboo Moo
170	Ritika Lepcha	10	F	Do	IV	Do	--
171	Nitika Lepcha	8	F	Do	III	Do	
172	Pema Lepcha	34	M	Do	--	Agriculture	..riboo Moo
173	Lakit Lepcha	33	F	Do		Household	--
174	Dawa Lepcha	18	M	Do	VII	—	Joriboo Moo

Source: Field Survey

Table – 3

C. Name of the Village : KHAMDUNG

Sl No	*Name*	*Age*	*Sex*	*Religion*	*Education*	*Primary Occupation*	*Moo*
1	*2*	*3*	*4*	*5*	*6*	*7*	*8*
1	Bir Sing Lepcha	34	M	Buddhist	VIII	Agriculture	Shyok Moo
2	Passangkit Lepcha	26	F	Do	V	Household	Saongtyen Moo
3	Ongdup Lepcha	7	M	Do	II	Student	Shyok Moo
4	Tshedup Lepcha	5	M	Do	LKG	Do	Do
5	Tendup Lepcha	3	M	Do	—	—	Do
6	Budhamit Lepcha	66	F	Do	—	Household	Malaom Moo
7	Budha Tsh Lepcha	40	M	Do	VIII	Agriculture	Shyok Moo
8	Nima Lepcha	21	M	Do	BA	Student	Do
9	Lakpa Lepcha	16	M	Do	IX	Do	Do
10	Nigen Lepcha	35	M	Do	VIII	Carpenter	Do
11	Samala Lepcha	28	F	Do	VIII	Household	—
12	Gyan Tsh Lepcha	8	M	Do	V	Student	Shyok Moo
13	Beep Tsh Lepcha	6	M	Do	IV		Do
14	Madina Lepcha	12	F	Do	VII	Do	Do
15	Prem Tsh Lepcha	65	M	Do	—	Carpenter	Sambo Moo
16	Nimthi Lepcha	49	F	Do	—	Household	Lik Moo
17	Prem Chung Lepcha	23	M	Do	IX	Agriculture	Sambo Moo
18	Nunimit Lepcha	19	F	Do	VII	Student	Lik Moo
19	Pemu Lepcha	15	F	Do	IX	Do	Do
20	Budumit Lepcha	34	F	Do	—	Household	Arampucho Moo
21	Saongay Lepcha	45	M	Do	VIII	WB Police	Yung Moo
22	Budumit Lepcha	33	F	Do	—	Household	Malaom Moo
23	Den Lepcha	13	M	Do	IX	Student	Yung Moo
24	Kapgen Lepcha	11	M	Do	VII	Do	Do
25	Priyankit Lepcha	9	F	Do	IV	Do	Malaom Moo
26	Alyon Sing Lepcha	64	M	Christian	V	State Gvt Job	Phepon Moo
27	Dinamit Lepcha	55	F	Do	V	Household	Naamchu Moo
28	Lhadup Lepcha	37	M	Do	BA	Agriculture	Phepon Moo
29	James Lepcha	35	M	Do	VI	Do	Do
30	Joshep Lepcha	27	M	Do	BA	Do	Do
31	Michiel Lepcha	18	F	Do	XII	Student	Naamchu Moo
32	Sammuel Lepcha	31	M	Do	BA	Agriculture	Phepon Moo
33	Birkha Lepcha	28	F	Do	IX	Household	—
34	Sinimic Lepcha	5	F	Do	UKG	Student	—
35	Phurba Lepcha	31	M	Buddhist	IV	Agriculture	Sambo Moo

(Contd...)

1	2	3	4	5	6	7	8
36	Sanchamit Lepcha	19	F	Do	IV	Household	Malaom Moo
37	Yougel Lepcha	1	M	Do	—	—	Sambo Moo
38	Phensol Lepcha	25	M	Do	HS	Agriculture	Do
39	Lhamu Lepcha	24	F	Do	MP	Household	Sadaa Moo
40	Shalmu Lepcha	4	F	Do	UKG	Student	Do
41	Shalonkimit Lepcha	2	F	Do	—	Do	Do
42	Marbu Tsh Lepcha	64	M	Do	VIII	Retd	Malaom Moo
43	Chungkit Lepcha	53	F	Do	IV	Household	Sungoot Moo
44	Norgen Lepcha	26	M	Do	X	Driver	Malaom Moo
45	Pema Lepcha	21	F	Do	VIII	Household	—
46	Ongden Lepcha	25	M	Do	V	Agriculture	Malaom Moo
47	Mina Lepcha	21	F	Do	MP	Household	—
48	Ongchu Lepcha	3	M	Do	LKG	Student	Malaom Moo
49	Dawa Lepcha	57	M	Do	IV	Agriculture	Yung Moo
50	Ongmit Lepcha	45	F	Do	—	Household	Shyok Moo
51	Rajen Lepcha	23	M	Do	V	Agriculture	Yung Moo
52	Phurden Lepcha	15	M	Do	IX	Student	Do
53	Indu Lepcha	50	M	Do	VIII	Agriculture	Do
54	Amit Lepcha	44	F	Do	V	Household	Naom Gye Chuchu Moo
55	Nimkit Lepcha	21	F	Do	MP	Do	Do
56	Mikma Lepcha	17	M	Do	VI	Student	Yung Moo
57	Tshering Lepcha	60	M	Do	V	Agr; Bongthing	Do
58	Ash Laxmi Lepcha	55	F	Do	—	Household	—
59	Durga Lepcha	43	F	Do	III	Do	—
60	Chunden Lepcha	25	M	Do	III	Agriculture	Yung Moo
61	Passangkit Lepcha	21	F	Do	III	Household	Malaom Moo
62	Yougen Lepcha	2	M	Do	—	—	Yung Moo
63	Nim Tsh Lepcha	43	M	Do	II	Agriculture	Fonyoong Rungsaong Moo
64	Nagarmit Lepcha	36	F	Do	—	Household	Emsaong Moo
65	Sonam Lepcha	18	M	Do	IV	Agriculture	Fonyoong Rungsaong Moo
66	Premkit Lepcha	16	F	Do	IV	Do	Emsaong Moo
67	Karmit Lepcha	13	F	Do	VI	Student	Do
68	Anumit Lepcha	10	F	Do	I	Do	Do
69	Prem Tsh Lepcha	47	M	Do	I	Agr; Bongthing	Shyok Moo
70	Lamit Lepcha	45	F	Do	IV	Household	Simik Moo
71	Ingkit Lepcha	15	F	Do	IX	Student	Do

(Contd...)

1	2	3	4	5	6	7	8
72	Ramden Lepcha	13	M	Do	IV	Do	Shyok Moo
73	Saongden Lepcha	11	M	Do	IV	Do	Do
74	Marden Lepcha	9	M	Do	III	Do	Do
75	Margen Lepcha	7	M	Do	III	Do	Do
76	Mongmit Lepcha	6	F	Do	II	Do	Simik Moo
77	Sankit Lepcha	4	F	Do	I	Do	Do
78	Ram Tsh Lepcha	2	M	Do	LKG	Do	Shyok Moo
79	Kuber Lepcha	64	M	Do	—	Agriculture	Tingboo Moo
80	Likmaya Lepcha	59	F	Do	—	Household	—
81	Suk Tsh Lepcha	34	M	Do	IX	Agriculture	Tingboo Moo
82	Sumitra Lepcha	28	F	Do	X	Household	—
83	Niden Lepcha	3	F	Do	—	—	—
84	Mangal Tsh Lepcha	23	M	Do	BA	Agriculture	Tingboo Moo
85	Premkit Lepcha	46	F	Do	I	Household	Malaom Moo
86	Punam Lepcha	26	M	Do	HS	Agriculture	Shyok Moo
87	Sukden Lepcha	20	M	Do	HS	Household	Do
88	Nima Tsh Lepcha	39	M	Christian	IX	Agriculture	Naamchu Moo
89	Aimit Lepcha	36	F	Do	VIII	Household	Ethan Moo
90	Issac Lepcha	15	M	Do	X	Student	Naamchu Moo
91	Topesh Lepcha	13	M	Do	VI	Do	Do
92	Kapgay Tsh Ronjii Lep	46	M	Buddhist	IV	Agriculture	Fonyoong Rungsaong Moo
93	Lagay Tsh Ronjii Lep	19	M	Do	VII	Do	Do
94	Yankit Lepcha	17	F	Do	X	Student	Malaom Moo
95	Markit Lepcha	15	F	Do	X	Do	Do
96	Lha Tsh Ronjii Lepcha	12	M	Do	IX	Do	Fonyoong Rungsaong Moo
97	Alina Lepcha	9	F	Do	VI	Do	Malaom Moo
98	Ram Sing Lepcha	64	M	Do	I	Agriculture	Shyok Moo
99	Phol Maya Lepcha	53	F	Do	—	Household	—
100	Daniel Lepcha	49	M	Christian	III	Carpenter	Naamchu Moo
101	Anila Lepcha	45	F	Do	II	Household	—
102	Alia Lepcha	15	M	Do	III	Student	Naamchu Moo
103	Alisa Lepcha	14	M	Do	III	Do	Do
104	David Lepcha	9	M	Do	I	Do	Do
105	Bir Sing Lepcha	66	M	Do	VII	Agriculture	Do
106	Budumit Lepcha	60	F	Do	I	Household	Simik Moo
107	Simon Lepcha	30	M	Do	VIII	Agriculture	Naamchu Moo
108	Jukden Lepcha	27	M	Do	MP	Driver	Do
109	Budeumit Lepcha	23	F	Do	IV	Household	Pothyaang Moo

(Contd...)

1	*2*	*3*	*4*	*5*	*6*	*7*	*8*
110	Abhigel Lepcha	5	F	Do	I	Student	Do
11	Abhishek Lepcha	4	M	Do	UKG	Do	Naamchu Moo
112	Pemba Lepcha	42	M	Buddhist	II	Agriculture	Shyok Moo
113	Laden Lepcha	24	F	Do	—	Household	—
114	Bunchu Lepcha	16	F	Do	I	Do	—
115	Birkit Lepcha	12	F	Do	V	Student	—
116	Bunu Lepcha	9	F	Do	III	Do	—
117	Aimit Lepcha	7	F	Do	II	Do	—
118	Passangkit Lepcha	1	F	Do	—	—	—
119	Dawa Tsh Lepcha	54	M	Do	I	Agriculture	Naamchu Moo
120	Sanumit Lepcha	44	F	Do	—	Household	Malaom Moo
121	Domit Lepcha	18	F	Do	IX	Student	Do
122	Premkit Lepcha	14	F	Do	VI	Do	Do
123	Chot Tsh Lepcha	16	M	Do	VI	—	Naamchu Moo
124	Lachung Lepcha	12	M	Do	II	Student	Do
125	Ong Tsh Lepcha	10	M	Do	II	Do	Do
126	Som Tsh Lepcha	8	M	Do	UKG	Do	Do
127	Nima Tsh Lepcha	38	M	Do	VII	WB Police	Shyok Moo
128	Rinjii Lepcha	30	F	Do	MP	Household	—
129	Chimed Rigfin Lepcha	10	M	Do	V	Student	Shyok Moo
130	Pema Hashel Lepcha	4	M	Do	LKG	Do	Do

Source: Field Survey.

Table – 4

D. Name of the Village : LOWER BEYONG

Sl No	Name	Age	Sex	Religion	Education	Primary Occupation	Moo
1	2	3	4	5	6	7	8
1	Sukman Lepcha	62	M	Buddhist	IX	Ex Army	Tangee TaamMoo
2	Chyongkit Lepcha	60	F	Do	II	Household	Songmooce Moo
3	Kul deep Lepcha	24	M	Do	XII	Student	Tangee TaamMoo
4	Budha Lepcha	14	M	Do	IX	Agriculture	Do
5	Kumar Lepcha	38	M	Do	—	Do	Looyi Moo
6	Chanchalmit Lepcha	38	F	Do	—	Household	Sambar Gen Moo
7	Sarmit Lepcha	13	F	Do	VI	Student	Do
8	Chyomit Lepcha	12	F	Do	V	Do	Do
9	Tashi Lepcha	11	M	Do	IV	Do	Looyi Moo
10	Aiti Lepcha	9	F	Do	III	Do	Sambar Gen Moo
11	Samten Lepcha	8	M	Do	I	Do	Looyi Moo
12	Aman Lepcha	70	M	Do	—	Agriculture	Do
13	Pumthi Lepcha	70	F	Do	—	Household	Sampo Moo
14	Panzan Lepcha	29	M	Do	III	Agriculture	Looyi Moo
15	Ong Tsh Lepcha	27	M	Do	IV	Do	Do
16	Atyong Lepcha	65	F	Do	—	Household	Saongmoo Sheemoo
17	Purnamit Lepcha	30	F	Do	V	Agriculture	Do
18	Pema Lepcha	26	M	Do	VI	Do	Goulook Moo
19	Chinlop Lepcha	16	M	Do	X	Do	Do
20	Purna Sing Lepcha	46	M	Do	II	Agriculture	Do
21	Samkit Lepcha	46	F	Do	—	Household	Koorook Moo
22	Mangalmit Lepcha	22	F	Do	VI	Agriculture	Do
23	Chanchalmit Lepcha	21	F	Do	VIII	Do	Do
24	Chyomit Lepcha	15	F	Do	VII	Student	Do
25	Junmit Lepcha	12	F	Do	V	Do	Do
26	Nurmit Lepcha	10	F	Do	III	Do	Do
27	Aitamit Lepcha	9	F	Do	II	Do	Do
28	John Sing Lepcha	40	M	Do	I	Agriculture Bongthing	Goulook Moo
29	Normit Lepcha	39	F	Do	—	Household	Bri Moo
30	Chozong Lepcha	9	M	Do	III	Student	Goulook Moo
31	Nurzong Lepcha	8	M	Do	IV	Do	Do
32	Eyongdup Lepcha	7	M	Do	III	Do	Do
33	Nur Pandi Lepcha	4	F	Do	UKG	Do	Bri Moo
34	Karma Tsh Lepcha	68	M	Do	—	Agriculture	Goulook Moo

(Contd...)

1	*2*	*3*	*4*	*5*	*6*	*7*	*8*
35	Ongmit Lepcha	65	F	Do	—	Household	Saongmoo Sheemoo
36	Birmit Lepcha	42	F	Do	IX	ICDS	Do
37	Songmit Lepcha	28	F	Do	VIII	Agriculture	Do
38	Budhamit Lepcha	23	M	Do	V	Do	Goulook Moo
39	Sonam Lepcha	35	M	Do	VIII	Do	Do
40	Budhamit Lepcha	32	F	Do	I	Household	Sambar Gen Moo
41	Nuozong Lepcha	10	M	Do	V	Student	Goulook Moo
42	Ripsong Lepcha	8	F	Do	III	Do	Sambar Gen Moo
43	Sukman Lepcha	59	M	Do	—	Agriculture	Tahitaong Moo
44	Nimkit Lepcha	59	F	Do	—	Household	Simik Moo
45	Tendup Lepcha	25	M	Do	IV	Agriculture	Tahitaong Moo
46	Imit Lepcha	26	F	Do	IV	Do	Simik Moo
47	Sukden Lepcha	23	M	Do	IV	Do	Tahitaong Moo
48	Suk Tsh Lepcha	22	M	Do	IV	Do	Do
49	Budhi Sing Lepcha	54	M	Do	—	Agriculture	Do
50	Sukmaya Lepcha	41	F	Do	—	Household	Chaong Moo
51	Premkit Lepcha	16	F	Do	I	Agriculture	Do
52	Chyokit Lepcha	15	F	Do	I	Do	Do
53	Rongkit Lepcha	12	F	Do	II	Student	Do
54	Songkit Lepcha	7	F	Do	I	Do	Do
55	Ongkit Lepcha	5	F	Do	I	Do	Do
56	Gendup Lepcha	6	M	Do	UKG	Do	Tahitaong Moo
57	Ripdup Lepcha	2	F	Do	—	--	Chaong Moo
58	Sonam Lepcha	53	M	Do	—	Agriculture	Tahitaong Moo
59	Man Sing Lepcha	49	M	Do	—	Do	Do
60	Roman Lepcha	51	M	Christian	VI	Do	Do
61	Ayaknesh Lepcha	50	F	Do	—	Household	Yari Moo
62	Christo Lepcha	29	M	Do	IX	Agriculture	Tahitaong Moo
63	Jyokhim Lepcha	25	M	Do	VII	Do	Do
64	Jeeni Lepcha	21	F	Do	VIII	Do	Yari Moo
65	Joshna Lepcha	17	F	Do	XII	Student	Do
66	Pendi Lepcha	19	F	Do	VII	Do	Taakmaan Moo
67	Suk Sing Lepcha	34	M	Buddhist	VII	Agriculture	Malaom Moo
68	Puspa Lepcha	33	F	Do	X	Household	Naomfaok Moo
69	Nurgen Lepcha	8	M	Do	III	Student	Malaom Moo
70	Chyogen Lepcha	3	M	Do	—	—	Do
71	Tharten Lepcha	26	M	Do	IV	Agriculture	Do
72	Gen Tsh Lepcha	25	M	Do	IV	Do	Do

(Contd...)

1	2	3	4	5	6	7	8
73	Mangalmit Lepcha	18	F	Do	X	Student	Faokli Moo
74	Mangal Lepcha	43	M	Do	—	Agriculture	Looyi Moo
75	Urmila Lepcha	40	F	Do	—	Household	Saongmoo Sheemoo
76	Manyos Lepcha	17	M	Do	II	Agriculture	Looyi Moo'
77	Somit Lepcha	15	F	Do	IV	Do	Saongmoo Sheemoo
78	Chyoden Lepcha	13	M	Do	VI	Student	Looyi Moo
79	Nerkit Lepcha	9	F	Do	III	Do	Saongmoo Sheemoo
80	Song Kit Lepcha	8	F	Do	II	Do	Do
81	Tshering Lepcha	29	M	Do	IX	Agriculture	Tangee Taam Moo
82	Samit Lepcha	26	F	Do	II	Household	Tingboo Moo
83	Sakchen Lepcha	4	M	Do	UKG	Student	Tangee Taam Moo
84	Saknon Lepcha	2	F	Do	Infant	—	Tingboo Moo
85	Sebastine Lepcha	64	M	Christian	II	Agriculture	Looyi Moo
86	Monika Lepcha	57	F	Do	I	Household	Raongding Sundyaang Moo
87	Silbester Lepcha	36	M	Do	BA	Ch Rev.	Looyi Moo
88	Raseline Lepcha	26	F	Do	XII	Household	Raongding Sundyaang Moo
89	Dawa Tsh Lepcha	79	M	Do	—	Agriculture	Fodaong Moo
90	Ayongmit Lepcha	79	F	Do	—	Household	Yari Moo
91	Monika Lepcha	52	F	Do	X	Teacher	Do
92	Leezu Lepcha	40	F	Do	X	Household	Do
93	Angu Lepcha	38	F	Do	IX	Do	Do
94	Sinamit Lepcha	29	F	Do	X	Do	Do
95	Chen Tsh Lepcha	14	M	Do	VIII	Student	Fodaong Moo
96	Sonarip Lepcha	13	F	Do	VII	Do	Soongoot Moo
97	Mongrip Lepcha	10	F	Do	IV	Do	Do
98	Nermit Lepcha	46	F	Do	—	Household	Yari Moo
99	Samrit Lepcha	27	F	Do	XI	Do	Do
100	Tshering Lepcha	25	M	Do	IV	Driver	Tahitaong Moo
101	Anju Lepcha	24	F	Do	V	Household	—
102	Simik Lepcha	9	F	Do	I	Student	—
103	Penjoo Lepcha	3	M	Do	Infant	Do	Tahitaong Moo
104	Som Tsh Lepcha	1	M	Do	—	—	Do
105	Jeena Lepcha	21	F	Do	VIII	Agriculture	Yari Moo
106	Bar Sing Lepcha	18	M	Do	XII	Student	Tahitaong Moo
107	Saongita Lepcha	16	F	Do	X	Do	Yari Moo

(Contd...)

1	2	3	4	5	6	7	8
108	Pempo Lepcha	46	M	Do	VII	Driver	Taamsaang Moo
109	Nerkit Lepcha	45	F	Do	XII	Teacher	Yari Moo
110	Advin Lepcha	44	M	Do	II	Agriculture	Looyi Moo
11	Simon Lepcha	40	M	Do	II	Do	Do
112	Amrush Lepcha	31	M	Do	VI	Do	Do
113	John Lepcha	29	M	Do	VI	Do	Do
114	Nim Tsh Lepcha	55	M	Buddhist	III	Agriculture	Tangee Taam Moo
115	Mangalmit Lepcha	42	F	Do	—	Household	Saongmoo Sheemoo
116	Samkit Lepcha	15	F	Do	IX	Student	Do
117	Nimkit Lepcha	10	F	Do	IV	Do	Do
118	Samrip Lepcha	8	F	Do	II	Do	Do
119	Nima Tsh Lepcha	53	M	Do	—	Agriculture	Looyi Moo
120	Premit Lepcha	40	F	Do	—	Household	Saongmoo Shemoo
121	Kamit Lepcha	25	F	Do	III	Do	Do
122	Dawa Tsh Lepcha	20	M	Do	IV	Driver	Looyi Moo
123	Songkit Lepcha	18	F	Do	X	Household	Saongmoo Shemoo
124	Cheo Tsh Lepcha	13	M	Do	VI	Student	Looyi Moo
125	Ribamit Lepcha	11	F	Do	IV	Do	Saongmoo Shemoo
126	Suk Sing Lepcha	52	M	Do	IV	Agriculture	Looyi Moo
127	Napti Lepcha	52	F	Do	—	Household	Chang Moo
128	Aita Lepcha	27	M	Do	IV	Agriculture	Looyi Moo
129	Sanu Lepcha	16	F	Do	VI	Do	Chaong Moo
130	Suksuk Lepcha	10	M	Do	VI	Student	Looyi Moo
131	Ongzom Lepcha	7	M	Do	III	Do	Do
132	Cherman Lepcha	31	M	Do	III	Agriculture	Do
133	Lamit Lepcha	31	F	Do	VI	Household	Soongoot Moo
134	Lyangdop Lepcha	3	M	Do	LKG	Student	Looyi Moo
135	Lyangrip Lepcha	2	F	Do	—	—	Soongoot Moo
136	Ongthi Lepcha	30	M	Do	IV	Agriculture	Looyi Moo
137	Phulmit Lepcha	28	F	Do	II	Household	Tingboo Moo
138	Karmit Lepcha	6	F	Do	II	Student	Do
139	Karchen Lepcha	5	M	Do	II	Do	Looyi Moo
140	Dorjee Tsh Lepcha	84	M	Do	—	Agriculture	Do
141	Prem Tsh Lepcha	61	M	Do	IV	Do	Do
142	Phulmit Lepcha	52	F	Do	—	Household	Taamsaang Pajyeng Moo
143	Ongdup Lepcha	26	M	Do	XII	Agriculture	Looyi Moo
144	Gyandup Lepcha	18	M	Do	III	Do	Do
145	Dan Sing Lepcha	50	M	Do	IV	Do	Tahitaong Moo

(Contd...)

1	2	3	4	5	6	7	8
146	Liki Lepcha	35	F	Do	—	Household	Soongoot Moo
147	Suk Tsh Lepcha	8	M	Do	IV	Student	Tahitaong Moo
148	Lyangmik Lepcha	7	M	Do	III	Do	Do
149	Lyandong Lepcha	6	M	Do	II	Do	Do
150	Ripayong Lepcha	. 3	F	Do	Infant	Do	Soongoot Moo
151	Lyangoom Lepcha	1 m	M	Do	—	—	Tahitaong Moo
152	Tshering Dorjee Lepcha	74	M	Do	IV	Agriculture Bongthing	Goulook Moo
153	Cremu Lepcha	66	F	Do	—	Household	Bri Moo
154	Landop Lepcha	26	M	Do	XII	Indian Army	Goulook Moo
155	Songrip Lepcha	24	F	Do	X	Household	Chaong Moo
156	Lasong Lepcha	1 m	M	Do	—	—	Goulook Moo
157	Dup Tsh Lepcha	25	M	Do	VIII	Agriculture	Do
158	Harkamit Lepcha	24	F	Do	IV	Do	Bri Moo
159	Namgong Lepcha	65	M	Christian	II	Do	Looyi Moo
160	Veronica Lepcha	65	F	Do	—	Household	Naomfaok Kooraok Moo
161	Issac Lepcha	36	M	Do	IX	Pvt Job	Looyi Moo
162	Songmit Lepcha	30	F	Do	VIII	Agriculture	Simik Moo
163	Laeria Lepcha	7	F	Do	III	Student	Do
164	Lyaksong Lepcha	4	M	Do	LKG	Do	Looyi Moo
165	Ansalam Lepcha	30	M	Do	IX	Agriculture	Do
166	Suprina Lepcha	21	F	Do	VIII	Do	Keyoungrip Yokchom Moo
167	Philip Lepcha	45	M	Do	III	Agriculture	Looyi Moo
168	Sihilia Lepcha	45	F	Do	I	Household	Simik Moo
169	Sabina Lepcha	21	F	Do	XII	Ttc	Do
170	Sarina Lepcha	11	F	Do	VI	Student	Do
171	Sophia Lepcha	10	F	Do	V	Do	Do
172	Rizard Lepcha	7	M	Do	II	Do	Looyi Moo
173	Pema Lepcha	52	M	Buddhist	IV	Agriculture	Do
174	Mangalmit Lepcha	48	F	Do	—	Household	Tingboo Moo
175	Passangkit Lepcha	19	F	Do	X	Student	Do
176	Youngkit Lepcha	17	F	Do	X	Do	Do
177	Lakra Lepcha	15	M	Do	III	Do	Looyi Moo
178	Genmit Lepcha	13	F	Do	II	Do	Malaom Moo
179	Marina Lepcha	10	F	Do	III	Do	Naomfaok Kooraok Moo
180	Pandi Lepcha	7	F	Do	II	Do	Do
181	Nama Tsh Lepcha	63	M	Do	—	—	Do

(Contd...)

1	*2*	*3*	*4*	*5*	*6*	*7*	*8*
182	Nur Sing Lepcha	37	M	Christian	V	Agriculture	Munsaong Moo
183	Matilda Lepcha	37	F	Do	IV	Household	Naomfaok Kooraok Moo
184	Mayal Christina Lepcha	13	F	Do	VI	Student	Do
185	Laerip Sabastina Lepcha	4	F	Do	UKG	Do	Do
186	Komit Lepcha	55	F	Buddhist	—	Household	Munsaong Moo
187	Azyam Lepcha	19	F	Do	I	Agriculture	Do
188	Som Tsh Lepcha	26	M	Do	IV	Do	Taamsaang Moo
189	Norkit Lepcha	25	F	Do	II	Household	Munsaong Moo
190	Kyal Sing Lepcha	13	M	Do	VII	Student	Taamsaang Moo
191	Aita Lepcha	12	M	Do	IV	Do	Do
192	Ugen Lepcha	65	M	Do	—	Agriculture	Do
193	Laymit Lepcha	50	F	Do	—	Household	Saongmoo Shemoo
194	Sukmit Lepcha	41	F	Do	X	Teacher	Do
195	Pema Lepcha	31	M	Do	X	SSB	Taamsaang Moo
196	Phamit Lepcha	25	F	Do	IX	Household	Rongding Moo
197	Zurip Lepcha	1	F	Do	—	—	Do
198	Palden Lepcha	45	M	Christian	III	Agriculture	Gangtok Moo
199	Clara Lepcha	37	F	Do	—	Household	—
200	Anzyal Lepcha	18	M	Do	IX	Student	Gangtok Moo
201	Banden Lepcha	17	M	Do	IV	Agriculture	Do
202	Nyalson Lepcha	16	M	Do	IX	Student	Do
203	Looyisce Lepcha	50	M	Do	—	Agriculture	Sadaa Moo
204	Mitik Lepcha	40	F	Do	—	Household	Naamchu Moo
205	Simon Lepcha	18	M	Do	IX	Agriculture	Sadaa Moo
206	Sammuel Lepcha	17	M	Do	VIII	Do	Do
207	Peter Lepcha	16	M	Do	—	Do	Do
208	Simson Lepcha	10	M	Do	V	Student	Do
209	Richard Lepcha	9	M	Do	III	Do	Do
210	Mikma Lepcha	59	M	Buddhist	—	Agriculture	Taamsaang Moo
211	Sukmit Lepcha	51	F	Do	—	Household	Tingboo Moo
212	Buddha Lepcha	29	M	Do	V	Agriculture	Taamsaang Moo
213	Premit Lepcha	27	F	Do	BA	Do	Tingboo Moo
214	Yok Tsh Lepcha	24	M	Do	X	Do	Taamsaang Moo
215	Nerkit Lepcha	22	F	Do	IX	Do	Tingboo Moo
216	Shyomit Lepcha	17	F	Do	X	Student	Do
217	Rema Lepcha	16	F	Do	IX	Do	Do
218	Ugen Tsh Lepcha	56	M	Christian	—	Agriculture	Malaom Moo

(Contd...)

1	2	3	4	5	6	7	8
219	Mangalmit Lepcha	51	F	Do	—	Household	Chong Yaoksaom Moo
220	Triza Lepcha	26	F	Do	HS	Teacher	Do
221	Makdoline Lepcha	25	F	Do	V	Agriculture	Do
222	Kanchimit Lepcha	63	F	Buddhist	—	Household	Tingboo Moo
223	Shermit Lepcha	32	F	Do	—	Agriculture	Do
224	Chedup Lepcha	24	M	Do	VII	Driver	Malaom Moo
225	Man Sing Lepcha	75	M	Do	—	Agriculture	Tahitaong Moo
226	Sermit Lepcha	63	F	Do	—	Household	Naomfaok Kooraok Moo
227	Denishka Lepcha	40	M	Do	IV	Driver	TingboogbooMoo
228	Rita Lepcha	36	F	Do	III	Household	—
229	Ugen Lepcha	14	M	Do	VI	Student	Tingbo Moo
230	Nurgen Lepcha	1	M	Do	—	—	Do
231	Sukman Lepcha	33	M	Do	VIII	Agriculture	Gangtok Moo
232	Clara Lepcha	27	F	Do	VI	Household	Saompa Moo
233	Susang Lepcha	6	F	Do	III	Student	Do
234	Kusaong Lepcha	4	F	Do	LKG	Do	Do
235	Sam Pandi Lepcha	2	F	Do	Infant	Do	Do
236	Phulmit Lepcha	40	F	Christian	—	Business	—
237	Agyan Pandi Lepcha	12	F	Do	VII	Student	—
238	Asho Tsh Lepcha	12	M	Do	VII	Do	Sadaa Moo
239	James Lepcha	47	M	Do	—	Agriculture	Kaabo Moo
240	Sisilia Lepcha	42	F	Do	—	Household	Keng Moo
241	Tashi Lepcha	22	M	Do	IX	Do	Kaabo Moo
242	Tachen Lepcha	17	M	Do	IX	Student	Do
243	Andras Lepcha	45	M	Do	VIII	Agriculture	Sadaa Moo
244	Sophia Lepcha	38	F	Do	IV	Household	Taamsaang Moo
245	Anand Lepcha	17	M	Do	XI	Student	Sadaa Moo
246	Shilvia Lepcha	14	F	Do	X	Do	Taamsaang Moo
247	Targay Lepcha	45	M	Do	III	Agriculture	Sadaa Moo
248	Roja Lepcha	45	F	Do	II	Household	—
249	Anup Lepcha	19	M	Do	XII	Student	Saongma Moo
250	Edward Lepcha	16	M	Do	IX	Do	Do
251	Som Tsh Lepcha	42	M	Buddhist	VI	Agr Labor	Gangyong Sumbor Moo
252	Barmit Lepcha	36	F	Do	—	Household	Shara Moo
253	Pema Lepcha	17	M	Do	VI	Agriculture	Gangyong Sumbor Moo
254	Munna Lepcha	16	F	Do	IX	Student	Shara Moo

(Contd...)

1	*2*	*3*	*4*	*5*	*6*	*7*	*8*
255	Junna Lepcha	13	F	Do	VII	Do	Do
256	Jelu Lepcha	12	M	Do	VI	Do	Do
257	Sankit Lepcha	11	F	Do	III	Do	Do
258	Lina Lepcha	3	F	Do	I	Do	Do
259	Laden Lepcha	52	M	Do	X	WB Police	Bri Moo
260	Sumitra Lepcha	40	F	Do	IX	Household	—
261	Chitus Lepcha	12	M	Do	VIII	Student	Bri Moo
262	Tshering Ongmu Lepcha	10	M	Do	VII	Do	Do
263	Ongmit Lepcha	62	F	Do	—	Household	Sungdyaang Moo
264	Sukmit Lepcha	30	F	Do	IX	Do	Do
265	Mangalmit Lepcha	28	F	Do	VII	Business	Do
266	Suk Tsh Lepcha	21	M	Do	XII	Student	Bri Moo
267	Passaongkit Lepcha	20	F	Do	XI	Do	Sungdyaang Moo
268	Pandu Lepcha	19	M	Do	X	Do	Do
269	Pasa Tsh Lepcha	72	M	Do	—	Agriculture	Goulook Moo
270	Kenga Lepcha	35	M	Do	—	Do	Do
271	Bimla Lepcha	26	F	Do	—	Household	—
272	Susmita Lepcha	7	F	Do	I	Student	—
273	Saongden Lepcha	3	M	Do	Infant	Do	Gangtok Moo
274	Norden Lepcha	1	M	Do	—	—	Do
275	Bir Sing Lepcha	26	M	Do	IX	Agriculture	Do
276	Benu Lepcha	25	F	Do	—	Household	—
277	Ong Tsh Lepcha	55	M	Christian	IV	Agriculture	Saongmaa Moo
278	Irun Lepcha	50	F	Do	II	Household	Saompa Moo
279	Barnabad Lepcha	30	M	Do	V	Agriculture	Saongmaa Moo
280	Sujata Lepcha	18	F	Do	—	Household	Saompa Moo
281	Ranjana Lepcha	15	F	Do	VII	Student	Do
282	Annamika Lepcha	11	F	Do	V	Do	Do
283	Emil Lepcha	12	F	Do	I	Do	Do
284	Maroline Lepcha	10	F	Do	V	Do	Do
285	Nuel Lepcha	8	M	Do	III	Do	Saongmaa Moo
286	Joshina Lepcha	7	F	Do	III	Do	Saompa Moo
287	Caroline Lepcha	24	F	Do	XII	Ch Sister	Do
288	Launath Lepcha	50	M	Do	—	Agriculture	Malaom Moo
289	Veronica Lepcha	31	F	Do	—	Household	—
290	Normit Lepcha	4	F	Do	LKG	Student	—
291	Peter Lepcha	3	M	Do	Infant	Do	Malaom Moo
292	Bimiyan Lepcha	23	M	Do	I	Agriculture	Do

(Contd...)

1	2	3	4	5	6	7	8
293	Herman Lepcha	42	M	Do	VII	Do	Do
294	Trisa Lepcha	37	F	Do	—	Household	Sungdyaang Moo
295	Royal Lepcha	21	M	Do	III	Pvt Job	Malaom Moo
296	Sammuel Lepcha	19	M	Do	VIII	Agriculture	Do
297	Phabian Lepcha	17	F	Do	V	Household	Sungdyaang Moo
298	Jasinta Lepcha	13	F	Do	VI	Student	Do
299	Man Sing Lepcha	75	M	Do	—	Agriculture	Malaom Moo
300	Narkit Lepcha	80	F	Do	—	Household	Saompa Moo
301	Fedrik Lepcha	42	M	Do	X	Agriculture	Malaom Moo
302	Albina Lepcha	35	F	Do	—	Household	Raongding Moo
303	Chyogyel Lepcha	10	M	Do	IV	Student	Malaom Moo
304	Elisa Lepcha	12	F	Do	III	Do	Raongding Moo
305	Sabastine Lepcha	9	M	Do	I	Do	Malaom Moo
306	Juli Lepcha	46	F	Do	XII	Ch. Sister	Saompa Moo
307	Laku Tsh Lepcha	50	M	Buddhist	—	Pvt Job	Looyi Moo
308	Ongmit Lepcha	38	F	Do	—	Household	—
309	Palden Lepcha	13	M	Do	IV	Student	Looyi Moo
310	Tshering Lepcha	8	M	Do	LKG	Do	Do
311	Mikma Lepcha	35	M	Do	X	Pvt Job	Do
312	Sunil Lepcha	19	M	Do	XI	Student	Do
313	Dhiren Lepcha	15	M	Do	IX	Do	Do
314	Ongmu Lepcha	83	F	Christian	—	Household	Brisaong Moo
315	Prem Tsh Lepcha	59	M	Do	IX	Ex CRPF	Naomfaok Moo
316	Ruth Lepcha	45	F	Do	V	Household	—
317	Rabika Lepcha	22	F	Do	XII	Student	—
318	Lodrik Lepcha	16	M	Do	X	Do	Naomfaok Moo
319	Renol Lepcha	9	M	Do	IX	Do	Do
320	Nimtondu Lepcha	77	M	Buddhist	—	Agriculture, Bongthing	Tahitaong Moo
321	Rinchen Lepcha	35	M	Do	V	Agriculture	Do
322	Ganga Lepcha	30	F	Do	IV	Household	—
323	Shalina Lepcha	11	F	Do	V	Student	—
324	Nuzong Lepcha	6	F	Do	I	Do	—
325	Monjyor Lepcha	4	M	Do	UKG	Do	Tahitaong Moo
326	Panjo Lepcha	1	M	Do	—	—	Do
327	Santa Rajmit Lepcha	22	F	Do	IX	Agriculture	Bri Moo
328	Mangal Lepcha	32	M	Do	VII	Do	Tahitaong Moo
329	Indra Lepcha	25	F	Do	IV	Household	—
330	Simron Lepcha	6	F	Do	I	Student	—

(Contd...)

1	*2*	*3*	*4*	*5*	*6*	*7*	*8*
331	Soochen Lepcha	4	M	Do	UKG	Do	Tahitaong Moo
332	Kamal Lepcha	48	M	Do	VII	Driver	Do
333	Maina Lepcha	44	F	Do	---	Household	—
334	Bimla Lepcha	21	F	Do	IX	Agriculture	—
335	Rip Pandi Lepcha	18	F	Do	VII	Do	---
336	Nigen Lepcha	13	M	Do	VI	Student	Tahitaong Moo
337	Susang Lepcha	8	M	Do	III	Do	Do
338	Thamas Lepcha	77	M	Do	--	Agriculture	Malaom Moo
339	Lhamit Lepcha	58	F	Do	---	Household	Songmoo Shee Moo
340	Paskal Lepcha	28	M	Do	IV	Missing	Malaom Moo
341	Amash Lepcha	26	M	Do	VII	Agriculture	Do
342	Solaman Lepcha	17	M	Do	IX	Student	Do
343	Kap Sing Lepcha	28	M	Do	III	Agriculture	Goulook Moo
344	Charan Sing Lepcha	26	M	Do	I	Do	Do
345	Susan Lepcha	19	F	Do	VI	Household	Yari Moo
346	Gen Tsh Lepcha	17	M	Do	VI	Agriculture	Goulook Moo
347	Rup Tsh Lepcha	9	M	Do	IV	Student	Do
348	Peter Lepcha	38	M	Do	XI	Agriculture	Sambar Moo
349	Reena Lepcha	38	F	Do	IX	Household	Tahitaong Moo
350	Tresa Nisa Lepcha	14	F	Do	IX	Student	Do
351	Aniset Lepcha	1	F	Do	---	—	Do
352	Andru Lepcha	32	M	Do	BA	Agriculture	Kaabo Moo
353	Secelia Lepcha	30	F	Do	X	Household	Naomfaok Moo
354	Briman Lepcha	8	M	Do	III	Student	Kaabo Moo
355	Branden Lepcha	5	M	Do	UKG	Do	Do
356	Ambruse Lepcha	28	M	Do	Mgt Dip	Pvt Job	Do
357	Ledia Lepcha	33	F	Do	BA	Ch Sister	Tahitaong Moo
358	Regina Lepcha	44	F	Do	BA	Do	Do
359	Benifar Lepcha	39	M	Do	VIII	Ex Army	Kaabo Moo
360	Sukmit Lepcha	30	F	Do	XII	Houschold	Goulook Moo
361	Refer Lepcha	8	M	Do	II	Student	Kaabo Moo
362	Renal Lepcha	5	M	Do	UKG	Do	Do
363	Sugan Lepcha	43	M	Do	V	Agriculture	Tahitaong Moo
364	Rosy Lepcha	43	F	Do	VII	Household	—
365	Lewis Lepcha	18	M	Do	XI	Student	Tahitaong Moo
366	Lelicia Lepcha	15	F	Do	IX	Do	—
367	Ledia Lepcha	12	F	Do	VII	Do	—
368	Bangamit Lepcha	73	F	Do	V	Household	Sungdyaang Moo

(Contd...)

1	2	3	4	5	6	7	8
369	Jana Lepcha	40	M	Do	IX	Agriculture	Tahitaong Moo
370	Honak Lepcha	30	M	Do	V	Do	Do
371	Seena Lepcha	35	F	Do	IX	Teacher	Sungdyaang Moo
372	Sonam Lepcha	81	M	Do	VIII	Agriculture	Tahitaong Moo
373	Manica Lepcha	60	F	Do	V	Household	—
374	Grashi Lepcha	28	F	Do	BA	Nurse	—
375	Aluise Lepcha	26	M	Do	VIII	Agriculture	Tahitaong Moo

Source: Field Survey

Appendix - II

STATE-WISE LIST OF SCHEDULED TRIBES IN SIKKIM, TRIPURA AND WEST BENGAL

Sikkim:

1. Bhutia, (including Chumbipa,Dopthpa,Dukpa, Kagetey, Sherpa, Tibetan, Tromopa, Yolmo).
2. **Lepcha**
3. Limboo
4. Tamang.

Tripura:

1. Bhil.
2. Bhutia.
3. Chaimal
4. Chakma
5. Garoo
6. Halam, Bangshel, Dub, Kaipeng, Kalai, Karbong,Lengui, Mussum, Rupini, Sukuchep, Thangchep
7. Jamatia
8. Khasia
9. Kuki, including the following sub-tribes:
   (i) Baite
   (ii) Belalhut
   (iii) Chhalya
   (iv) Fun
   (v) Hajango
   (vi) Jangtei

(vii) Khareng

(viii) Khephong

(ix) Kuntei

(x) Laifang

(xi) Lentei

(xii) Mizel

(xiii) Namte

(xiv) Paitu, Paite

(xv) Rangchan

(xvi) Rangkhole

10. Lepcha

(xvii) Thangluya

11. lushai

12. Mag

13. Munda, Kaur

14. Noatia, Musrashing

15. Orang.

16. Raing.

17. Santal.

18. Tripura, Tripuri, Tippera

19. Uchai.

West Bengal:

1. Asur
2. Baiga
3. Badia, Bediya
4. Bhumij

5. Bhutia, Sherpa, Toto, Dukpa, Kagatay, Tibetan, Yolmo
6. Birhor
7. Birjia
8. Chakma
9. Chero
10. Chik Barak
11. Garo.
12. Gond
13. Gorait
14. Hajang
15. Ho
16. Karmali
17. Kharwar
18. Khond
19. Kisan
20. Kora
21. Korwa
22. **Lepcha**
23. Lodha, Kheria, KhAeria
24. Lohara, Lohra
25. Magh
26. Mahali
27. Mahli
28. Mal PahAeriya
29. Mech

30. Mru
31. Munda
32. Nagesia
33. Oraon
34. Parhaiya
35. Rabha
36. Santal
37. Sauria PahAeria
38. Savar
39. Limbu (Subba)
40. Tamang

Index

Colour Plates

Young Lepcha Girls relaxing by taking tea.

Boys and girls of a Lepcha Night School

Enjoying and separating paddy from paddy straw by dancing circularly on them.

Lepcha girls enjoying a picnic.

Young girls coordinating ethnic function.

Hand tc hand in protest rally.

Men and Women in Protest rally

Children performing Cultural Program

Female Mun, Lepcha priestess.

Girls & boys reading Naamthaar, holy book.

Protest rally

Female Mun, Lepcha priestess.

Girls reading Naamthaar before Bongthing.

Girls are taught to take care of plants.

Girls reading Naamthaar before Mun.

Girls reading Naamthaar with Bongthing

Girls ready for cultural program.

Groom party in a marriage function.

Some items of Bride-price.

Women busy in cooking, carrying luggage, separating paddy by dancing

Punishment & road blocked for a groom party due to their late arrival.

Bride Groom Party carrying bride price at the back

Offerings to nature by all.

Fun & punishment to groom party.

Fire wood in front of marriage gate.

Male Mun

Older generation

Woman carrying luggage at the back.